TO THE GLORY OF GOD

To/ Major Heather Poxon,

May God continue to bless + use you in your service, especially in your present role as you seek to love + serve the poor.

Ray. Oakley

September 2015.

Information on Cover Picture Painting

The pictures on the cover to this book are taken from a lithographic print of an original painting by Michael John Ewins, ASAI, a well known Hertfordshire artist. He was commissioned to paint it as a permanent reminder of some of the buildings and events significant in Salvation Army history as well as depicting the developing mission and uniform of the Army. The artist was advised by the International Heritage Centre and it is dedicated to The Salvation Army of today.

The buildings can be identified from left to right as follows:

The Vine Public House in Whitechapel Road

The Blind Beggar Public House in Whitechapel Road

Mission Hall in Whitechapel Road

Men's Social (City Colony) Headquarters with food & shelter Depot & People's Mission

Headquarters in Whitechapel Road

Clapton Congress Hall & Training Garrison

Eagle Tavern & Grecian Theatre

International Headquarters in Queen Victoria Street in ruins after May 1941

Trade Headquarters – SP&S in Judd Street, Kings Cross

1965 International Headquarters

Territorial Headquarters (1998) for the United Kingdom Territory in Newington Causeway

The individuals and representative groups of people in the picture can be identified from left to right as follows:

1. William Booth beginning alone in Mile End waste, in July 1865.
2. Catherine Booth – circa 1865.
2a. Brigadier William Lord – circa 1899.
3. A group of local Salvationists – circa 1910.
4. Boy selling Salvation Matches – circa 1890.
5. Cycle Brigade – circa 1910.
5a. William John Colley – Sent to Australia as reinforcement in 1882.
5b. Albert James Bettes – Sent to Australia as reinforcement in 1882.
6. Mobile food kitchen – Sunderland circa 1930.
6a. Boy with bowl of food – circa 1930
7. General Booth's motor campaign passing through Watford, on 18th July 1908.
7a. Household Troops Band – circa 1890.
8. Women officers – circa 1950.
9. Searching the ruins of the bombed headquarters building in 1941.
10. Mobile canteen outside ruins of the IHQ building 1941.
11. First aid van in Kent hop fields – circa 1940.
12. Household Troops Band – 1985.
13. Open-air meeting group – circa 1970.
14. New-style uniform – 1970.
15. Summer uniform – 1990.
16. Majors Robert & Muriel McClenahan with the Prince of Wales in July 1996.
17. Emergency Unit from Hoxton Centre – 1996.

TO THE GLORY OF GOD

A HISTORY OF THE DEVELOPMENT OF THE SALVATION ARMY
IN THE BRITISH ISLES AS EXPRESSED, ILLUSTRATED AND SYMBOLISED
THROUGH ITS BUILDINGS AND SOME PAINTINGS.

RAY OAKLEY

Published privately in June 2011 with re-print in November 2011
by Ray Oakley
Leamington Spa, Warwickshire

ISBN: 978 0 85412 827 3

Book Design: Ian Hughes, www.mousematdesign.com
Book Production: Graham Cook

Printed and Bound in Singapore

CONTENTS

FOREWORD

Can bricks and mortar speak? Any archaeologist will tell us that the answer is yes. Even from the merest potsherd dramatic accounts of past civilisations have been built. These pages have no need to resort to such speculation. Within them is told the stirring flesh and blood story of The Salvation Army in Britain, based not on fragments of stone but as seen and expressed and symbolised by the buildings that Salvationists have used during the past 145 years to save souls, grow saints and serve suffering humanity.

We watch as our early-day fortress and castle corps buildings become citadels. The word barracks, we are told, was soon abandoned because people thought all Salvationists slept there! We see even the concept of citadels becoming outmoded as our buildings become ever friendlier – not there to repel invaders but to attract into them seekers after truth and those in need of practical ministry. We observe how they are adapted to increased community service – with the debate now being whether it is the worship hall or the community rooms that visitors should first see as they enter. We discern why the term church is no longer considered inappropriate for these church buildings with a difference.

The dramatic story of how the Army's social work in Britain has developed over the years is even more clearly symbolised by the changing face of the buildings it has used for its mission. Early-day hostel dwellers, sleeping in coffin-like beds, would be amazed to find their counterparts of today living in en suite bedsits. Past residents of our children's homes would be astounded to see their former dwelling adapted and re-adapted and adapted yet again to meet new needs and seemingly ever-changing social philosophies and government legislation.

Included are fascinating nuggets of information about special buildings like the William Booth College. When economies had to be made to the design of the college, its world-renowned architect, Sir Giles Gilbert Scott, suggested that the tower should be sacrificed. Denmark Hill without its tower? Unthinkable!

This account also puts on record the achievements 'to the glory of God' of the Army's architects office and introduces us to the notable personalities that have bestridden the scene. It is a unique story for no other part of the Army world has had an in-house architects department whose accumulated experience saved the Army from re-inventing the wheel whenever a new building was needed.

The author of this remarkable and beautifully designed book is himself a remarkable person. Lieut-Colonel Ray Oakley, M.Sc, RIBA, FRICS embodies those many virtues that have characterised the architects office throughout the years. Having worked with him on a number of property projects, I have watched with admiration as with unbounded optimism and patience he has deployed his creative, technical, business, diplomatic and problem-solving skills to turn unformed dreams into tangible reality. We Salvationists of Britain stand indebted to him, and even more so now that he has written this admirable work.

John Larsson
General (Retired)

Dedication

The motivation for this book arises from a number of personal factors. I discovered in my work as a Salvation Army officer-architect the plan of God for my life. By God's grace, trained and equipped with the necessary skills for this special role, I found deep satisfaction in contributing in this way to the development of The Salvation Army. I also discovered numerous predecessors who shared similar convictions and who served God and the Army in a similar role. This book is therefore dedicated to the many people who have devoted a major portion of their lives to providing The Salvation Army with appropriate environments to fulfil its God-given mission of 'saving souls, growing saints and serving suffering humanity'. Of the long line of architects who have directed this work special mention needs to be made of Lieutenant-Colonel David Blackwell RIBA, Chief Architect at International Headquarters from 1967 to 1990, who was a major influence on myself and others, motivating us and providing a role model for us to follow.

Acknowledgements

This book would not have been possible without the help and encouragement of many people. I would like to acknowledge the help provided by some individuals and thank them all for their contributions:
• Alf and Valerie Youell, for their encouragement and generous financial support.
• David Greenwood, my friend and colleague with whom I spent many years in The Salvation Army Architects Office, has given me much advice and supplied many of the photographs and illustrations.
• Colonel Margaret White and Colonel Trevor Tribble, former leaders of the UK Territory Social Services, have both contributed much information about the history of the Salvation Army's social work.
• Gordon Taylor, archivist at The Salvation Army International Heritage Centre, and his colleagues for their guidance in researching so much of the history of the Army.
• Dr. Mike Sinclair in the Property Department and Lynn Rust in the Photographic Unit of THQ.
• The many friends and colleagues who have supplied information and photographs that I requested.
• My wife, Brenda, for her skills in editing the draft manuscript and making it more readable.
• Major David Dalziel for his skill and patience in guiding the writer and editing the final draft of this book.
• Graham Cook for his help, knowledge and experience in getting the book published privately.

Copyright Acknowledgements

The majority of the images used in this book have been provided by the author, his friends and colleagues with other material provided by The Salvation Army UK Territorial Headquarters and The Salvation Army International Heritage Centre. For images taken from other sources, every effort has been made to obtain permission from the original source and to acknowledge copyright, where appropriate. The following is a list of those images, and copyright owners where known:

• Cover picture from the painting 'A Pictorial History of The Salvation Army' © Michael John Ewins. http://www.blue-lampprints.co.uk/otherpics.htm (prints still available from SP&S, 1 Tiverton Street, London SE1 6NT)
• Image 3; London's Canary Wharf © The Docklands Development Corporation / Canary Wharf Contractors Group.
• Image 5; Durham Cathedral – from *Durham Cathedral* © Jarrold Publishing 2005.
• Images 6 and 7; Liverpool Anglican Cathedral Church of Christ – from *Liverpool Cathedral Calendar* 1998 © Carr Fox Photographs 1987.
• Images 8 and 9; Liverpool Metropolitan Cathedral – from Liverpool Cathedral brochure special issue *Liverpool 67* © City of Liverpool Public Relations Office.
• Image 45; Painting of William Booth by W.J. Carroll, hanging in William Booth Memorial Halls, Nottingham.
• Images 61, 62 and 63; Albert Orsborn Memorial Halls, Bournemouth © The Brick Development Association.
• Images 69, 70 and 71; Chelmsford Corps Halls © Hudson Architects. http://www.hudsonarchitects.co.uk/#hudson-architects
• Image 83; Chester-le-Street hall ©Architect Tony Burns
• Image 109; Tom Raine Court © Architect Tony Burns
• Image 131; Riverside House © Graeme Ackroyd/Swanke Hayden Connell International Ltd.
• Image 160 &165–172; The Salvation Army International Headquarters © Architects Sheppard Robson http://www.sheppardronson.com/projects/page.cfm?projectID=100026
• Image 179; Painting 'Carols at Judd Street' © Martin Sexton http://www.martinsexton-artist.co.uk (prints still available from SP&S, 1 Tiverton Street, London SE1 6NT)
• Image 25, 65, 106, 151, 173 and 175 all from paintings © Rosa Branson. http://www.theworlingtonmovement.co.uk

PREFACE

The history of the development of The Salvation Army, from a small open-air evangelical Christian Mission in the East End of London in 1865 to the present worldwide organisation it is today, has been faithfully recorded and the story told from a variety of perspectives. However, the development of its mission, especially in the British Isles where it commenced, as reflected and symbolised in its buildings, has not previously been recorded except in a few fragmentary academic dissertations, and some articles in Salvation Army publications.

Archaeologists have discovered how artefacts of any culture or civilization can reveal a great deal about the beliefs, faith and activities of the people who created them. Buildings are, of course, some of the most significant and symbolic artefacts in this regard which provide tangible evidence of how ideals and ideas have been translated into action. The historic records of the development of Salvation Army buildings and the personal knowledge of the author mean that this account does not need to rely on the findings of archaeologists. However, the principle remains true that its buildings tell us much about the organisation that created them.

In relation to The Salvation Army's evangelical mission the work commenced in a tent on Mile End waste, following open-air meetings. The mission, as it developed into 'the Army', then made use of hired music halls, circuses and skating rinks and eventually developed purpose-built places of worship with significant community service facilities. Much of the residential social work commenced in warehouses and workhouses where only minimum facilities could be provided for the maximum number of people. However, the importance and uniqueness of each individual finds expression today in individual care plans and private rooms or suites within the Army's residential buildings. The development of The Salvation Army's administrative structure and of the business processes appropriate for this unique section of the Christian Church which has also become a major social agency, is reflected in the provision of the various headquarters and other buildings related to its regional, national and international activities.

William Booth, early in his ministry, became aware of the contribution that buildings could make to aid or hinder his mission. In 1880 he founded The Salvation Army's own architects' office, to guide and direct the design and development of all new Salvation Army buildings. This office operated within International Headquarters until 1990, then within the newly formed United Kingdom Territorial Headquarters for a further 12 years. A number of very different people directed this office throughout its 122 year history, each making their own significant contribution, as their personal profiles will reveal.

The Salvation Army has always prided itself on being a people-focused organisation and would therefore still claim that it can carry out many of its activities without buildings of its own. A review of the current Salvation Army property portfolio in the United Kingdom would however show that in the main this has not been the approach pursued. A history of the development of

Salvation Army architecture will help present-day readers to understand how the design of its buildings has reflected the application of William Booth's vision in ways appropriate to each new generation. Similarly, it is hoped that this story will also provide insights into how and where buildings influenced the success of The Salvation Army's mission with lessons from the past hopefully informing the present and influencing the future.

The phrases 'Kingdom of Heaven' and 'Kingdom of God' used throughout the gospel records, appear to be synonymous with each other. This kingdom is of course spiritual in character. It was originally intended to call this book 'Building the Kingdom', but as the contents of the book focus on man-made buildings, that title seemed inappropriate and misleading. The book is principally about the development of The Salvation Army's mission of proclaiming the good news, combined with the prophetic actions of showing mercy and fighting for social justice.

The buildings which the Army has developed are symbolic of this mission and are a testimony to those spiritual ideals. This book aims to show, from a historical perspective, how spiritual goals have been and are being translated into bricks and mortar in order to aid the objectives of changing people's lives and seeking to transform society at large.

The mission of The Salvation Army is to bring 'Glory to God' through its worship, its activities and its influence on people's lives. Its buildings therefore seek to enhance and reflect this mission. Every building opened by The Salvation Army since its commencement has been built 'TO THE GLORY OF GOD', and often those very words are carved on foundation stones or on commemorative plaques to mark the building's completion. It seems appropriate therefore to entitle this book 'TO THE GLORY OF GOD' to reinforce the purpose behind the design and construction of these buildings.

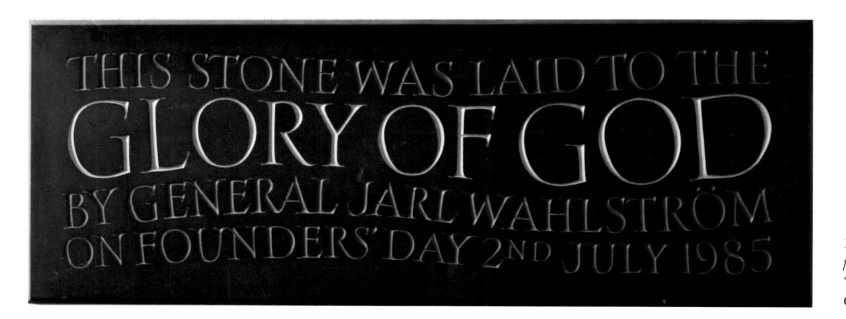

1. Example of a foundation stone: 'To the Glory of God'

INTRODUCTION

Actions speak louder than words! The Salvation Army has been most effective in its mission to show God's love to the world by showing it in action in countless different ways. One of its slogans 'Heart to God and Hand to Man` seeks to reflect a church with its sleeves rolled up. This is symbolised in two of its emblems, the SA crest signifying faith and worship and where the shield is used it signifies action in service. In pursuing its mission since its commencement in 1865 The Salvation Army has acquired, adapted and designed a large portfolio of buildings. These buildings, as with many artefacts, symbolise the aspirations, values and activities of this branch of the Christian Church, as it has responded to the evolutionary changes in the culture of the British Isles over the last 145 years or so.

Before the industrial revolution in England, the tallest, most prominent features of most towns and villages were church steeples, like fingers pointing to heaven. At that time, worship of God and church activity were at the centre of community life. During the Industrial Revolution large cotton and woollen mills or coal pithead buildings became the dominant features of the townscape, signifying the prime place of work and the production of goods in the lives of those communities, especially in the north of England. In the 21st century the tallest buildings in our cities are office blocks, such as Canary Wharf in London, often owned by banks and building societies. Some dominate the skyline even around St Paul's Cathedral within the City of London. The buildings covering the largest site areas tend to be indoor shopping centres. The importance of money and the material nature of our present society are graphically illustrated and symbolised in these buildings.

2. Slimbridge Village Church Spire

3. London's Canary Wharf

In his book: *How to Read a Church*, Richard Taylor describes the numerous symbols and images that were intentionally created in church architecture. For example he states:

Churches and cathedrals are packed with meaning. Outside, the spire points to heaven; the carvings around the entrance announce the holiness of the space inside; the aisle draws you to the altar, with the ranks of pews on either side, is the gangway of a ship carrying worshippers to God; the altar, the whole heart of the building, is contained in a separate and sacred space; all around, numbers, colours, the animals and plants in the stonework, and the scenes in the stained glass, point to aspects of Christian teachings about God.

During the Victorian era, however, churches built in the more affluent areas of towns were magnificent Gothic or classical structures which spoke of wealth and appeared unrelated to the lives of poorer citizens. The 'medieval' interiors of many of those churches failed to communicate a God of love who was relevant to the lives of the poor. Consequently the poor were generally antagonistic to religion, as symbolised by the established church and its buildings. The aim of the more evangelical Christian denominations, however, was to change the lives of individuals and so to change society. This was the environment into which The Salvation Army was born and the section of the Christian Church to which it belongs.

This branch of the Christian Church developed along military lines and military metaphors were used in the new symbols it created to illustrate the tenets of its faith and practices. This new set of symbols included flags, uniforms and bands instead of incense, cassocks and organs. Salvationists sang songs to well-known secular tunes and used simple language to express their faith. The interiors of their citadels resembled music halls rather than traditional churches. The main colour of their flag was red to symbolise the blood of Jesus and often the exterior walls of their citadels were built in red brick. Some felt this too was intended to reflect the blood of Jesus which was a central theme of The Salvation Army, though it was more probably chosen so that the buildings reflected the local vernacular architecture. Some saw The Salvation Army as a bastion against revolution by the discontented masses, as it redirected their energies into spiritual warfare and thus improved society by peaceful means.

The historical development of Salvation Army buildings provides an interesting and challenging story illustrating the adaptation of its mission to changes both within and outside the organisation. A number of excellent source documents help us to understand these changes. Sources used are listed in the bibliography, with The Salvation Army Heritage Centre a prime resource for this information. These documents, together with the author's personal knowledge throughout more than 40 years of Salvation Army development in the United Kingdom, have provided the main material for this story.

In one of Charles Wesley's songs, much loved by Salvationists, he writes: 'To serve the present age my calling to fulfil' (The Song Book of The Salvation Army 472 v.2). These words describe one of the main motivating themes that have required The Salvation Army to adapt its tactics and methods in order to remain relevant to the changing lifestyles and cultures of this country for almost 150 years. This has been particularly important as the speed of change has greatly accelerated since the Army came into existence. While it would claim that its *purposes* have not altered, it commenced as a mission, then became a Christian army; it's also described as an organisation and is now recognised as a denomination of the Christian Church. All these labels reflect ways in which the movement, which is yet another description of it, has developed.

The Salvation Army has generally been led by pragmatic people who have not been inhibited by the absence of resources, but have commenced their work within the limitations prevailing at that time. While it is amazing how God has provided The Salvation Army with the resources it needs, nevertheless it is inevitable that the work has been influenced by the limitations of those resources in terms of personnel, finance and property. The constraints of those limitations can be seen in the type and design of the buildings used at different stages in this Salvation Army story, but especially in the initial years.

The Salvation Army and its buildings have also been affected by other changes in the external environment. Changes in government policy and in social priorities have greatly affected both the resources available and the expectations of how The Salvation Army should respond, particularly in relation to its residential social services and its community work. The minimum standards required in these buildings, in terms of space and amenities, have increased dramatically. While the increased cost of raising these standards has exercised the Army, it has always welcomed policies that improve the quality of life for everyone, especially for the poorest members of society. It has often led the way in setting model standards of excellence in its service and in the accommodation provided.

Throughout Britain and Europe many beautiful cathedrals are admired by worshippers and visitors alike. Some of these buildings took about 100 years to complete and in spite of adaptations and additions many have lasted almost 1,000 years. The names of the people who created these places of inspiration are largely forgotten, with a few notable exceptions. The craftsmen who carved and fashioned the stonework and woodwork often spent all their working lives creating a single building. They took the same care with every detail whether it was in the roof vaulting or on the altar. The motivation of both designer and craftsmen were expressions of love and devotion, principally to bring 'Glory to God'.

Architects employed by The Salvation Army have never been required to produce cathedrals. Their design projects have usually been to create appropriate, simple buildings for worship and community service or residential centres for the provision of some form of social service. For the 122 years that The Salvation Army had its own architectural staff however, their motivation was the same as the cathedral builders, to bring 'Glory to God'.

During the Second World War, Winston Churchill said to the people of the United States of America, prior to US entry into the war: '*Give us the tools and we will finish the job*'. Salvation Army architects saw their role in similar terms; that is to provide The Salvation Army with the necessary tools, in terms of appropriate buildings, to continue and win its spiritual warfare.

At the foundation stone-laying ceremony for the new International Headquarters building on 5 May 1962, conducted by General Wilfred Kitching, the programme notes included these words:

Quite naturally, there have always been those who lamented the necessity of steel and concrete as part of the Kingdom of God on earth. How much better it would be if prayer alone could suffice, with the hymns of saints and the songs of Salvationists. But alas, spiritual reflections, sermons, poetic cadences of the Bible, blessed retreats of pious Christians are not enough. The Salvation Army has been forced to accept its God-given destiny but this presents practical and urgent administrative problems that have to be housed in man-made walls.

Clearly, similar sentiments could be applied to the necessity for all Salvation Army buildings.

ARCHITECTS AND ARCHITECTURE

4. Aerial View of St Paul's Cathedral with The Salvation Army International Headquarters (1963 building), in the foreground

Introduction

Architecture has been called the mother of the arts. From time immemorial buildings have been a lasting record of man's achievements and aspirations. From ancient times man has used his imagination and ingenuity to erect an edifice around an altar in his endeavour to express the Glory of God. We can be 'lost in wonder, love and praise', as we admire monasteries and cathedrals; places such as Westminster Abbey, the renaissance of Greek temple architecture in St Paul's Cathedral in London or the relatively modern miracle of Coventry Cathedral, rising from the remnants of the original Gothic cathedral destroyed in the Second World War. Durham Cathedral is the nation's best-loved building, according to a nationwide poll in 2001 and is also the greatest Norman building in Britain and perhaps in Europe. For 900 years it has stood, in the words of the Dean: 'as a sign of our human search and of divine welcome and hospitality'.

It is, however, in the City of Liverpool that the faith of Christians has been most clearly expressed in the building of cathedrals during the 20th century. At either end of a street named HOPE are two cathedrals, just half a mile apart, built during the last 100 years. At one end is the Anglican Cathedral of the Church of Christ, the largest cathedral in Britain, and at the other end is the Roman Catholic Metropolitan Cathedral of Christ the King.

The Anglican cathedral was designed by Giles Gilbert Scott (who later designed The Salvation Army's William Booth College) when he was only 21 years of age. It houses 3,000 worshippers, is designed in a traditional Gothic style, built of sandstone, and it took 75 years to build.

5. Durham Cathedral (far left)

6. Liverpool's Anglican Cathedral of the Church of Christ

7. Nave of the Church of Christ Cathedral

8. Liverpool's Roman Catholic Metropolitan Cathedral of Christ the King (far right)

The Catholic cathedral is a complete break with convention, with a central altar and the congregation seated in circular fashion, all facing the altar, the symbol of God's presence. This cathedral housing 2,000 worshippers took only four and a half years to build, possibly the fastest that any cathedral has ever been built. It was designed by Sir Frederick Gibberd and built in modern materials with reinforced concrete ribs surmounted by a huge lantern of coloured glass. Three luminous orbs in this glass lantern in yellow, red and blue, are intended to represent the Trinity. Interestingly these same colours are also used in The Salvation Army Flag to represent aspects of the Trinity. Coloured or stained glass has been used in churches from medieval times to depict Christian saints or tell Biblical stories. The light shining through the glass is used to symbolise the Light of the World (Jesus) shining through our lives, giving a glimpse of the Glory of God.

where individuals experienced the presence of God, often in the most dramatic fashion. As the Jewish and, later, Christian religion developed, the concept of 'holy' things became associated with artefacts separated from common use and consecrated or set apart for a sacred purpose related to God. For the Israelites there were initially the Ten Commandants on tablets of stone, then the scrolls on which the law, their traditions and the prophets' messages were written. The Ark of the Covenant, which contained those tablets of stone, itself symbolised the presence of God in their midst, particularly in the space between the wings of the cherubim above the mercy seat. These artefacts were housed initially in the tabernacle (a tent) and later in Solomon's magnificent temple in Jerusalem. Even the remaining portion of wall of the temple that was later built on that site is today still held in great reverence by the Jews.

In the Christian faith, the places of Jesus' birth, death and burial are deemed to be sacred places. Great cathedrals, such as St Peter's Basilica in Rome and Canterbury Cathedral in Kent, have been centres of Christian worship for more than a thousand years and hence are viewed as holy places and sacred buildings. As stated previously, their religious significance relates to their association with spiritual experiences in the past. Even within church buildings some artefacts, such as the altar signifying the presence of God, are considered more sacred than other parts.

When Jesus was asked a question by a Samaritan woman, 'Where should we worship God?' he replied: 'God is Spirit, and only by the power of his Spirit can people worship him as he really is' (John 4:23, 24 GNB). These words seem to suggest that the place is relatively unimportant compared to the spirit of one's worship. However, later in Jerusalem Jesus took great exception to the Temple precincts being used for unprincipled trading

9. Huge lantern over altar to Christ the King Cathedral

Sacred Places

Most religions have places they deem to be sacred, usually associated with some religious experience which has taken place there. The Old Testament records numerous places which the Jews considered 'Holy', and the extortionate exchange of local currency into temple currency, all in the name of religion. A place and building which symbolised the presence of God was being used, not for worship, but for the exploitation of poor people.

The Salvation Army, when it commenced as the Christian Mission, had no access to any sacred buildings, i.e. those used exclusively for worship. Services or meetings, as they called them, were held in a tent and later in music halls, skating rinks or any manner of building available. They did not consider sacred buildings were necessary for the worship of God nor for the 'saving of souls'. The emphasis of their preaching and teaching was on holy living rather than on holy places. Consequently when they did commence to acquire or build their own premises, they used them for all manner of activities as well as for worship.

The Salvation Army taught and proclaimed, like many other Christians, that if people lived every aspect of their lives 'to the glory of God' then there was no division between the sacred and the secular activities of every-day life, as exemplified in Horatius Bonar's words:

So shall no part of day or night
From sacredness be free;
But all my life, in every step,
Be fellowship with thee.
(*The Song Book of The Salvation Army* 7 v. 4).

Salvationists' emphasis on action and service, especially to the poor, is both an expression of their faith and a reflection of this conviction. Similarly their belief that the Spirit of God can be present in every person reflects their emphasis on holy *people*, rather than holy things.

As far as worship halls were concerned, the essential elements of those first Salvation Army halls were specified as:

- A platform from which the Scriptures, 'The Word', could be preached, where converted individuals could give their personal testimony on how God had changed their lives and from where the leader could lead the singing of Gospel songs.
- A penitents' form or mercy seat, in front of the platform, where seekers could publicly respond to the spiritual challenge 'to be saved'.
- Ample seating for the expected large congregation with clear views of the platform and sufficiently near to hear the message.

The mercy seat or penitents' form was originally an ordinary bench but this gradually changed to a more elaborate form as it became one of the principal focal points of the meeting. The association of this bench with spiritual decisions led to a desire to reverence it and treat it as sacred. For a period this led to a desire to protect it from improper use, resulting in the erection of posts and elaborate ropes in front of the mercy seat in some halls. This arrangement did not last long as it was felt important that the mercy seat should be available for use at any time and on any day.

Meeting halls were initially used for every kind of activity necessary in the life of a Salvation Army corps, from jumble sales to divine worship. In recent years, however, some corps view the main meeting hall, or church as it is now increasingly called, as a sacred space and wish to reserve it for divine worship alone. This is only possible where sufficient alternative spaces are available for all the other corps activities. While there may be practical reasons for reserving the main hall for more formal occasions, The Salvation Army still does not require the creation of separate sacred spaces used for worship only. It reiterates the scriptural teaching that the 'body of believers' is the Church and that people are the dwelling place of God's Holy Spirit, not the buildings. The scriptural basis for this view is contained in the following extract from Paul's letter to the Christians at Corinth: *'Surely you know that you are God's temple and that God's Spirit lives in you . . . For God's temple is holy and you yourselves are his temple'* (1 Corinthians 3:16–17, GNB).

The Jewish Tabernacle was a tent and The Salvation Army's first meeting place was also a tent, but it was not revered by Salvationists nor seen exclusively as the dwelling place of God. Some 145 years later, however, meetings (religious services) are now generally held in spacious and carefully designed halls.

Jonathan Meades, writing for the RIBA Journal in April 2007 controversially suggested that *'those faiths and cultures whose numbers are swelling hardly need bother with buildings* (but) *history shows us it is the failing denominations that require architectural support'*. A cursory review of Salvation Army history in the United Kingdom might seem to support that view. Of course many factors have impacted on the decisions to erect new Army buildings and have influenced the quality of their design as will be explored later.

When a spiritual revival first takes place, as was the case with the birth of The Salvation Army, the priority is to get as many people saved as possible through Gospel meetings, held in whatever places are available. Similarly in its social action The Salvation Army's emphasis was to feed and house as many as possible of the thousands of destitute people, at the lowest possible cost. In both aspects of this two-pronged approach, minimal funds were available for the work and initially both activities were seen to cater for people on a short term basis. It was initially expected that those converted would then attend their local churches and that the housing of the homeless would only be for a minimum period. Both of these assumptions proved to be wrong and therefore more permanent solutions were required.

In the case of the evangelical work it became necessary to provide not only halls for Gospel meetings but permanent places of worship where new Christians could be nurtured in their faith and find opportunities in the service of their fellow men. Greater funds became available as the general public learned the value of the Army's work in redeeming large numbers of the poorest members of society and thus helping to transform society. The families of those converts found that the benefits of a Christian lifestyle included an increase in their wealth as well as an improvement in their quality of life, especially in later generations. This change in circumstances among its members, linked to the tithing of their personal giving, resulted in substantially more funds being available for the work generally and for new buildings in particular. The aspirations of Salvationists also changed, so that their expectations of the quality of environment considered as an appropriate worship space has both evolved and greatly increased.

Greater concern with material things, such as buildings, can sometimes detract from the spiritual aspects of corps life, with material replacing spiritual priorities. While this danger is recognised, it is also true that buildings carefully designed to the glory of God can enhance worship, helping to create for many people an environment where God's presence is more easily experienced. This is generally the motivation of the architects who design places for divine worship.

The Physical Environment

Some would suggest that our environment determines our behaviour and that of our children. Christians believe that no matter what characteristics a person may develop as a result of heredity or environment, the grace of God can change them for the better. However, though we do not believe that the environment can *determine* human behaviour, it is generally accepted that one's environment will have a considerable influence upon it.

Buildings provide part of the physical environment in which we live and work, and the layout and character of buildings has a major influence on whether our lives and work are made easier or harder. The character and design of Salvation Army buildings can influence the success of its work and whether it is able to achieve its objectives. If a building's design correctly interprets the users' needs, whether that is corps or social centre, then it can operate more efficiently and successfully. Built form can help facilitate the development of community and social ideals or inhibit them. The success of a building largely depends on there being a good fit between the building and its proposed use, which is its function. The simpler the proposed function of a building and hence the design, the more easily this can be accomplished. If the building user is also the builder then it is likely that function and design will be well matched. Where this is not possible, as with more sophisticated buildings then the match depends upon the communication of the building's purpose to the designer and their ability to correctly interpret this information and translate it into a building design. In other words the buildings provided can either help or hinder The Salvation Army in its purpose of meeting specific needs, whether these are social, medical, educational or spiritual. In the case of a place of worship there is of course the desire for it to be inspirational as well as functional in terms of the atmosphere it creates. The accumulation of considerable knowledge and experience of the requirements and needs of all aspects of The Salvation Army was made possible by the retention of its own in-house Architects Office for 122 years of its history.

Environmental Psychology

The study of the interface between human behaviour and the environment is now a specialised branch of psychology known as environmental psychology. In the United Kingdom this subject became of particular interest following post-war building activity. The government of the day was determined to demolish the slum dwellings of the UK cities. Many closely packed houses were therefore demolished and tall blocks of flats erected to replace them. This idea of arranging domestic dwellings in a *vertical street* had been taken from a European model initially promoted by the famous French architect, Le Corbusier. However, in the United Kingdom those new buildings became associated with graffiti, noise, disturbance, intimidation and violence. People, who seemed to have enjoyed the close community relations of the terraced houses, now felt they were living in a hostile environment. Moving to a different form of built environment and the speed of change had apparently substantially changed people's behaviour and their sense of community. Other changes in society of course played their part as well. The study of environmental psychology has developed greatly since that initial interest to include all aspects of social and physical environments in micro and macro settings, ranging from individual rooms to whole countries and cultures. Interestingly, Le Corbusier was the design architect for *La Cité de Refuge*, The Salvation Army's large hostel for homeless people in Paris.

The current understanding of environmental psychology had not been developed when William Booth founded The Salvation Army. However, the impact of an environment on human behaviour was clearly evident to William Booth. He saw that most of the people in the slums were denied even the most basic of provisions, such as were provided for London cab horses – namely the provision of food, shelter and work. He coined the phrase the 'Cab Horse Charter' and then set out to provide these three basic essentials which he deemed necessary for human dignity. One of the ways that he sought to implement that charter was to move people from their present environment in a three-stage elevator system, consisting of a city colony, a farm colony and an overseas colony. The goal was to help people lift themselves by ever-widening opportunities. Each step involved the provision of food, shelter and work, including job training. All of these were provided in an environment created to reduce the temptations of alcohol and the influence of former companions on those being rehabilitated. Certainly, William Booth was fully aware of the importance of the appropriate social environment as well as the right physical environment for his social programmes to succeed.

The Role of the Architect

Like many human activities, building a structure is generally a response to human need and to an idea about how that need might be met. Shelter is one of the most fundamental of human needs. In many societies, people build their own shelter or house and turn it into their home. In these situations the same person is the client, designer (architect) and builder. The vast majority of buildings in the world today are still built according to established customs and traditions, where methods of construction and the requirements of the building owner change very slowly.

As society and buildings become more complex, there is need for an increasing division of labour and a need for the trained building designer, an architect. In Britain today architects design most new buildings, even though some of them are in the employ of builders or developers.

An architect is trained in the design of buildings and in all aspects of the built environment, able to analyse and define problems and suggest possible ways of dealing with them. The architect is generally a problem solver, who must have expertise to analyse and document a client's requirements and activities so that the designed building will meet all the environmental needs of that client. In analysing client requirements an architect should be able to offer alternative solutions and alternative ways of viewing the same problem.

An architect therefore combines creative ability, technical knowledge and managerial expertise to be able to interpret a client's requirements and translate them into built form. Architects take account of the characteristics and restrictions of the site, the financial budget, statutory regulations and the influence of climate and culture as well as the particular geographical setting in producing their design. A unique skill is the ability to visualise a building in three dimensions and produce a conceptual design for it.

In the United Kingdom the architectural profession is one of a limited number of professions protected by an Act of Parliament, namely the Architects Act 1997. No one is allowed to call himself or herself an architect unless he/she has completed a course of training and practice, usually over a minimum of seven years, to obtain the appropriate qualifications. They must be registered with the government body now known as the Architects Registration Board, formerly the Architects Registration Council of the United Kingdom. This registration thus provides protection for the public in appointing an architect, similar to that afforded by other registered professions, such as doctors of medicine and solicitors.

The Salvation Army Architects Office

In December 1999, an article in the *Architects Journal* acknowledged that The Salvation Army Architects Office was then one of the oldest architectural practices in London. The reason for this was that in 1880, two years after the Christian Mission became The Salvation Army, William Booth appointed his own in-house Staff Architect.

In 1882 a book entitled *The Salvation War* stated the following:

The Salvation Army has acquired more property in 1882 than in all the previous 17 years of its history.

This was just two years after William Booth appointed the first in-house Staff Architect. However, the quotation obviously refers back to 1865 when the organisation, initially called the East London Revival Society and later The Christian Mission, was founded. This statement is remarkable because the general policy at that time was to rent buildings wherever possible. The earliest recorded instance of Booth using a private firm of architects was the appointment of Messrs Habershon and Pite in 1870 to alter and adapt the People's Market in Whitechapel, which was to become the People's Mission Hall. The decision of William Booth in 1880 to appoint an in-house architect may have been because of the magnitude of the building programme, dissatisfaction with the private architectural firms or the speed with which he required his building projects to be completed. Whatever the reason,

10. *Original design drawing for York Citadel – 1882*

the Architects Office was to serve The Salvation Army for the next 122 years. A glimpse of the personal profiles and character of the principals who directed this office will follow later. Of course less is known about some of the earlier personnel than about those of more recent years.

Also in *Salvation War* William Booth writes:

We do not profess by any means to be satisfied, however, with our accomplishments in so far as the way of hall building. In this, as in everything else, we have had everything to learn. With the assistance of an architect and others connected with the building trade, who have devoted themselves to this department of the work for the love of it, we hope before another year is over to have made great progress in the discovery of that form of building capable of containing the largest number of people, to be erected at the lowest possible cost, in which any man or woman filled with the love of God may feel perfectly at home in addressing the assembled thousands with the greatest ease and comfort to himself and all about him.

Just one year later than this, Booth reported the following:

As a rule we have ourselves erected these buildings by contract, under the supervision of our own architect, Commissioner Sherwood.

Some of the earliest drawings, such as those for York Citadel dated 1882, bear the joint names of Sherwood and James Flint, who was an assistant to Sherwood. The foundation stone at York Citadel also bears witness to their involvement. However, the first person to be appointed Staff Architect to The Salvation Army seems to be this Edmund James Sherwood. A brief personal profile of him and of the subsequent staff or chief architects will follow, giving some indication of their contribution to the development of The Salvation Army and its buildings.

Edmund James Sherwood

In a list of the general staff attached to headquarters of The Salvation Army in 1880, E. J. Sherwood was listed as the Architect and Surveyor with Mr E. Searle as one of his assistants. Sherwood was immediately commissioned as an officer with the rank of Major but with an appointment where he was described as Commissioner for Property. However, he was subsequently referred to simply as Commissioner Sherwood. Early correspondence from him shows that he used the title E. J. Sherwood, Architect and Surveyor with his address as Superintendent, Architect's Department at International Headquarters, 101 Queen Victoria Street, London E.C. There is no mention of his rank in his correspondence, which may have been to emphasise his professional status or to avoid confusion over his rank. He was appointed at a time of phenomenal growth within The Salvation Army and the demand for

appropriate buildings was growing each year. A report in 1883 stated that 34 new buildings had been erected or purchased in that year with a further 16 planned.

As far as corps buildings were concerned the mandate for their design was very clear. This was to build by the cheapest methods to provide the maximum seating capacity possible. The 34 buildings completed that year seated a total of 46,900 people at a total cost of £22,000. The further 16 projects planned were to seat a further 20,000 people. A hectic programme of building development therefore took place under Sherwood's direction. An early drawing of a standard design for a Salvation Army hall with a barrel vault roof bears his name, E. J. Sherwood.

Sadly, Sherwood left the employment of The Salvation Army when he was dismissed as an officer in about 1890. A dispute had arisen over the payment of fees for design

11. Original drawing by Sherwood for a standard Hall design

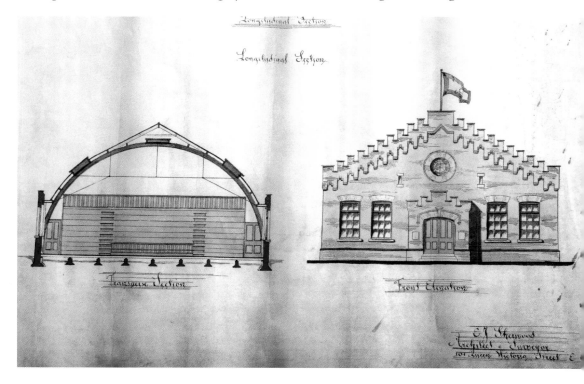

work for the Star Hall building in Manchester. The building was commissioned by Frank Crossley, a successful business man and devout Christian. A staunch supporter of William Booth, he had intended to hand over the completed building to The Salvation Army but then received a call from God to use the building himself to preach holiness.

Crossley paid Sherwood the sum of £134 for the architect fees for the design of the buildings with a further £100 to follow. Sherwood felt that the payment was to him personally. The Salvation Army however felt that all fees were due to them, as Sherwood was an officer in the Army. Sherwood appeared before a Commission of Inquiry and was subsequently dismissed. He initially took Booth to court for unfair dismissal, but on the morning of his appearance at the Assize Court, Sherwood withdrew his action on the advice of his legal counsel.

Sherwood later emigrated to South Africa as he had relatives in Johannesburg. He appears to have developed a successful architectural practice there, for he is mentioned as the architect who designed St John's Methodist Church, after his proposals in Gothic style won a design competition. The church accommodated 400 people with a gallery to seat 80 more with a large chancel window, tower and spire. It was opened in 1894.

Alexander Gordon

In October 1889 Alexander Gordon had been commissioned as a Salvation Army officer and commenced work at International Headquarters working initially in the Survey and Valuation Department. Internal reports to the Salvation Army's Chief of the Staff describe him as good, hard working and most painstaking, loyal and energetic with fair organisation and business skills and good all-round education.

For a time there appears to have been no principal in charge of the Architects Office. However, on 23 February 1893 Alexander Gordon was appointed as Head of the Architects' Department with the rank of Staff Captain. He continued in this post until 1903 with promotions firstly to Major and then to Brigadier. On 10 May 1901 he was elected a Fellow of the Surveyors Institute having completed the necessary professional studies. He was married with children but no further details of his family are known.

An interview with Major Gordon for *The War Cry* of 2 February 1895 reveals much about his personality and motivation as follows:

I was converted at 16 and my one great idea was to be a missionary. From the first I felt the necessity of a wholehearted service. I wanted to leave the profession to which I had been articled 12 months before, but my father did not see the same commercial value in soul-saving as in architecture and overruled my purpose. I thought my calling was mistaken and did not see that the experience I gained then was to be stored up for future usefulness for God.

After years of struggling, I made a definite calm surrender to God in my own bedroom. The architects of The Salvation Army needed more assistance and the position seemed made for me and I knew I was qualified for the post. It was not at the front of the battle, but I feel it none the less important. Sometimes when I speak to a crowd of people in one of our Army barracks I tell them: 'Somebody had to do the thinking before they could come here'. When I hear of glorious results seen in the newly opened barracks, I always feel justified to claim a share in the labours which are thus repaid. So perhaps after all, my early dreams are realised and I am yet something of a missionary. Praise God for an organisation where my technical training can be utilised for the salvation of sinners, instead of building up a personal reputation and a search for gold.

Sadly Alexander Gordon experienced continuing difficulties in managing on a Salvation Army officer's modest salary and on 1 July 1903 he resigned his officership. He continued, however, as an employee of The Salvation Army in the same architects' office.

Oswald Archer

A new Staff Architect was appointed in 1906, namely Oswald Archer, who served in this post until 1935. This was a period of very rapid expansion and a great number of new buildings were erected. These included the William Booth Memorial Corps Halls in Nottingham, William's birth place. The building was designed 'in-house' and a copy of the original drawings, bearing Oswald Archer's name, are still displayed and mounted in the present building. During his period of service many other Army buildings were designed by him personally, as the signatures on the original drawings testify. There are unfortunately few personal details of him in the historical records, possibly because he was an employee and never commissioned as an officer. However, he served in this capacity for almost 30 years, during which period James Vint, his successor, received his training as an architect.

James Henry White Vint

Born on 12 September 1878 to parents who were Salvation Army officers, James Vint came to work in The

Salvation Army Architects Office as a clerk on 16 April 1894 at the age of 15 years. He was commissioned as an officer on 5 November 1900 after six months training, and remained to serve a total of 52 years, the longest serving officer in the history of the Architects Office. He was elected a Fellow of the Surveyors Institute following his long experience and became principal architect to The Salvation Army in 1935. Having been gradually promoted through all the ranks of the time, he continued working in the Architects Office until he retired as a Colonel on 4 October 1946 after three years extended service. He had served in the Architects Office during two world wars and continued to serve on specific assignments after his retirement, in spite of deteriorating health. His commitment to The Salvation Army and this special role are a true example of dedication and hard work. This is particularly of note as the initial reports about him, when he was young, were rather dismissive of his abilities and potential. His long service covers a period of major change for The Salvation Army and for the world at large.

12. Original design drawing by Oswald Archer of Nottingham Memorial Halls

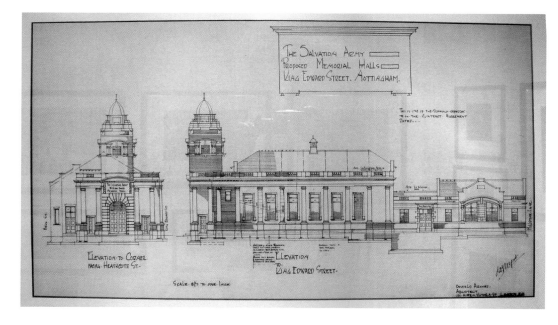

William Henry Charles, LRIBA

William H. Charles was born into a Roman Catholic family at Barrow in Furness, Cumbria on 10 February 1902. Upon leaving school he was unable to find employment in his home town and set off on foot to find work. He eventually walked all the way to Southport on the Lancashire coast. He found lodgings with a Salvation Army family and thus commenced his association with The Salvation Army.

He entered The Salvation Army Clapton Training Garrison in 1922 and was commissioned a Probationary Lieutenant on 10 May 1923 with an initial appointment to a corps, which lasted less than 12 months. Bill Charles, as he became known, was more than 6 feet 3 inches tall, and well built. A car driver by occupation before entering the training college, he was soon appointed to act as chauffeur and bodyguard to General Bramwell Booth, as Salvation Army personnel were still subject to hostility and violence at that time. This particular appointment left Bill with time on his hands, while he waited at various locations for the General.

Mrs General Bramwell Booth took an interest in Bill Charles, encouraging him to improve himself by study. She advised him that The Salvation Army would need specialists in the future and encouraged him to study building construction and architecture, which he did by attending night school classes. After a period in different appointments in both National and International Headquarters he was appointed to the combined Architects and Surveyors Department on 12 December 1932. His studies achieved their goal and Bill was elected a Licentiate of the Royal Institute of British Architects, the first chartered architect on the staff of The Salvation Army.

Bill Charles married Captain Ella Young in June 1927. They subsequently had two sons, one of whom became a chartered quantity surveyor. Bill was gradually promoted to the rank of full Colonel, after being appointed principal of the Architects Office in 1945. Following the retirement of Colonel James Vint, the Architects and Surveyors Department was once again split into two, much against the wishes of Bill Charles. An employee, Ernest Lipscombe, a chartered surveyor, became head of the Surveyors Section.

In addition to his role in the Architects Office, Bill Charles undertook other responsibilities including being the flag carrier for the International Staff Band with the added duty of making all the travel arrangements and organising the transport of instruments, music, etc. The band tours took him to many countries as well as numerous cities in the United Kingdom.

Bill took a special interest in the social work of The Salvation Army. He was known among women social services officers as the 'gentle giant', because of his size and courteous manner. He took a great interest in training the younger members of the Architects Office, such as David Blackwell and Ray Oakley and encouraged them to fully experience the environment of the residential social centres. He claimed that architects needed to sleep in the hostels, alongside the 70-100 men who occupied the large dormitories at that time, if they were to successfully design an appropriate environment for homeless people. He retired in 1967 after 34 years in the architects' office – the last 22 years as Staff Architect. He was succeeded by his assistant, David Blackwell.

David Benjamin Blackwell, ARIBA

As a young evacuee during the Second World War, David Blackwell's first ambition was to be a sea pilot and so to emulate the words of his favourite Army chorus:

> *I have a pilot who guides me*
> *Night and day;*
> *Through cloud and sunshine I trust him,*
> *Come what may.*
> *Dangers may threaten but I never fear;*
> *I'm full of confidence while he is near;*
> *I have a pilot who guides me*
> *Along life's way*
> (*The Song Book of The Salvation Army*, Chorus 132)

He went on to steer, not ships but Army buildings to completion (sometimes as many as 12 a year) in his capacity as Staff Architect then Chief Architect at IHQ and latterly as Senior Projects Manager at THQ. He was born to corps officer parents in 1932 at Braintree in Essex. Sixty years later the New Direction centre for homeless people in that town was named after him to mark his long-standing service as a board member and Chairman of The Salvation Army Housing Association. His flair for art and design became apparent while he was still a boy. Desiring to become an architect, he began work in the IHQ Architects Office when he left school and studied at college part-time for eight years. By his

teens David had become an accomplished euphonium player and was invited to join the International Staff Band. However, Bill Charles, the Staff Architect at that time, told David to make up his mind, to become either an architect or a musician. David therefore left the ISB to concentrate on his architectural studies and training. Wishing to be like Christ, the suffering servant, he believed he should practice non-violent resistance and became a pacifist. Therefore during the period when most 18-year-old men were called up for two years of National Service in the armed forces, David registered as a conscientious objector. He spent those two years working in the allied profession of Quantity Surveying.

Later, during two years in architectural private practice he used his spare time energies to engage in youth work at Catford Corps. David was fascinated by Army history and its unique balance of fervent evangelism allied to social concern. Although he felt called to be a Salvation Army officer, he deferred entering the training college for many years. His officer father, Benjamin Blackwell, had died unexpectedly when David was in his teens, so he stayed at home to support his mother, younger brother and sister. He eventually felt able to leave home to train as a Salvation Army Officer, entering the Heroes of the Faith Session in 1962. After commissioning in 1964, he returned to the Architects Office at IHQ as Assistant Staff Architect. With characteristic quiet enthusiasm he played a major part in the *For God's Sake Care!* programme to upgrade social centres throughout the UK.

His interest in London's youth was revealed through his leadership of the Regent Hall Youth Club, in Oxford Street. The new lieutenant possessed all the necessary qualities of genuine interest in the individual, a love of debate and a degree of flamboyancy and humour. In 1968 he married Lieutenant Elisabeth Kopp, the start of 30 years of marriage, raising three daughters. When their first child was born with Down's Syndrome he spontaneously told his wife, 'Then we shall love her even more'; an unperturbed attitude from which his wife derived much strength and which brought beauty into their initial sadness. The last suite of halls that Blackwell designed and completed before retirement was for Thornton Heath Corps, where he was a soldier, young people's worker and bandsman for many years.

During his time as Chief Architect, David provided many documents to assist corps in developing their client's brief before an architect was instructed to design their new buildings. These included a questionnaire to encourage corps to re-think the purpose and require-ments of the corps and a document entitled *Plan Your Hall's Kit*, which gave detailed information about activities to consider, their space requirements and costs. He made available alternative designs for items such as the penitents' form and platforms as well as examples of typical different sized halls. David left his particular imprint on many Salvation Army halls, reflecting changes of programme and styles of worship; such as flexible seating and a movable dais that brought the meeting leader closer to the congregation. Rooms formerly used solely by music sections became designed for multi-purpose usage. He felt that his work as an architect had a touch of the sacred in designing places where Salvationists were inspired to serve God more effectively. He was also immensely practical and introduced planned maintenance guidance, initially for all the Social Services buildings but later for corps buildings as well.

He found time to paint in water colour and to draw rather cheeky ink caricatures of people attending Salvation Army business meetings, whenever the agenda became tedious.

Within months of his retirement in 1990, David Blackwell was 'Promoted to Glory'. Long-standing business contacts then revealed that they always regarded him as a Christian in commerce. He was indeed an officer and a gentleman to all who knew him.

Ray Oakley, M.Sc, RIBA, FRICS

Ray was born on 28 February 1937 in Manchester and in his early years rarely saw his father who was serving in the Medical Corps of the British Army during the Second World War. Ray attended the Sunday School at the Star Hall Corps in Manchester, where his aunt was the Primary Sergeant for more than 40 years. During his later teenage years and early twenties Ray was involved in most of the corps activities. His particular love was work with the young people, both in the Sunday School and in the Torchbearer Youth Club, where he was the player-manager of their amateur football team. He met his wife Brenda through the youth club activities and was married in June 1961. Ray had left school at 16 years of age and worked for Sumner Smith & Partners, a firm of Quantity Surveyors in Manchester, studying part-time. He completed his training and became a chartered surveyor in the same year that he married. Just fifteen months later at the end of August 1962, he and Brenda entered the William Booth Memorial Training College in the Heroes of the Faith Session to commence training as Salvation Army officers and had their first contact with fellow cadet David Blackwell.

Brenda and Ray already had a three month old baby son, Paul, whom they had to leave with friends in Manchester before entering training. The William Booth College could not accept children, as they had no facilities at that time for them. After just nine months training they were appointed as corps officers to Yiewsley in West London. However, twins, Mark and Joy, were born just a month before that first appointment. They arrived therefore at their first corps with three children under 13 months of age. Sadly, one of the twins, Mark, died at the age of nine months from that mysterious illness described as a 'cot death'. Some three years later another child was born to Brenda and Ray, a girl whom they named April. She brought them much joy and her birth helped heal the pain of their earlier loss.

In November 1964, after only 18 months at Yiewsley Corps, Ray was appointed to the Architects Office at IHQ as he was already a Chartered Surveyor. This new appointment necessitated a further nine years in part-time studies for him to qualify as an architect. All of his 15 years of study to qualify both as a surveyor and an architect were undertaken part-time while he worked in a professional office. Ray became the IHQ Staff Architect in 1980, sharing this period of leadership with David Blackwell. In 1990, after the division of the administrations of THQ and IHQ, he became the Chief Architect to THQ, although he was retained by IHQ as their Consultant Architect.

In 1980 Ray achieved a Masters degree in Environmental Psychology, following one year's full-time study at the University of Surrey. He took homelessness as the topic for his dissertation, being anxious to understand more fully the experience of being homeless. He also wanted to ensure that the design of new centres would aid their therapeutic purpose. Following further extensive research on homelessness by Surrey University, he received a dual

appointment as Director of the London Homelessness Project in addition to his role as Chief Architect. In 1993 he became Director of Research and Development for The Salvation Army Social Services, a role later expanded to include corps community work. He remained in that appointment until retirement on 1 January 2003.

Ray remained a soldier – that is a member – of Catford Corps for 40 years, carrying out a variety of leadership tasks there. During his time at IHQ, Ray also undertook a number of special overseas tasks, including visits to resolve Salvation Army property and financial issues in Portugal, Brazil and Russia. He was involved in most of the major social projects developed in the United Kingdom over a period of 40 years, as well as many corps projects. He also advised on a variety of major projects for International Headquarters, including the new IHQ building opened in 2004.

Ray summed up his work in Winston Churchill's words: 'Give us the tools and we will finish the job' as he saw himself primarily as a provider of facilities to allow The Salvation Army to continue its mission.

David Greenwood, DipArch, RIBA, FCSD

David studied architecture at Manchester and Canterbury Colleges of Art, receiving his diploma in 1966. After working for two years in London and Bristol he joined The Salvation Army Architects Office in 1968.

His first task was to design a complex of buildings in Nottingham around the birthplace of William Booth, founder of The Salvation Army. The project included a homeless families hostel, a community centre, an elderly persons residential care home and a museum in the restored former home of William Booth, which became the focal point of the complex. Upon completion, the scheme received a Civic Trust Award and was featured in Nicholas Pevsner's *Buildings of England*.

Following completion of the Nottingham project in late 1971, David was recruited through the Ministry of Overseas Development to work for the Government of Zambia. During the next five years he designed a variety of government buildings throughout Zambia, together with High Commission projects for the Zambian Ministry of Foreign Affairs in the neighbouring countries of Malawi, Kenya and Tanzania. Through the Zambia Institute of Architects he organised and supervised preparatory courses in design and architectural history for Zambian students selected to study architecture in the UK.

On his return home in the late 1970s David rejoined The Salvation Army Architects Office and continued to design new major projects including social service hostels, churches/community centres and a conference centre. Many of these projects, which included Brighton Congress Hall and Sunbury Court Conference Centre were in conservation areas. This required sensitive negotiations where David was able to use his design and presentation skills to acquire planning approval. Several of these buildings have received national and local awards.

David was appointed Chief Architect at THQ in 1995 and continued until 2000, the first employee since Oswald Archer to be appointed to this position. When David relinquished this position he continued to work in the Architects Office as a part time consultant. During this period he prepared the master plan for the re-establishment of The Salvation Army's Training Project at Hadleigh in Essex. This involved obtaining planning approval within the green belt for a visitor centre and tea rooms overlooking Hadleigh Castle and the Thames Estuary. The designs also included a new church/community centre for Hadleigh Corps in the town centre.

In January 2003, after the closure of The Salvation Army Architects Office, David, with several of his colleagues, joined the private firm of Swanke Hayden Connell Architects, working as a part time consultant. Since retiring David continues his involvement with architecture through sketching buildings observed on his travels and painting in water colour.

Patrick Spears BA (Hons), DipArch, RIBA

Patrick studied architecture at Sheffield University, completing his Diploma in 1986. He initially worked for private architects, Carr Goldsmith and Fallek and for Elsworth Sykes Partnership in London, before joining The Salvation Army Architects Office in February 1988. Patrick was appointed Chief Architect at THQ in June 2000. Patrick's wife Doreen is an architect who also worked for a number of years in The Salvation Army Architects Office.

During his time in the Architects Office, Patrick specialised in the development of elderly care residential homes, designing centres at Southend-on-Sea, Glasgow and Coventry. His first elderly persons' care home at Southend-on-Sea won the inaugural, annual Borough Council Design Awards Scheme in 1994. Patrick also worked as design and project architect on a variety of other buildings including hostels in London and church/community centres in Sheffield, Doncaster, Deptford and Stowmarket. In addition he had overall responsibility for the design and delivery of all projects in the office during his tenure as Chief Architect.

Just prior to the intended closure of The Salvation Army Architects Office, Patrick joined the private architects firm of SHCA, in November 2002, as a Senior Associate together with other colleagues from The Salvation Army's office. Patrick continued the design work on schemes commenced at the Salvation Army office, including the new Hopetown Women's Hostel and Supported Housing Scheme in Whitechapel and the new Riverside Men's Hostel and Supported Housing Scheme in Docklands. Patrick was the last in-house chief architect to be appointed by The Salvation Army at Territorial Headquarters.

Comments on SA Architects Office

From 1880 until 1990 The Salvation Army Architects Office was part of IHQ, but the work undertaken was almost entirely concerned with Army buildings in the British Isles. As far as the international scene was concerned its only role was an advisory one although individual members were occasionally sent on trouble-shooting visits to overseas territories. No other territory had an in-house architect's office, although for short periods an architect was occasionally employed in an advisory capacity within some territorial property departments.

It is interesting to read a paper on 'Architectural Development for Salvation Army Buildings' presented at the Executive Officer Councils of the USA Eastern Territory by Lieut-Colonel George F. Russell on 16 November 1966. Having reviewed new Army corps schemes across the four USA territories, he was critical of the absence of any particular consistent Army style or character in these buildings, which in his view also failed to create an appropriate atmosphere for Christian worship. He quotes the findings of a Commissioner's Conference that 'the place of worship is second only to conduct' and in conclusion states that 'building a place of worship, a sanctuary, is the most important building task we have to face'. It seems therefore that at this time the Army leaders in other countries were conscious of the contribution that building design could make in aiding or hindering worship. In his presentation Colonel Russell also set out a process of development control which he hoped would overcome many of the concerns he had over the way new schemes in the USA were organised at that time. The principles of that process appear to be based on those used in the UK by the Architects Office at IHQ.

All new building projects and major extensions or alteration schemes in the British Isles were organised by the Architects Office within the IHQ Property Department. Some projects would be designed and supervised by the in-house architects and others delegated to private architects, but still under the supervision of the in-house staff. There were many periods of intense activity but probably the most productive was between 1980 and 1990 when some 16 staff in this office were not only responsible for all of the Salvation Army projects but also for most of the Salvation Army Housing Association schemes, during a period of major housing association development. The Salvation Army Architects Office was one of the few architectural practices designing new hostels at this time, so the Salvation Army Staff Architect was used as a consultant to the UK government's Department of Environment to establish the required standards and cost yardsticks for all new government-funded hostel buildings.

A number of major capitalization schemes were undertaken during this period to raise funds for new social projects. Planning permission for a change of use was required in order to realise the maximum capital returns on three sites. In two of the following schemes it was necessary to appeal through a public inquiry and in the other to undertake long and delicate negotiations with the City of London planning office.

The projects concerned were:
- For the site of the Red Shield Hostel in Westminster to be used for offices.
- For part of the farm land at Hadleigh to be developed for housing.
- For the site of the Middlesex Street Hostel and Men's Social Services HQ to be used for offices.

Each proposal was successful and the sale of these three sites raised about £25 million for The Salvation Army Social Trust. Other schemes which The Salvation Army intended to develop themselves which also necessitated a planning appeal and a public enquiry included:
- Redevelopment of the Spa Road site in Bermondsey
- New family flats for cadets at the William Booth College at Denmark Hill.
- Redevelopment of the Regent Hall site in London's Oxford Street.

David Blackwell and Ray Oakley conducted the delicate planning negotiations and acted as expert witnesses for The Salvation Army in these appeal cases with Slaughter and May acting as solicitors and the same barrister, Anthony Dinkin QC, presenting the Salvation Army case.

During this decade a large proportion of the major schemes, particularly those schemes for the social work and SAHA, were designed by the in-house staff. The fees charges were generally 1% below those recommended by the RIBA and charged by private architects. As VAT was not applicable to in-house services a further 1% of the building cost was also saved on those fees. In spite of charging these reduced fees, the Architects Office made sufficient profit in some years during this period to cover the total operating costs of the whole IHQ Property Department.

Sadly with the closure of the Architects Office on 1 January 2003, the considerable knowledge, expertise and experience in relation to Salvation Army buildings, particularly for social developments, was lost together with this fee earning capacity. The intellectual capital built up over those 122 years had been considerable and the Salvation Army buildings developed over that period had benefitted from William Booth's foresight in establishing this office. The Salvation Army at both IHQ and THQ would in future have to depend primarily on outside consultants for advice, although after the closure of the Architects Office, an architect was appointed as advisor on new developments. This architect, Thomas Burfitt-Williams, has now become the Head of Major Development Projects at THQ.

William Booth had discovered the value of research data to aid in his proposals to tackle some of the social evils of his day, as described in his book *In Darkest England and the Way Out*. He wanted the Army to keep informed about social needs to ensure that its plans and actions were similarly based on up-to-date information. He therefore set up an Intelligence Department for this purpose. By the 1970s however this role had been largely forgotten with the last semblance of it on International

Headquarters being the title of 'Intelligence Officer' added to the job description of the General's chaffeur. There was therefore in some areas of social concern, especially regarding homelessness, a paucity of information available to the Army. The Salvation Army Architects Office therefore took the initiative to encourage its staff to research many of these issues whenever they had opportunity, such as during academic studies for their professional qualifications, as listed in later chapters. But it was not until the 1990s, after the establishment of a separate UK Headquarters, that a specific Research and Development Unit was set up. This was initially for the Social Services but it soon became available to all Army programmes, with the Army's chief architect appointed as its director soon after it had been established.

The profiles of those who have directed The Salvation Army Architects Office show how God can take ordinary people and do extraordinary things for them and through them; a comment that could apply to so many people who serve God in The Salvation Army. Of course many others gave years of service in the Architects Office, in such roles as assistants and project managers, as well as those in the surveyors and conveyancing sections who also contributed immensely to the development of Army buildings. Valuable contributions have also been made by innumerable private architects to whom the functions of the staff architects have been delegated.

The Salvation Army Architects Office was always part of the Property Department and the heads of that department, the Property Secretaries and their assistants, were very supportive, generally allowing architects a great deal of freedom and autonomy in their activities, especially when it was part of International Headquarters. It was a period in Army history when significant progress was made in the quantity and quality of the buildings developed within the British Isles. The international Army also benefitted from shared property expertise used in the vetting of major overseas projects and the development of property approval systems.

CORPS BUILDINGS

13. Aberdeen
Citadel

Introduction

Corps buildings serve local branches of The Salvation Army as evangelical mission stations, places of worship and centres for community service. Some aspects of Salvation Army corps and their requirements have changed dramatically since The Salvation Army commenced, while other aspects remain basically the same.

As previously mentioned, Booth's plan to convert people to a vibrant Christian faith and then direct them to attend their local church services proved to be unworkable for a variety of reasons. Many 'respectable' members of the established churches considered the converts from Booth's Mission to be uncouth and undesirable.

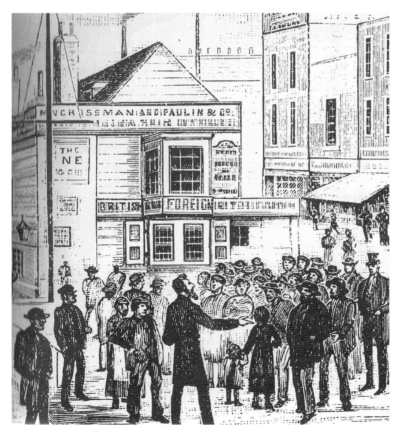

Furthermore, the formal church services were in total contrast to the form of mission meetings led by William Booth, added to which, church buildings were often austere in appearance and cold in atmosphere. William also needed some of his new converts to help him in his work and by their testimonies to influence others from a similar background to commit themselves to Christ.

In an Open University course on Religion and Society, John Kent stated:

> *The medieval interiors of the churches failed to communicate a God of love relevant to the lives of poor people. Consequently the poor were generally antagonistic to the religion as symbolised by the established churches. This was the environment into which The Salvation Army was born. They had a new set of symbols in flags, uniforms and bands instead of crosses, incense, cassocks and organs. They sang songs to well-known tunes and used simple language to express their faith. The interior of their citadels resembled music halls rather than traditional churches.*

The rejection of Booth's converts by the established church seems to have resulted in Booth feeling that anything labelled '*church*' was a hindrance to his mission. Booth had already adopted a style of meeting which was more closely aligned to the characteristics of a music hall than the typical church service and he initially made use of music halls and other secular buildings. Therefore both the settings and form of these meetings were in surroundings familiar to those attending and of a style where his 'congregation' felt at home. One of his best known sayings is: '*Why should the devil have all the best tunes?*' However, this quotation reflected Booth's general approach to spiritual warfare, as he seems to have also

14. Drawing of open-air meeting led by William Booth

wondered why the devil should have all the best methods to win people's allegiance!

His evangelical meetings contained hearty singing with a variety of musicians taking part, personal testimonies to God's power to change lives and fervent preaching and prayers. They contained a rich variety of entertainment and challenge, as well as providing the offer of a better life to people who had few prospects of improvement in this world. Booth's aim was not just to change individuals but also to change society.

Kent also stated that:

Some saw The Salvation Army as a bastion against revolution by the discontented masses, as the efforts of The Salvation Army redirected their energies into spiritual warfare and into improving society by peaceful means.

The nature of these meetings and Booth's apparent dislike of 'churchy' things no doubt played their part in The Salvation Army creating its own symbols of religious faith, as Kent mentioned, in the crest, flag and penitents form, and their buildings' resemblance to music halls, rather than church buildings. In fact it has taken almost 100 years for the term 'church' to be applied to Salvation Army halls in the United Kingdom, presumably because the term had been seen by Booth as a stumbling block to The Salvation Army's early mission. In some other parts of the world, where The Salvation Army has spread, the term does not appear to have evoked the same prejudicial associations, and the term 'Salvation Army Church' has been used for a long time in relation to Salvation Army corps buildings. However, today, even in the United Kingdom the main hall is sometimes described as a church and the meetings as services.

The absence of this label 'church' has greatly affected the design of Salvation Army halls in the UK. Until recent years, the principal criterion affecting decisions, relating both to Salvation Army activity as well as the design of its buildings, was not *'is this appropriate for a Christian church?'* but *'is it Army?'* This emphasis was presumably in order to retain many of the unique features of The Salvation Army's work and worship, which were seen as distinct from those of other Christian denominations.

Christian Mission Days

For the working-class people of the mid-nineteenth century, living conditions were deplorable and those of the inhabitants of London's East End were among the worst. Dwellings were cramped and insanitary, with unemployment and starvation rife. When work was available, conditions were arduous and hours long. More often than not, the meagre earnings received were squandered on alcohol from the cheap beer shops or gin palaces. It was to these people that William Booth's heart went out in 1865, and their needs inspired him to commence the Christian Mission. He realised that 'salvation of the soul' was the key to salvation of the body.

Few churches of the day had room for the poor or the outcast, and they in turn despised religion. Going out on the street and presenting the gospel message in ways which they could understand was the only way to get a response. Many were attracted by this approach to evangelism, as well as by the offer of a better way of life. Notorious characters were reformed and they testified to a change of heart. They then, in turn, attracted their friends and people of a similar disposition, who only knew that they wanted to get what their friends had received.

One great problem was to find premises suitable to

house the large number of people who flocked to hear the message. Any building was welcome that offered a large floor space and a fair degree of protection from the weather, as well as from opponents of the Mission. A variety of places were therefore commandeered. The first, a large dancing saloon at 23 New Road, Whitechapel, known as the Assembly Rooms, was rented for a guinea a day. In those early days it seated 350 people and the seats were carried in each Sunday morning after the dancers had left. Theatres and music halls were often hired for the occasion, especially on Sundays, when licensing laws prohibited public performances.

A CHANGE OF PERFORMANCE!
WANTED:
3,000 TO FILL THE EFFINGHAM THEATRE.

These were the words which formed part of the advertisements when, in February 1867, Sunday meetings were transferred from the dancing saloon. The layout of the theatre with its galleries and stalls encircling the stage was ideal for these meetings and visitors felt at ease in such familiar surroundings. The leaders of the mission

were seated at the rear of the stage with the front occupied by a long bench or penitents form. William Booth believed in potential converts making a bold and public declaration of their intentions, so that they would be invited to come forward and kneel at this bench.

The use of these premises and other theatres, such as the Portsmouth Music Hall, had a considerable influence in determining the layout and character of the early meeting halls which were to follow. An early Mission leader advocating the use of such public buildings stated:

15. *Drawing of Effingham Theatre. (far left)*

16. *Drawing of meeting in Portsmouth Music Hall*

What more suitable building could we possibly have for close, thorough dealing with the heart? Every eye can see the preacher's face, every ear could catch his slightest whisper and the people seemed all close around him, piled together like an open-air crowd. Everyone seems to be facing you, as if there were only two of you present.

Smaller meetings of the missioners and converts were held in other premises. The first week-night meeting had been held in an old wool store in Satchwell Street, Bethnal Green. Other premises used included a stable entered through an open court off Whitechapel Road and a hayloft off Mile End Waste. Various chapels were tried, but were not considered to be very suitable, because of the reluctance of people to enter a church building. Sunday schools for children were held in one or two places, but were not generally encouraged in those early days. In 1866 the Christian Mission acquired its first building, a wool store off Cambridge Road, Bethnal Green, which later became a carpenter's shop.

New preaching stations were set up in 1867 and a variety of premises with rather distinctive characteristics were adapted and used. The Union Temperance Hall, in the High Street, Poplar was one such place, separated from stables and pigsties only by a wooden partition, through which the stench of the animals would freely permeate. Use was also made of the Alexander Hall, a covered skittle alley attached to a public house in Raven Street, Whitechapel. Here it was necessary to board over the ninepin frames to form the platform. That place later became a printing workshop. Another mission room was situated behind a 'pigeon shop', where noisy animals and birds were bartered while the meetings proceeded. Other buildings such as the Edinburgh Castle Tavern in Stepney and a room in a factory were similarly used as preaching stations.

During that year the Mission's first headquarters was established in a former beer shop called the 'Eastern Star', in Whitechapel Road. The American-style bowling alley there was adapted to seat 300 people and its shop was used for the sale of religious literature with the parlour as a reading and refreshment room. Mothers' meetings and Bible classes were held in the concert room. These facilities were very suitable for new members who wished to escape the wrath of their families and former acquaintances.

17. Eastern Star 1867

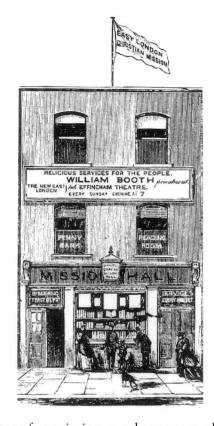

Living quarters for mission workers were also provided, although this practice was not widely adopted. A similar centre was set up for a short time in a converted but previously infamous coffee house in Shoreditch.

Continued unemployment at this time had intensified distress and the Mission began to distribute food and clothing to the poor. Soup kitchens were also opened and free teas provided. This service operated in Poplar and also in Shoreditch. Plans were formed to build a new meeting hall to seat 1,000 people. It was to be a plain hall and the cost of construction was estimated at £500. This was the first recorded design of a proposed new building scheme but no evidence is available that it was ever built.

Early in 1868 the Apollo Music Hall in Hare Street, Shoreditch with a seating capacity of 600 became available and was used until the activity was later transferred to 'the old pudding shop'. In October of that year a 'penny gaff', known as the 'Eastern Alhambra', opposite Limehouse Church, was also converted for use as a Mission Hall. During the following year a tin plate factory in Bethnal Green was adapted to provide two halls, one seating 300 people and the other 200, as well as a soup kitchen and other facilities. A railway arch, at the East End of Bethnal Green Road, was also taken over and five years later lengthened to accommodate 400 people as well as to provide a vestry and other rooms. That building was the home of Bethnal Green Corps for some time. Its shape possibly influenced the concept used in the design of several early halls, such as the design for a standard hall, previously illustrated. Those halls had a barrel-vaulted ceiling, resembling the railway arch, but supported on semi-circular timber trusses.

The rapid expansion of the Christian Mission and the need for a central focus made it essential to establish a central meeting hall. A commercial developer had erected a building to house a People's Market in Whitechapel, but this venture had proved unsuccessful. The building was offered for sale and seemed ideal for the purposes of the mission. William Booth eventually negotiated the

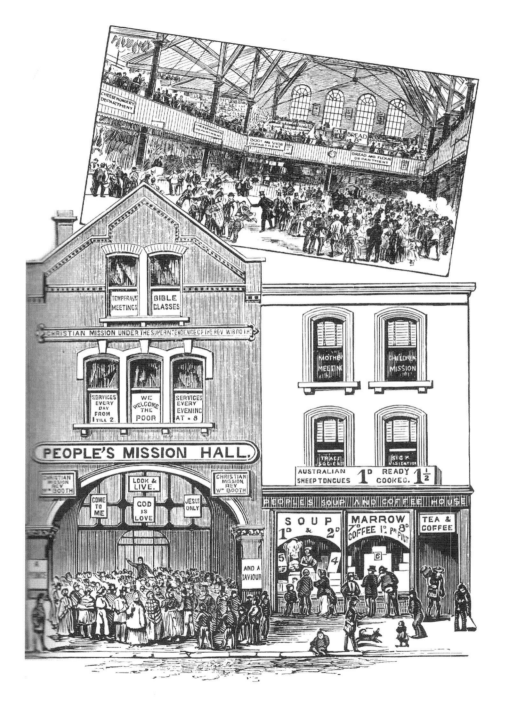

purchase of a 29-year lease for £1,750.

In order to carry out the necessary alterations, Booth decided to appoint architects. This was the first recorded use of architects, namely Messrs Habershon and Pite, who supervised the alterations costing £1,500. The Market Hall was reported to seat 1,500 people comfortably and 2,000 people if crowded in. Ten other rooms, a large shop and a soup kitchen were also included. Recorded comments about the hall included: *'It had been ascertained that the acoustic properties of the building gave no reason for fear'*. In adapting the premises it was suggested that the stone paved floor should be asphalted. To this approach William Booth replied quickly: *'No! Poor people feel the cold quite as much, if not more, than rich people do. We shall have a wooden floor and the place shall be heated by hot water apparatus'*. On Sunday 10 April 1870, the occasion of William's 41st birthday, he opened the People's Mission Hall, just five years after the first tent meeting had taken place.

By 1870 the Mission's efforts in East London were concentrated upon securing buildings that would be entirely for the Mission's use, whether they were rented, purchased or purpose-built. The formation of its forces into self-contained units showed that the organisation was acquiring a more definite and permanent structure. In the Mission's first constitution, provision was made for all property to be held in trust by 12 people. However, that arrangement did not continue for long and was later rescinded.

Expansion outside the East End of London was inevitable. Already in 1867 the Assembly Rooms at Margate had been hired for Mrs Booth's campaign and in 1869 the work was established in Croydon at the Workmen's Hall which seated 700 people. New corps buildings were built there soon after, in 1887. Efforts

were made to commence mission stations at Brighton in 1869 and Tunbridge Wells in 1872. The first new hall erected by the Christian Mission at Ninfield in Sussex had been completed in 1871 then later, in 1907, it became a United Methodist chapel which is still in use today. In 1877 a 'Salvation Warehouse' was opened in Leicester, while at Bradford, Saturday evening salvation meetings were held in the Pullen's Theatre of Varieties.

The assorted buildings which were adapted and used in this early period have been described at length in order to illustrate the dynamic nature of the early Christian Mission. The creativity involved in making use of these buildings for the Christian Mission's purpose is typical of the ingenuity and strength of purpose which resulted in the rapid expansion of the movement during the next quarter of a century.

A New Name: 'The Salvation Army'

Militant Christianity was much in people's minds in the late 19th century. The north of England was being 'attacked' by the Christian Mission and in October 1877 a certain Elijah Cadman had 'opened fire', calling for volunteers to join 'The Hallelujah Army'. During his campaign at Whitby, meetings in the local 'Congress Hall' were regularly attended by 3,000 people, about one in seven of the population of that town. The idea caught on and about May 1878, the Mission became known as 'The Salvation Army'. Military ranks and emblems were instituted, orders and regulations issued and flags and brass bands introduced. The first use of the term 'barracks' as applied to the Army's halls appeared in January 1879.

The following facts give some idea of the amazing expansion which the Army was undergoing. At the beginning of 1881 there were 172 corps, but by the end of 1883 that figure was 528. Up to this time meetings had been held in small buildings with public buildings hired as required for large gatherings and special campaigns. However, it became obvious that if corps were to be established permanently they would need premises of their own and of sufficient size to accommodate large numbers.

The harvest of these ready-made halls began in earnest the following year. In York, the Gillygate skating rink was used, seating 4,000 people. A second corps in York was soon operating in a circus building at Fishergate. A second corps also opened in Hull, leasing a former icehouse as its permanent premises, where the corps naturally became known as 'Hull Icehouse'. In order to create a large meeting hall there, a wall through

20. Drawing of Bristol Circus exterior. (Far left)

21. Drawing of Bristol Circus interior

A few years earlier a craze for roller skating had swept through England, so that most towns and cities had their own skating rinks. Other large buildings were erected to house circuses, but neither of those ventures had proved popular for very long. In August 1880, Herbert Booth, a son of the Founder, was sent to open a corps in Bristol. In his search for suitable premises he found a dilapidated building, which had previously housed a circus. It was called Backfields in the district of St Paul's. It required some £200 to be spent on renovations, but it then provided seating capacity for 2,250 people. From then on this corps was known as 'Bristol Circus' until the building burnt down in 1893.

the middle of that building was replaced by pillars with a gallery to give a total seating capacity for 3,000 people. A rink hall at Chester and a circus building in the same town were simultaneously used and filled to their respective capacities of 2,000 and 3,000.

At Oldham in Lancashire a contemporary evening newspaper reported:

The notorious Salvation Army stormed Oldham yesterday and effected a lodgement at the Skating Rink where Mr Butterworth has, at great expense, thrown up breastworks and fortifications.

22. Converted Skating Rink at Oldham, Lancashire

The rent was £200 per annum plus gas. These buildings were admirably suited to the purposes of the Army. The tiered seating permitted an excellent view of the arena and at one end a platform and penitents' form were erected. This was a pattern of design which architects and builders of future Salvation Army halls would adopt.

The year 1882 proved to be eventful. Not only was the movement rapidly growing throughout the country, but in London four important buildings were acquired. In March, the General opened one of those buildings, namely the Regent Hall near Oxford Circus. This is perhaps the most familiar of the converted skating rinks still being used and is known universally as 'The Rink'. An insignificant entrance on to Oxford Street leads to the large meeting hall, which originally seated 1,000 people, but was later enlarged with a gallery around its three

sides. This tunnel entrance has an interesting history in that it was originally just the means of access into the open yard of livery stables beyond. After this yard was converted to a skating rink and then into the Army hall, there was a dispute over the nature of the ownership of this tunnel. William Booth fixed posters to the side walls advertising the meetings but the building's owners objected. It went to court and William Booth was not only successful in his legal action but he established a very unusual, if not unique, classification of ownership called a 'flying freehold'. This was unusual because at that time the Army did not own the basement or ground beneath, nor the walls at the side, nor the space above. It is from this tunnel that every Sunday a 30–35 piece brass band still forms up and commences to play rousing marches as it emerges onto the busy and perhaps the most famous shopping street in Britain, to the amazement of the crowds of shoppers who come to Oxford Street from around the world. In recent years a well-known artist, Rosa Branson, painted six pictures in oils, depicting and symbolising the corps activity, to hang on these walls and thus enhance this passage to help attract visitors to enter the main worship hall and the other facilities beyond.

In 1882 a building was also urgently required for use as a national centre for training new officers. The opportunity was quickly seized when the London Orphan Asylum at Clapton became available. This building, erected in 1821 at a cost of £60,000, had previously housed 600 children in wings around a quadrangle. The Army provided a roof over this area and a timber floor to create a spacious hall, which could accommodate up to 5,000 people. Other meeting halls and classrooms were provided in the wings and 300 cadets could be housed in the home at any one time. The total cost of this building was £15,000 purchase price bought at auction plus £23,000 for the necessary alterations.

23. Tunnel
entrance to
Regent Hall. (Far
left)

24. Regent Hall
interior (Left)

25. Rosa
Branson's oil
paintings
symbolising
Regent Hall
Corps activity.
(Only two
shown of the six
donated for use
in entrance
tunnel)

26. Clapton Congress Hall and National Training Barracks. (Above)

27. Drawing of the Eagle Tavern, after takeover by The Army 1882. (Right)

This National Training Barracks and Congress Hall were opened, amid great celebrations, on 13 May 1882. The buildings were used as a training centre until the William Booth Memorial Training College in Denmark Hill was opened in 1929. The Clapton Congress Hall Corps continued to operate from within this building for 40 years after the cadets had left, but it was sold in 1969 to the local authority. The remaining portions of the building have now been carefully repaired and restored to form part of Clapton Portico, a new learning centre for children and young adults.

In 1882 another conquest was made when the Army purchased the remaining 16 years of the lease of the 'Eagle', a famous public house with theatre attached, in London's City Road. This was the building made famous by the song 'pop goes the weasel'. The tavern was fitted out as a hostel for 70 persons and the 'Grecian' Theatre there served admirably as a meeting hall.

The following is an extract taken from a letter dated 5 July 1882 written by William Booth, presumably, to potential donors to whom he appeals for help to cover the costs as follows:

Purchase of the Eagle, the Grecian Theatre and Dancing Grounds

My dear friend,

We have secured the Lease of the above notorious premises for £16,750. The Grecian Theatre, the Dancing Pavilion, the Dancing Saloon, and the Assembly Room will seat 10,000 persons; so that we shall be able to accommodate congregations of 10,000 at once besides having the "Eagle" house, another dwelling house and stables. Standing amidst a dense working-class population five minutes walk from the Hall of Science and known far and wide, the building will give us an opportunity far superior to any we have hitherto of gathering tens of thousands of the worst of people together, and we trust that a great many of those who have formerly been seen there dancing their way to destruction will be found on the same spot rejoicing in the Lord and leading others to follow Him.

WE HAVE ONLY THREE WEEKS in which to complete payment, so that we must have help at once. The Archbishop of Canterbury was almost the first to assist us in the matter, His Chaplain writes us – His Grace has no hesitation in approving the acquisition by you of premises at present used for so different a purpose and although his contribution can be only a nominal one, I am authorized to say that you can put down the Archbishop's name as a subscriber of £5, for which I enclose a cheque.

Her Most Gracious Majesty the Queen (Victoria), the Bishop of London, the Right Hon. Earl Cairns, the Lord Mayor, the ex-Lord Mayor, and others of influence have also expressed their warm sympathy with us,

Surely this scheme must commend itself to all lovers of morality, and those who are heartily with us must still more rejoice at the prospect of seeing so great a work of Salvation established on the Devil's own ground.

It is hard for us now to appreciate the excitement, turmoil and opposition that the acquisition created in 1882. The acquisition of the Eagle Tavern by a temperance movement caused great concern that 'the poor man would be robbed of his beer', perceived to be the limit of human hardship that it was possible to impose. The violence was more massive and concentrated than encountered anywhere else previously with a mob, estimated at 30,000, thronging the nearby streets at one time. It was only by the intervention and skilful use of a large contingent of police that serious injuries and deaths were avoided amongst the Salvationists. It was not only in the streets that William Booth encountered determined opposition to this acquisition but also in the law courts. Eventually most of the legal battles were also won, but Booth was forced to accept that the Eagle Tavern would have to continue as a public house selling alcohol; otherwise he would be forced to forfeit the lease to the whole premises. Although the Eagle Tavern was managed by another tenant, this situation caused William Booth much pain that he was technically the licensee and it left him open to much criticism of hypocrisy. The period of the lease expired in 1898 and so the whole property then passed from the Army's ownership.

At Camberwell a large meeting hall was acquired, which had been built for the activities of an evangelist, Ned Wright. It was considered to be very suitable and with various improvements and alterations, it remained in use until 1994, when it was replaced by a much smaller

Salvation Army building and some flats for resettling homeless men.

The Salvation War 1882 contained a section about property and gave this view on important aspects relating to the design and use of buildings at that time:

The Army has acquired more property in 1882 than in all the previous seventeen years of its history. We never build except where it is impossible to rent buildings large enough for our purposes and we spend no money on needless ornamentation. It will be seen at a glance that the form we give to our buildings, as well as the name barracks, as far as any arrangement can, ensures neither being nor appearing to be intended for any other purpose than that for which they are at present used. We do not profess by any means to be satisfied, however, with our accomplishments so far, in the way of hall building. In this, as in everything else, we have everything to learn. But with the assistance of an architect and others connected with the building trade, who have devoted themselves to this department of the work for the love of it, we hope before another year is over to have made good progress in the discovery of that form of building capable of containing the largest number of people to be erected at the lowest possible cost. We hope to build Salvation warehouses everywhere, as commodious and strong as our present barracks, yet capable of accommodating a given number of persons at a much lower cost than our present average of £1 per person. It will be remembered this is a much lower rate of expenditure than is commonly approved of nowadays in connection with ecclesiastical architecture.

At this time, all property was held in trust by William Booth or his successor on behalf of The Salvation Army.

Corps Halls 1883–1900

The main factors which influenced the design of many of the new 'barracks', built during the remainder of the 19th century can be summarised as follows:

A change of policy was made to secure or construct permanent buildings for all corps. The idea was to obviate the uncertainty associated with short-term leasing of premises. Flourishing corps needed large halls to accommodate the maximum number of people at the least possible cost. Local Building Scheme Companies were formed and shares sold with attractive rates of interest to raise the necessary capital for the development. Shop premises or dwellings were often incorporated into the development to increase the investment potential.

Secondly, a distinctive appearance was required so that Salvation Army buildings could be easily recognised for what they were. Military forms had been adopted for other purposes and this seemed to be the obvious choice for the style of architectural treatment. The idea for the buildings to resemble barracks, fortresses, castles and citadels seemed the logical approach. Interiors were arranged after the manner of the theatre, skating rink or music hall. Wooden forms were used as they could seat the maximum number of people.

A third factor arose from the employment of a staff architect to be responsible for most of the new buildings throughout the country. This policy resulted in a consistency and uniformity in design. However, the architectural fashion of the period, the Victorian era, with its hybrid of ornamentation did affect the design of some detailing.

Military imagery permeated the early purpose-built halls, which often had red brick façades with battlemented parapets and flanking towers decorated with crusader cross openings. Photographs of halls at Sheffield, Edmonton and Rochdale illustrate some of these aspects. In the 1980s the Salvation Army's own architect's office adopted as its logo a drawing of the Sheffield Citadel building, because of the historical importance of these designs.

28. Edmonton Citadel front facade. (Far left below)

29. Sheffield Citadel Hall. (Left)

30. Rochdale Citadel Hall

The initial use of theatres and music halls by the Christian Mission and for early Salvation Army meetings had an equally important influence on the design of new halls. The layout of these theatres which centralised performers with wrap-around audiences influenced the design of most of the larger meeting halls. The floor plans of both Sheffield and Rochdale halls show this typical theatre type layout. It is obviously impossible to provide a comprehensive description of all corps buildings but those described or illustrated later are typical of this period.

31. First floor plans of Sheffield and Rochdale Citadel Halls

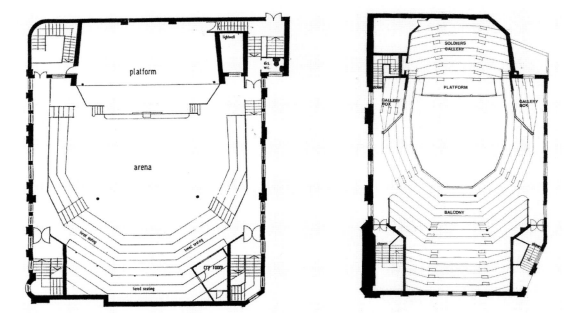

By 1885 clear guidance was being given on the importance and character of Salvation Army corps buildings in *Orders and Regulations for Divisional Officers*, as follows:

The experience of the Army has gone to prove, so far, that there lies a very close connection between a good building and a prosperous corps:

a) By a good building, is simply intended a commodious room, capable of containing from 400 to 3,000 people, according to the population of the town or neighbourhood where it is situated.

b) By a comfortable building is intended one that is warm in winter, tolerably ventilated in summer, fairly lighted, good for speaking and hearing, and seated throughout.

c) By a building fairly situated is intended one in a good thoroughfare and not far from a working-class neighbourhood.

Nevertheless, the Army has in the past been remarkably successful (even) in buildings of a very wretched character and the probabilities are that much of the world around us will have to be brought to Christ in even more unfavourable conditions still in this respect.

There can, however, be no question that a good comfortable Barracks is favourable to the spread of Salvation. Such must be deemed an advantage, and must be sought after and any reasonable effort made to obtain it.

Guidance was also given on the kind of Barracks to build and on the character of the building to be achieved. There was detailed guidance given on very many other aspects including the size and the proportion of the main hall, the type of outbuildings and ante-rooms, entrances and lobbies, the height of the ceiling and galleries, the construction of walls and roof, the floor, the platform, staircases, the type of finishes, signs, decoration, seating, lighting, heating and ventilation as well as all the other materials for the building. Nevertheless there was a preamble that stated, 'it is hoped that architects, builders and friends will improve upon these suggestions'.

Under the section on advice about the 'style of buildings' it stated:

Buildings intended for Barracks should be as unlike churches and chapels as possible, because this style appears cold and stiff, and to the masses of people in most English-speaking countries is unattractive. Our halls should be made more after the fashion of theatres and places of amusement, seeing that these are usually more cosy and comfortable-looking. In appearance at least, they may be made more in accordance with our military system. This can be carried out at a trifling extra expense by a little castellated work on the elevations, or by turrets, or the like.

It seems that the Army leadership did not see any conflict between a fortress-like exterior and a cosy interior. The extra cost involved in this treatment was 'played down' as it was the military image that was required externally. The hall at Camborne in Cornwall, built in granite with red

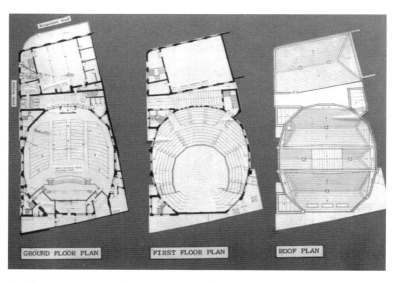

33. Drawing of front façade of Bristol Citadel. (Above)

34. Floor plans of Bristol Citadel – circus shape? (Left)

brick piers, window surrounds and castellations to the parapets shows clearly the exterior treatment required.

In Aberdeen, however, The Salvation Army erected a very distinctive building, which was opened in 1896 and unlike any other built specifically for The Salvation Army at that time or later. The local town council was justly proud of Union Street, the main thoroughfare of the city, and of its Town House building, built 20 to 30 years before the Citadel. The Town Council decreed that whatever was built on the Castlegate site, which faced down the mile long Union Street, must be of a style and

32. Camborne Hall, Cornwall. (Far left)

35. Interior Bristol Citadel. (Right)

Local oral history says the design came about after William Booth's visit to the city when he was taken up to Royal Deeside and saw Queen Victoria's Balmoral Castle, which was by then about 30 years old. He is reported to have said: '*If it's good enough for Queen Victoria it will be good enough for Aberdeen Council*'. So the new plans incorporated some aspects of Balmoral Castle into the design, such as the tower of the Citadel building which bears a strong resemblance to the tower at Balmoral. The Citadel is built of Kemnay granite, quarried about 10 miles from Aberdeen, in the Scots Baronial Style. The architect was James Soutter who had built two similar buildings in the city, immediately before working on the Citadel. Both these buildings still survive due to their architectural merit, as does Aberdeen Citadel. The total cost for The Salvation Army complex was £23,000. It consisted of the main worship hall, ancillary halls and divisional headquarters offices plus shops on the ground

design in keeping with the rest of the granite built premises of that street. The first two plans submitted by The Salvation Army were rejected because they did not meet the above requirements, but the third set of plans was accepted for the reasons now described.

36. Aberdeen Citadel. (Right)

37. Main Hall interior Aberdeen Citadel. (Far right)

floor and 21 residential flats. The rent from the shops and flats was intended to offset the cost of upkeep of the building.

Another unusual building was the Star Hall in the Ancoats district of Manchester, designed by the first Salvation Army architect Edmund Sherwood for Frank Crossley, a Christian engineer and philanthropist. Crossley had provided Booth with substantial funds for the expansion of the work of the Army, although he never became a Salvationist himself. On the site of this building was the original Star Music Hall, which had been hired for the first Salvation Army meeting in Manchester, as music halls were prevented by law from operating on a Sunday. Crossley however, whose engineering firm was located nearby, considered that this music hall was the centre of the social evils affecting the poor of the district. He felt compelled by God to purchase the Star Music Hall and then had the building completely demolished. Sherwood designed a new suite of buildings on this site for him and Crossley initially intended to hand the completed buildings over to The Salvation Army for its use. However, he received a call from God to move from his home in the picturesque village of Bowdon in Cheshire into Ancoats, one of the poorest areas of Manchester, and there to manage the Star Hall centre himself, including undertaking the preaching role and leading the evangelical services.

The building was opened on 4 August 1889 and had a main hall seating 1,000 people furnished with purpose-made heavy pine seats, apparently intended to prevent them being thrown around if there was a riot. There were many other facilities including a large lecture room and a basement community room where meals and clothing could be distributed. However, on 24 October 1918 the building was handed over to The Salvation Army '*in sacred trust for the preaching of Full Salvation*'. The congregations of the Star Hall and the members of two Salvation Army corps in the district, Every Street and Bradford Road, were joined to form the new Star Hall Corps. On a personal note and years later, the author of this book was converted in the Star Hall and later he and his wife went from there to the William Booth Training College to be trained as Salvation Army officers.

Congress Halls

The Clapton Congress Hall, mentioned earlier, was considered to be excellent in its plan form, being ideal for a large congregation to see and hear the speakers on the platform. It was thus regarded as a model for large halls to seat between 2,000 and 4,000 people. At Brighton, where activities had been recommenced in 1882, a new hall was planned on similar lines to that at Clapton and it was opened 1883. Initially it seated 3,500 people. The first drawings submitted to the planning office described the building as an Assembly Hall and stated that the

38. Manchester Star Hall interior. (Left)

39. Brighton Congress Hall (with entrance porch added and parapet reduced)

stepped right down to the speaker's platform. In that section of the platform there would be seated the soldiers, with the remainder of the seating intended for newcomers and the remainder of the congregation. The hall was of sufficient size to allow central gatherings to be held there for Salvationists from the whole district. Space for some rooms was provided under the soldiers' platform, while other rooms and a small hall were situated behind the platform. No provision for heating seems to have been made at that time. This Plymouth Congress Hall was demolished by enemy bombs during World War Two and new buildings were later constructed in Armada Way.

Two months after the original Plymouth Congress Hall buildings were opened, the Salvation Army publication *The War Cry*, published a description of a similar building at Oldham in Lancashire, which would seat 3,000 people:

applicant was a Mr George Buster. Although the words Congress Hall were inscribed above the entrance door, no mention was made of The Salvation Army. Whether the nature of the application was to avoid controversy in an area of Regency housing is not known. That Brighton Congress Hall building was later modernised before being finally replaced at the start of the 21st century.

In February 1886, General William Booth opened the new Plymouth Congress Hall. The words 'Salvation Barracks' and a five feet diameter Army crest were prominently incorporated in relief onto the façade. Imitation battlements and slit windows adorned the gable and sturdy square towers flanked the triple arched entrance. Stone copings, string mouldings, quoins and other decorations contrasted with the red brickwork. Entry was gained through a lobby with access to the gallery up a staircase in each tower. The hall, rectangular in plan, contained lower tiered seating with a gallery above on three sides. At the opposite end, the gallery

As the site is located at the corner of two streets, no difficulty has been experienced in providing those two essentials, light and air, which so materially add to the comfort of frequenters of public halls. There is to be a coved ceiling panelled out with marginal lights, the margins being filled with bright ruby glass and the corners with blue cut stars, thus producing a pleasing effect. Externally, the front is of red brick with stone dressings, with a tower running up each side of the main hall finished with battlements. Tudor Gothic (style) has been adopted for the architectural treatment, which style is considered by the architect as less cold and more appropriate than others usually employed for mission purposes: great care has been taken to secure, as far as possible without any lavish expenditure on details, a generally picturesque outline. 'The Salvation

Army Barracks Building and Property Company Ltd' sold 5,000 shares at £1 each with 5% interest guaranteed. The Army's Architect, Commissioner E.J. Sherwood of Headquarters, prepared plans and quantities.

Oldham was the first of many places where development companies were formed to raise the price of the tender, here amounting to £4,300. The Army architect mentioned is almost certainly the architect referred to in the publication *The Salvation War 1882*. Original drawings of other buildings designed between 1882 and 1889 also bear his signature.

Often existing properties were acquired and converted or extended to meet the new requirements. Alterations to a Temperance Hall building at Exeter completely transformed it into a typical barracks, but it was given the name 'Exeter Temple' by the Army and has remained so ever since. No sympathy was shown for the style of the old building, which was Greek revival. Instead a new façade with battlements and turrets was added as well as a gallery all round the inside.

Other Halls and Citadels

Mention should be made of some of the unusual forms given to halls at this time. Several halls were built which were semi-circular in roof section and rectangular in plan. No firm evidence is available but it seems reasonable to suggest that the inspiration for this idea had a direct link with the Railway Arch Hall at Bethnal Green. They generally had a tiered platform and seated in total about 750 people. They were built with semi-circular trusses about 300mm deep and at 3.2m centres supporting purlins and a roof of boarding and slates

which incorporated roof lights. A small pitched roof externally surmounted the curved roof. It was set tangential to the arc of the trusses, which partly overcame weathering difficulties. The new barracks designed in 1884 for Wisbech, with others at Battersea and Castleford, were constructed in this manner. Constructionally this type of building did not prove altogether satisfactory, so that the later insertion of tie rods was found necessary to stabilise the structure. Similar problems were experienced at Castleford, where buttresses were built in 1936 to resist the thrust of this roof and the slating replaced by built-up felt roof covering to lighten the loading.

Most corps did not require buildings as large as the congress halls and in many places an auditorium to seat about 500 people was adequate. Many buildings of this capacity were built before the end of the century and although at first they were known as barracks or fortresses, they were soon renamed citadels, with just a few buildings keeping their original title. This change happened because the earlier use of the name 'barracks' had given rise to a great deal of misunderstanding and scandalous rumours about their use circulated among the general public, who wrongly assumed that the Salvationists all slept there together. The name 'barracks' was not really appropriate as nobody lived in these buildings. Cradley Heath halls in Birmingham had the words 'The Salvation Army Fort' carved into the front façade on the main hall of 1893 and 'The Junior Barracks' on the young people's hall of 1900.

In the main, the plan layout of citadels was a miniature version of the larger congress halls, with the exception of the platform arrangement. In citadels the stepped soldiers' platform was situated behind a proscenium arch and was usually contained by a lean-to roof structure with the sidewalls splayed out. The main speakers occupied an 'apron' stage in front of the arch. Boxes in two tiers flanked the platform while the space on either side of the rear platform provided a useful area for the location of the officer's room and tea-room, which had by now become essential requirements. This new arrangement was obviously a direct adaptation of the theatre plan. The boxes were nicknamed 'Glory Boxes' because here the reformed characters, many of whom were former drunkards or criminals, would be seated until called upon to testify as to their conversion. Communication with and access to the speakers platform were necessary so that they could quickly reach the rostrum.

The ground floor by then had no banked seating but instead the floor had a slight slope towards the platform. On three sides of the hall the gallery was provided as before and supported on iron columns. However, these galleries stopped short of the platform, abutting the boxes. Generally the roof trusses spanned the full width of the hall, obviating the need to extend the iron columns up to ceiling level. Low relief mouldings divided the flat ceiling into panels, which contained laylights and ventilation grilles. The staircases and entrance lobby generally followed a similar pattern to the previous halls.

A citadel building in Tottenham, London was

40. *Tottenham Citadel.*

designed by architect W. Gilbert Scott (not to be confused with the later Sir Giles Gilbert Scott). The illustration shows the typical treatment of these halls with square towers at the corners, incorporating battlements and Crusader crosses. It was built by Frederick J. Coxhead, a builder who had joined the Christian Mission at the Millwall Candle Factory. He also built many other Army halls in North London.

A similar building was erected at about the same time at Wood Green for £2,100 to seat 800 people. Twenty-two different foundation stones were laid when the building of that hall commenced. A report at the time stated, '*Ventilation will be a special feature; nevertheless it will probably be magnificently warm on Sunday night, especially about 10pm*'. This comment alludes to the atmosphere generated in Army gospel meetings of that period. Most of these buildings, however, were by now provided with central hot water heating, although even some large halls still managed with a couple of the 'tortoise' stoves. These stoves used slow combustion but had long flue pipes. A self-rotating roof ventilator extracted the warm air through the ceiling grilles.

At Middlesborough, building operations were planned in phases. The first phase was to include the new fortress building which would be set back from the road frontage. The later second stage was built in front, consisting of a row of cottages with a central entrance archway to the hall. The façades to these buildings were given the full military treatment. The reaction of the tenants to the cottages is not known!

In about 1895 when Alexander Gordon succeeded to the position of staff architect, one of his first jobs was the design of the new Salvation Army citadel at Grantham. The word 'citadel' is actually used on the elevation there. Similar in many respects to previous designs, these buildings differed in their platform arrangement.

platform. This new set-up for the platforms was a reversion to the congress hall plan, which overcame most of these difficulties.

It is significant to note that Junior Soldiers' halls were not initially included in most schemes – Grantham was one of the exceptions – although some young people's meetings had commenced as early as 1880. Sunday schools for children had not so far been encouraged for fear that these additional activities would detract from the main purpose of getting the adults converted. However, a longstanding belief that children were also in need of spiritual guidance, the sympathetic approach of some leaders and agitation from Salvationist parents led to the formation of young people's corps and associated activities. These activities were similar to those of the senior corps but separate buildings were set apart for this purpose. Young people's facilities were therefore added to many of the existing halls as the need arose.

Salvation Army halls of this period, and even into the early part of the 20th century, were designed to accommodate the maximum number of persons possible, but the seating arrangements allowed at that time would be considered very cramped by present day standards. The floor area was calculated at between four and five square feet per person, which is less than 0.5 square metre. Wooden forms or benches with a plain rail as a back support became the traditional means of seating. Simple in construction, they were cheap, durable and allowed the occupants to squeeze together as necessary. They were not very comfortable but were in keeping with the definite intention of preventing people from feeling too relaxed either in body or soul in those gospel meetings. Rows of these forms were spaced at about 2' 3" centres (700mm) and stepped tiers were arranged to comply with this distance. The aisles between benches varied from three to four feet wide (900-1200mm).

41. Grantham hall

Probably the disadvantages of the 'theatre stage' layout had become apparent. These problems included the tortuous access to and from the boxes, the restriction in seating area, the poor natural light and the projection of the proscenium arch walls limiting views to and from the

Smaller Halls 1901–1914

42. Cirencester Hall – temporary home for 51 years! (Below)

43. Former Temperance Hall used by Cirencester Corps before and after temporary home. (Below right)

With the turn of the century came other influences which made a difference to the basic design of corps buildings. During the previous years the Army had built its congress halls and citadels in the cities and large towns. Meanwhile corps were being opened in the suburbs, in smaller towns and in villages and these also needed new premises. They did not need to accommodate the masses but needed to be of sufficient size for the soldiery and for as many 'new-comers' as could be brought in. In the immediate future therefore the majority of new buildings would be small to medium-sized halls. They usually bore the words 'The Salvation Army' and were known simply as halls.

Semi-permanent buildings were often built in the villages and smaller towns, where funds were not available for more ambitious schemes. These halls were typically built with a timber structure and clad with asbestos sheets. However, the one illustrated for Cirencester Corps, was not built until 1926 but was used by the corps until 1977 when they returned to the Temperance Hall (also shown) which had been their first home from 1881.

Often a small hall would be built on a site with space left for an extension when the corps expanded, which it was generally assumed would happen. The original hall would later be used for young people's work while a new building would be erected for the adults.

Provision for eventual expansion was not always possible, as often the sites available were too small. It was quite usual to build over the whole site area with small light wells and roof lights to provide the daylighting. Senior and Young People's halls often had to be planned on two storeys. Young People's work was now considered important and the proportion of accommodation for its

sole use increased.

In the main hall the tiered platform arrangement proved quite unsuitable for the seating of the bands, which had by now become an integral part of most corps. Difficulty was also experienced when pageants and plays were enacted. The flat platform therefore superseded the old ramped arrangement and eventually the majority of the tiered constructions were altered to provide a level platform.

The type of architectural treatment that originated under Staff Architect Oswald Archer's control can be seen on buildings throughout this period, although various assistants contributed new ideas. Certain common characteristics in the design of halls of this period were apparent:

- **In the elevational treatment.**
  This was mainly governed by the form of the hall. As the site was frequently restricted, there often remained only the street façade to be treated. Simplified classical ornamentation was adopted with the parapets and gables being treated in a variety of ways.
- **In the construction methods.**
  Simplicity and cheapness were the essentials of construction. Load bearing brick walls, with brick arches over timber windows, supported the roof construction. This form of construction remained basically the same for many years. A timber roof truss centred every 10 to 12 feet (3–3.2m) carried purlins, rafters, boarding and slates. Timber-framed platforms and floors were boarded, with dado match boarding to walls becoming a traditional feature. Large conical metal ventilators were fixed at ridge level with trunking connected to the ceiling grilles. Heating was from a central boiler and heating coils or by slow combustion stoves.

The new citadel built at Ilford could be regarded as typical of medium-sized halls of that time erected on long and narrow sites. The senior hall occupied the front of the site with a side passage giving access to junior halls on two stories at the rear. A tea room and officers' room were located either side of the platform. The platform was arranged in two areas, the upper part being recessed in an alcove, an idea reminiscent of the citadel platform arrangement. The front elevation had a restrained classical appearance. In 1937 the buildings were greatly enlarged by the addition of a gallery and the roof heightened with additional rooms and an enlarged Junior Hall at the rear.

The following two 'Mission Room' type buildings are representative of the many small halls built at that time. The layout, construction and finish were kept extremely simple. One was at Goodmayes, where allowance was made in siting the small hall to permit a larger hall to be built in the future. Another was the Raynes Park Mission Hall, which was sited 'broadside' on to the road. The interiors were simply furnished with a small dais, benches and heating stove.

An article entitled 'New Halls for Old' appeared in October 1909 in the Salvation Army international magazine *All the World*. It expressed the need for a three-part property programme for the British Isles, as follows:

1. To provide more suitable buildings in London.
2. To carry out enlargements, renovations and improvements to existing halls.
3. To clear existing debts on corps building schemes.

In referring to the design and finance of new projects the article stated:

Let there be no mistake about it, the Army does not spend a single sovereign upon any ornamentation inconsistent with reason, but it does not believe in erecting buildings which have the appearance of an old-time Dotheboys Hall, or a place suggestive of that in which the ever-lamented Bumble spent his declining days. The money is spent with a due regard for all essentials, common sense dictating according to local needs. The size and position are gauged by actual requirements and the size of the purse at the disposal of the Army.

The halls at Thetford in Norfolk illustrate another common type of hall. Designed for a narrow, confined site the two halls were placed side by side. This 'man and boy' arrangement seemed unavoidable where a pair of

44. Nottingham Memorial Halls

halls was required on such sites. Usually a central passage permitted some side lighting, but at Thetford even this refinement was not possible.

In August 1912, the Founder, General William Booth, died – 'promoted to Glory' in Salvation Army terminology and his son, Bramwell, was appointed his successor. A scheme was inaugurated for new halls to be erected in Nottingham in memory of the Founder in the city of his birth. On 18 July 1914 the foundation stones of the Nottingham Memorial Halls were laid. In its description of the halls, the *Nottingham Guardian* newspaper wrote:

A one storey building in red brick and Ancaster stone, the imposing main entrance is to face St Ann's Well Road. The entrance is semi-circular in design and on either side of the massive door are a couple of stone columns. A short square tower surmounts the whole. A series of stone columns, together with a heavy stone cornice with dentil course and a stone plinth stand out in relief on King Edward Street. Through a spacious crush lobby, one passes into the senior hall where accommodation is afforded for 1,000 worshippers. This hall is 70ft x 48ft. A large gallery at the rear of the hall will be on the cantilever principle, thus obviating the use of columns. The acoustic properties should be good, the ceiling being slightly domed. At the rear of the hall is the young people's hall, about 40ft. x 34ft. affording accommodation for 500 children. This hall can be converted into eight classrooms by utilising portable partitions.

These halls, designed by the Salvation Army Staff Architect, Oswald Archer were in the manner of much civic architecture of the time. An oil painting of William Booth by artist W. J. Carroll was presented to the Army at the opening of the new hall. Its completion coincided with the commencement of the First World War and a break in the continuity of building new Army corps halls. During the war years, much of The Salvation Army's efforts were diverted to provide aid for its service to support British troops and their families in Britain.

A Steady Building Programme 1920–1940

After that war many corps continued to expand and new permanent buildings were needed. The challenge of new housing estates called for new initiatives and foresight in the location of new corps buildings. The military imagery of the facades was either simplified or omitted altogether. The space requirements gradually became more complex due to the variety of activities that needed to be accommodated. For the musicians' use a band room and sometimes a songster room would be required in addition to the officers' room and tea room. Better toilet facilities were also needed and young people's activities as well as other new developments all required consideration.

The expanded basic components for new Salvation Army buildings were now a senior hall with its ancillary rooms and a young people's hall with its own associated rooms. It was considered desirable to arrange links between each part and essential to allow direct access between certain rooms and the platform of the main hall, but the senior and junior aspects of corps activity were kept separate.

Restricted sites were still commonly used due to the high cost and limited availability of land. This factor in most cases led to the adoption of one of three basic approaches to the planning problems:

1. Halls behind each other.
2. Halls side by side.
3. Halls, one on top of the other.

Building byelaws were by now applied quite stringently. The means of escape requirements in particular, had a significant effect on the design of new Salvation Army halls. This was especially so in London which had its own

45. Oil painting of William Booth by artist W. J. Carroll

legislation, known as the London Building Acts. These reflected concerns which had arisen centuries before this, after the Great Fire of London. New materials were also by now being used both for structural purposes and for finishes. A different character to hall interiors resulted from the use of steel roof trusses, usually concealed by a suspended ceiling. Asphalt or built-up bituminous felt roofing became commonly used, allowing the provision of flat roofs in lieu of the traditional pitched roofs. Cavity wall construction was adopted, giving the fabric increased thermal and weather-proofing properties. A central heating system was by now a standard requirement.

Elevations during this period were treated in a style that became traditional for Salvation Army buildings with its bold and rather grotesque classic detailing. However, before the middle of this period a new nondescript, but more refined, treatment of elevations was employed.

In 1935 Oswald Archer retired and James Vint took over as staff architect. He had already worked in the department for many years.

Mention has already been made of the semi-permanent type of hall that was developed. This was used where finance was limited and a cheaper type of building was acceptable. Many of these buildings were designed and erected under the direction of National Headquarters, without any input from the IHQ staff architect. Some were an imitation of the traditional type of hall but were of a lower standard of construction and finish, with some halls constructed with asbestos-clad timber framing resting on a brick plinth wall.

Various alterations were made to existing properties to meet changing demands. For instance, in October 1923, Brighton Congress Hall was reopened after reconstruction with the capacity of the main hall reduced to 1,600 in order to provide sufficient space for two young people's halls, each seating 500 children. The tiered platform was partially levelled and new rooms provided underneath the new platform. A report at the time made special mention of the sound-proofing of the floor separating the two sections.

In 1922, new buildings were erected at Tuebrook in Liverpool, accommodating 350 seniors and 550 juniors. This was an indication of the emphasis on young people's activities by that time, with requirements differing with location. This will be apparent by comparison of that Liverpool hall with the new centre built at nearby Seacombe, some three years later. Here the main hall had a gallery and seated 600 people while the junior hall held only 275. The design was for two halls side by side with rooms behind.

At Catford a new corps had commenced in 1919 in an old tin hut. In 1925, the tin hut was replaced by a permanent building on the same site which, apart from the usual accommodation, included offices for the divisional headquarters. These were provided over the front part of the main hall, which had a flat concrete roof broken by long lantern lights. The elevation is typical of the 'traditional' Army style of treatment of that period. The hall remains largely unaltered to this day. A similar façade would have been given to halls where a gallery was incorporated, in lieu of the divisional offices.

When a new hall building was being planned the issue which always arose related to the size of the main hall. Should the hall accommodate the larger crowd who wished to attend the occasional special meeting or musical festival, or should it provide just sufficient capacity for the maximum weekly attendance? If no local hall was available for hire, it might be necessary to cater for larger congregations but this generally would leave the Sunday preacher with a half-full hall. For smaller

corps there were also financial restrictions which obviously affected the hall capacity. Some flexible arrangement to overcome these issues was therefore necessary.

One solution to this problem was attempted at Aspley, where a small hall was to be erected in 1933. The plan was to provide a side 'aisle' alongside the hall as a lean-to addition. This could provide extra seating capacity but when this was not required then folding screens separated this area. This 'side aisle' area could then be used as classrooms. The two sections could be used together for other activity, such as the Sunday school or for youth club activities.

Another innovation common to these halls was the addition of an external porch or lobby. Although not a

new feature in chapel designs and even of some rural Army halls, it had usually been omitted to allow Salvation Army halls to take advantage of all the space behind the street building line. This meant bringing the main face of the building up to that line, with the entrance lobby incorporated into the building envelope. External lobbies, however, usually resulted in an improved appearance to the front elevation.

In 1934, a 'big push' was organised to house some of the 494 corps still without their own halls. At this time 23 building schemes were in progress or had been approved. There were 45 other prospective schemes and 76 sites had been secured for future development.

Although planned in 1929, the new halls at Douglas in the Isle of Man did not materialise until five years later. These halls can be regarded as illustrative of the third basic plan type. This scheme involved a small site area having reasonable daylighting. The halls were planned on two storeys. In this case the senior hall occupied the ground floor and was entered from the corner. A side staircase led to the young people's hall and classrooms above the main hall. This arrangement was not considered ideal, as insufficient room was available to allow for ancillary rooms to be located in their preferred location, such as the band room to adjoin the platform.

A change of external treatment came about just before the war. A desire was expressed that the back wall to the platform should not contain any windows. This resulted in the type of elevation used at Bromley in Kent, completed in 1939. The usual problem of a restricted site resulted in a long narrow plan arrangement in this building. It is interesting to note, however, the improved standard of finish and refinements to the interior that had by then become common, such as hardwood wall panelling, double-glazing and seating with chairs (rather than benches) in the main hall, adding to both its appearance and the worshippers' comfort.

When war came again in 1939, new hall schemes were abandoned or postponed and building work was not generally resumed for a further ten years.

Post War Buildings 1945–1953

In 1945 a new staff architect was appointed, Colonel William H. Charles. A great amount of building work was required owing to the break of building activity during the war years. However, licensing restrictions on building materials prevented rapid advance at first. The building programme of this period included four types of projects:

'War Damage' rebuilding. Many buildings had been totally or partially destroyed by enemy action and needed reinstatement. Meanwhile, corps affected were housed in temporary buildings or in alternative premises. In many cases Army corps activities were severely restricted during this period.

Replacement of old premises. Some corps had schemes pending since before the war, while others were rapidly expanding and needed new and larger halls.

Extensions to existing halls. Demands were being made for better accommodation and facilities. The improvements required included the addition of extra rooms, a new young people's hall or even a senior hall where the intention was to make the existing hall solely for use by the junior corps.

Buildings in new locations. There were new towns and new housing estates where the Army wished to establish its work. Some existing corps halls, affected by inner city redevelopment, had to be re-sited. New corps in new locations, established to meet growing demands, now needed halls. Many of the new sites were of limited size. This still created design problems, which could only be solved by one of the old basic arrangements. In other cases however, large open sites were made available and these presented scope for a completely new approach.

These new situations on open sites had the following impact. The buildings had to be designed as a total composition with each block and all elevations carefully considered for the first time. There now remained for the first time on Salvation Army sites some undeveloped area, which needed to be landscaped, often with parking facilities provided.

At first the designs were simple and unpretentious, with no radical departures from the pre-war traditions. Permanence and economy were still the fundamental necessities. Load-bearing brick walls with pitched, tiled or slated roofs were still considered the most durable construction and therefore they were generally the solutions used. Internally this meant using either timber trusses with an open roof structure or steel trusses with a suspended ceiling. Both of these methods proved reasonably economical.

One major difference particularly noticeable in new designs was the use of shallow pitched roofs. This feature became a basic characteristic of Army halls of this period. Non-traditional methods of construction were by then also being employed. However, a reduction of building costs was often required during the design process and changes were made at the expense of the quality of finishes to walls, floors and ceilings. These decisions to reduce the quality of materials had their effect on the later maintenance and servicing of new halls. Upon completion, responsibility for these aspects passed to the individual corps. Very often voluntary or casual labour had to be relied on for the upkeep of buildings. Anything that required further expenditure or labour was regarded with suspicion. Even such things as window cleaning, preservation of joinery and floors, maintenance of light fittings and the operation and servicing of heating plant was given insufficient care in many cases. Even the maintenance of grassed areas was seen as a problem at that time. Such points as these, if they did not receive sufficient thought in the planning and design had in some measure an adverse effect on the resulting appearance of the building once it was occupied. Window areas were required to be no larger than considered necessary to provide good daylighting to the building. Operating gear to windows had to be simple and sturdy with wall finishes required to be washable.

One of the earliest post-war schemes that proceeded was the building of a new young people's hall at Gillingham. This had been part of the original design but was not built when the main hall was erected, owing to financial limitations. It had been postponed further due to the war and was eventually built in 1949.

At Staines the old chapel building was demolished and new halls erected on the same site. The site there was rather small but the maximum accommodation possible was required because of the large size of the corps. The simple front elevation was a carefully expressed gable and the hall roof construction involved steel trusses with suspended ceilings of fibreboard.

Several properties in Plymouth suffered war damage and the first to be reconstructed in 1951 was the Exeter Street Hall. The remnants of the existing fabric were used and this dictated the plan form. The opportunity was taken however to modernise the elevation and to add a large classroom. Some existing buildings were acquired in

the same year, such as a Methodist Church property at Clacton-on-Sea. Alterations were carried out resulting in a property reasonably well suited to post-war Army requirements.

An extension to an existing hall was undertaken at Malvern in 1953 which provided a large schoolroom on the ground floor seating 150 people with a residential flat above for the corps officers. It was not customary to have the commanding officer's living quarters on corps premises, although there were some obvious advantages. The general Army policy was to keep living quarters separate from halls, to allow the officers some degree of respite from the demands of the corps and local community. A residential flat for the corps officers was however incorporated in the new Hull Central Corps building, where divisional offices were also included.

In 1952 the proposed development of Hemel Hempstead town centre made it necessary for the corps to be transferred from their existing small premises on The Marlowes. The advent of this scheme for the new

47. Hemel Hempstead Hall – front view.

town at Hemel Hempstead was to have long-term repercussions. The Hemel Hempstead Development Corporation had made available a large site, located on one corner of the proposed market square. This resulted in the building design being handled in a contemporary manner, which other new halls later followed on similar sites. The Army leaders responsible for approving schemes found this departure acceptable and did not discourage the new design approach or the use of new materials and construction methods.

The new halls at Hemel Hempstead included a senior hall with gallery to seat 370 people, a young people's hall and classrooms accommodating an equal number of children, and other facilities. Good linked access between rooms was provided and the hall was very satisfactory acoustically. Ample facilities were allowed for the future expansion of the corps.

48. Hemel Hempstead Hall – rear view.

The Army authorities then made a request for the design of a small standard type of hall that could be cheaply constructed in various places where requirements were simple and similar. The first of these was erected at St Albans, mainly to accommodate activities for young people from a housing estate. This building provided seating for 140 persons and contained the very minimum of facilities. The type of roof construction used was a new feature for Salvation Army halls. Exposed steel lattice trusses carried purlins onto which panels of a proprietary brand of strawboard were nailed. Unfortunately this material was later found to be unstable and tended to grow shoots if persistent leaks allowed the entry of moisture. The shallow pitch roof was covered with bituminous felt roofing. The hall was heated by a slow combustion convector type stove with electric heaters in the smaller rooms. Externally 'Tyrolean' rendered panels gave a contrasting appearance to the red brown brickwork. A similar small hall accommodating 200 was later planned for the Bedwell area of Stevenage New Town.

Corps Buildings 1954–2010

Salvation Army architect Gerald Norwood wrote in his RIBA thesis in 1954:

When designing a Salvation Army hall, the particular form of worship, and the activities which will take place in it must be studied in some detail. The main function is that of a meeting place for a Christian community, whose main aims are to serve and worship God, and to spread the Gospel of Jesus Christ throughout the world. Their gatherings are called 'meetings' instead of 'services' for liturgy plays no part in their worship. In common with the Society of Friends (Quakers) 'the sacrament of Holy Communion' is not celebrated in Salvation Army halls; the Salvationists regard every meal as a sacrament,

although Salvationists sometimes join with other Free Churchmen in this heart-searching ceremony, as a symbol of spiritual unity.

Meetings are essentially of a 'free and easy' nature and do not conform to a rigid programme. Music and song play a great part in these meetings. The right of anyone in the meeting to address the congregation is greatly exercised; personal testimony or witness has played an indispensable part in the development of The Salvation Army. The whole body of membership is encouraged to take an active part in the life of the corps. An extremely high proportion of Salvationists are active workers. The hall is not always used as a preaching hall but is multi-purpose in nature. It is often used for musical concerts, dramatic presentations, demonstrations, sales of work and for religious and educational film shows. As the use of film is being greatly increased, this fact must be considered. Everything which takes place in the hall must be in full accordance with the purposes and principles of The Salvation Army and it must have an evangelical appeal.

To sum up, an evangelical centre (referring to Salvation Army halls) should be: 'An outward and visible sign of an inward and spiritual grace'. It should fulfil the functional requirements of the community which it serves. Its design should reflect something of the faith and life of a Salvationist by its simplicity and the truthful expression of structural form. The skilful use of colour, materials and textures should help to show that the Christian life is not one of drab piety and gloom, but of happiness to be part of God's creation. Today there is a great need for new evangelical centres and this need will become even more pressing as the years go by. Although a large number of evangelical centres have been built since the war, this has only scratched the surface of the problem. There is considerable scope for young designers, especially now that 'contemporary' architectural design is

beginning to be appreciated by The Salvation Army. The architecture of the evangelical centre stands waiting for development.

Before 1950 there had been little scope for The Salvation Army to allow new approaches to the design of their corps halls – with a few notable exceptions. Restricted sites and limited funds had severely limited the opportunities for new approaches. However, the time was now right and the new halls at Hemel Hempstead opened in 1954 illustrated some of these possibilities. A further impetus for a change of approach in the design of new Salvation Army corps buildings commenced in 1956 when a Salvationist architect, Wycliffe Noble, was appointed to design the new halls for the corps at Hendon. He commenced with a design analysis of the pattern and liturgical nature of worship in Salvation Army halls, which he described as follows:

The pattern of Salvation Army worship as expressed through the eleven points of the doctrine within the Holiness and Salvation Meetings (mean that) the Services can be divided into two parts:

(a) That part of the Service devoted to the personal expression of worship during prayers, singing and testimony.
(b) That part of the Service devoted to teaching the Gospel.
From analysis it can be seen that a greater proportion of the Service is formed by the spoken word, rather than by music – the oratory being directed from the platform and at other times from the congregation, during prayers and testimony.

This pattern of worship does not require the establishment of a singular object as the visual

49. Hendon Corps Hall – exterior and interior views.

centre of the Service, nor are there any religious rites which are required to be performed before the congregation. Indeed, the Gospel itself in its abstract sense is the powerful medium upon which the Salvationist builds his hope and The Salvation Army service develops.

It follows that where no visual climax in a service exists, a psychological vacuum develops, and the mental powers of concentration during the services disintegrate, unless there is created an atmosphere singularly purist, where character is epitomised by simple geometric shapes, and unsophisticated detail, and the main architectural elements are grouped in a unified conception. Only in this way is space enclosed beautifully and the minds of men, devoid of external influences, can be guided in a true sense of worship through quietness and tranquillity. There is no attempt to create a hybrid of architectural conception and the building grows out of the idea of worship with the quality expressed in the simple design pattern.

The Hall of Worship is the larger element and dominates the other group which contains the Entrance Hall, Band and Songster rooms and officer's room. These smaller units, with the Entrance Hall as the hub of the group, are on a scale with that of domestic buildings. This developed from the idea of transition from the World, the street and the home, through a space which is neither dramatic nor restricted, but is warm, inviting and quietly dignified.

This new approach was greeted with enthusiasm both within The Salvation Army and by the architectural profession in general which featured this design in the *Architects Journal* and books on modern architecture.

The Hendon building did not provide any facilities for the young people's work nor community work as these activities continued in the original building at the rear of the new construction.

In Coventry, new halls were designed just a few years later by David Blackwell and completed in 1959. These halls, on a prominent corner in the central city area, were designed to reflect the new dynamic forms developed in the re-birth of a city largely destroyed by enemy bombing during the Second World War. The main hall had a

50. *Coventry Citadel 1959 building. (Far left)*

51. *Coventry Citadel 2004 building with interior view of café area. (Left and below)*

52. Bath Citadel Corps hall.

53. Bath main hall – view from platform.

illustrated, which was opened on 2 July 2005, reflecting new priorities within the corps activities.

A new suite of buildings was also designed by David Blackwell for a prominent corner site in Bath. This sought to reflect the architectural character of the locality and so was clad in natural stone. These halls were opened on 12 March 1964 and provided for all the various activities of the corps identified at that time. The building remains largely unchanged up to the present time.

Southwark Citadel hall deserves a mention as it was built with funds provided by the War Damage Commission. Opened in 1967, it was the last building in the United Kingdom to be funded in this way. The Government Office closed its operations after the completion of this hall and payment of the final tranche of compensation. The original Borough Corps hall had been destroyed by enemy bombing during the Second World War and the compensation funded the new hall. The Borough and Kennington Lane Corps were combined to form the new Southwark Corps in these

concrete portal frame structure expressed externally on the outside of both the walls and the roof, as illustrated. Over the years this treatment unfortunately created problems of moisture penetration, particularly through the roof. This building was replaced by a completely new suite of buildings of a very different design also

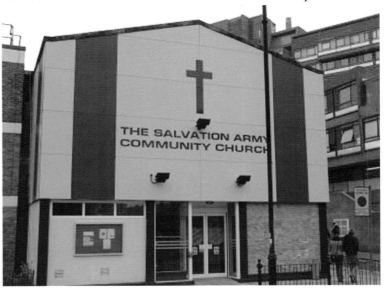

54. Southwark Corps hall – after 2005 ronovations.

premises. It was a traditional Salvation Army hall comprising main hall with gallery and built-in platform, youth hall, kitchen, office and some ancillary rooms all on the ground floor with a residential flat for the officer on the first floor. The exterior was in London stock bricks with reconstructed Portland stone cladding around the entrance porch on the front and side elevations. It was substantially renovated in 2005, which included recladding the front façade and adding the name 'Community Church'.

There were few directives from senior Salvation Army leaders during this period concerning the form that new corps buildings should take, so it was generally left to in-house architectural staff to take the initiative on how the new halls should be designed. The exception to this was Commissioner Will Cooper who, as British Commissioner, stated that the heart of any new corps building should be the kitchen – as a symbol of service. He felt that the location of the kitchen should reflect the important position that serving food and drink occupied within the life of a corps, as well as The Salvation Army's response to community needs. One of the new halls designed following this directive was Wood Green in Lymington Avenue where, in

1975, both the main kitchen and a tea-making kitchen were incorporated in central positions in the layout. This enabled the Tea Kitchen to be able to serve directly via a hatch into both the front lounge and the Community Hall.

Difficulties with the surrounding environment of a new site often produce the most interesting solutions. In the case of Wood Green the boundaries to site on two sides were roads, and a major relief road was planned for the third side. There was very little outlook and potentially a great deal of noise around the building. A landscaped garden courtyard was therefore created in the centre of the building containing a fish pond and cascade, intended as a natural place of quiet serenity on which to gaze when withdrawing from all the intense activity of urban life. It was fully glazed all round so the views into it could be enjoyed from both halls, as well as from the

55 Wood Green hall. (Below left)

56. Wood Green hall – landscaped courtyard. (Below)

57. L'Islet Fortress hall – 1889 building.

wide main corridor forming the spine of the building and a processional way between the main entrance and the worship hall. In the local area there was a shortage of nature areas, so that local schools often brought their pupils into the Army building just to see this feature and inspect the pond life. What was therefore designed as a solution to a noisy environment resulted in becoming an attraction to encourage people to visit the Army hall.

Among the major changes to building design generally, particularly in the elevational treatment was the desire to make the halls more inviting and visually open to the public. This resulted in the provision of larger foyers and transparent façades with large windows and glazed doors with clear glass replacing heavy masonry walls and obscured glass. This new image was intended to be an invitation for people to come in. The previous architectural treatment suggested a barrier of entry to the general public, as if there was a desire to keep them out or to provide protection for the Salvationists within.

Guernsey had long been known as a honeymoon island, and in 1855 William and Catherine Booth had visited the island for two weeks soon after their marriage. William was an ordained Methodist minister and each night he preached at the Clifton Hall, St Peter Port. In 1883 this same building was to become the first building on the island to be taken over by The Salvation Army for its meetings and the establishment of St Peter Port Corps. During the same year, the Grandes Rocques Corps was also opened, later to be known as L'Islet Corps. By 1889 a plot of land had been purchased in the sum of £60 for L'Islet Corps at Les Tracheries so the first purpose-built Army hall in Guernsey was erected there and named L'Islet Fortress. The Salvation Army continued to thrive on Guernsey and a third corps at St Sampson was later opened. Activities continued uninterrupted until after the German invasion of the island in January 1941, when The

Salvation Army was ordered to cease all operations. The halls were closed and Salvationists joined local Methodist churches for worship, until the liberation of the island in July 1945, when the three corps were re-opened.

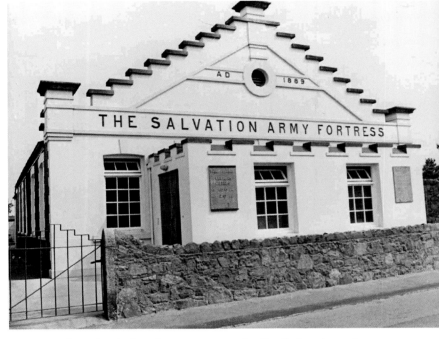

In July 1976 the first purpose-built Salvation Army hall in the Channel Islands since the turn of the century was opened on Guernsey by Sir John Loveridge, the Bailiff. It was on a new site located on Route du Picquerel. Again it was for the L'Islet Corps and it retained the original name of the previous building, 'L'Islet Fortress'. Initially, there were some difficulties in getting planning permission but when an architect's coloured perspective drawing (illustrated) showed how the design reflected the local vernacular architecture, it was approved. The new facilities provided a main worship hall which could be gradually enlarged by the use of sliding and folding screens to cater for the increasing congregations during the holiday period. Some

58. *Architect's perspective drawing of new L'Islet hall. (Opposite above)*

59. *L'Islet hall – 1976 building. (Opposite below left)*

60, *L'Islet Corps Corps main interior hall. (Opposite below right)*

61. *Albert Orsborn Memorial halls – Boscombe. (Below)*

doubts within the corps membership about the relocation of the hall as leaving their 'spiritual heritage' were resolved when it was agreed that they were building 'for generations yet unborn'. One interesting feature of this development was that the new halls were built on the site of former greenhouses where tomatoes had been grown. The rich top soil was a foot (300mm) thick across the site, with about another two feet (600mm) of good clean sand beneath. On such a relatively small island these materials had a high commercial value, so that the cost of the foundations and the stone sub-base for a car park was more than offset by their sale. In the building industry it is rare for the ground works 'to make a profit', but that is what happened here. The corps members also had to be convinced that building on the sand sub-soil, which covered this site, was quite safe because of the parable that Jesus had told of the foolish man who built on sand (Matthew 7:24-27). For interest, the story which Jesus used in the parable was a well-known story at the time, of a man who built his house on the sandy bottom of a dry river bed, which was fine until the rains came.

One suite of new halls designed in the 1980s by David

62. *Boscombe hall interior – view of platform. (Above)*

63. *Boscombe hall interior – view of gallery. (Below)*

Blackwell was the Orsborn Memorial Halls at Boscombe. As the name suggests it was built as a memorial to General Albert Orsborn, who became a soldier of that corps after retirement. It was opened on 24 November 1984 by Commissioner Howard Orsborn, the General's son. On the back wall to the platform The Salvation Army crest is created as an enlarged epaulet from the General's trimmings in plush velvet maroon material, some 20 feet (6metres) high, with the crest and laurel in gold. Boscombe is a large corps and consequently a large amount of accommodation was necessary to meet its needs on a rather restricted site with a limited construction cost of £500,000. The main hall alone required seating capacity of 600 with a community hall to seat a further 100 people and an even larger secondary hall plus the usual number of ancillary rooms. These factors had a particular effect on both the architectural design and the structural solution necessary. The main hall, measuring 20 by 15 metres, is traditional in shape with a large platform and gallery. To achieve the necessary volume for the correct acoustic effects the height of the hall internally is 7.8 metres to the underside of the beams. To reduce the apparent height of the façades to the adjacent street, the main hall and the building generally have a mansard roof slope around the perimeter. The designer also wanted to avoid large piers or a concrete frame projecting from the walls internally. The structural solution was to use 'post-tensioned' brickwork, a structural method developed by structural engineers W.G. Curtin and Partners. The roof structure consisted of steel beams cut and welded to form portal frames, thus minimalising their projection below the ceiling line.

The new suite of buildings for Hadleigh Temple designed by David Greenwood, a later chief architect, moved away from this traditional shape of hall. The main hall for worship and other formal occasions is octagonal in shape with a conical roof surmounted by a cupola of stained glass in Salvation Army colours of red, yellow and blue, all set in the centre of a beautiful pine wood ceiling. This approach had earlier been used in the design of Hereford hall, then subsequently in the new hall at Staines and also the Conference Centre at Sunbury Court. The Hadleigh main hall seats about 250 people with the ability to extend this by a further 140 seats into an adjacent multi-purpose hall by opening a moveable screen wall for such occasions as music concerts. Another general purpose hall and lounge can also be made into a

single space by opening a similar screen, thus giving the building great flexibility of use. The retention of a white, boarded, two storey building at the front provides both a link with the past and a contrasting element against the red brick main hall. The generous entrance foyer contains an oil painting by Rosa Branson depicting the history of the Salvation Army in Hadleigh creating an interesting welcome to the building.

The former congress hall in Brighton was demolished in 1999 to make way for another new design on the same site, which is in a conservation area. The new design therefore incorporated references to the Regency environment with zinc canopies and aprons to the slate roof, which helped to satisfy planning requirements. The plan form of the main hall is again octagonal in shape, doubling as a community centre during the week and a place of worship at weekends.

In designing the main meeting hall of any corps building to be used for worship and for musical festivals,

64. Hadleigh Temple Halls. (Above)

65. Rosa Branson's oil painting of Hadleigh. (Left)

66. Brighton Congress hall. (Right)

67. Brighton Congress hall interior. (Far right)

there is the problem of getting the correct balance in its acoustic properties. Halls of varying sizes need to cater for the spoken voice, usually amplified, at one extreme and a 30 piece brass band at the other. For all of these sounds the first requirement is to ensure that there are no sound reflections, that is echoes, which will affect the clarity of the sound as received by the listener. The second most important quality for each sound will be the reverberation time, which is the time it takes for the sound 'to die' or at least to become inaudible. For the spoken word the period required for this is very short, no more than one second and for amplified sound virtually none at all. In order to get the best from a brass band a period of about three seconds or more is preferred. Cathedrals often have a reverberation time of about five or six seconds, which suggests that the volume of the space is a major factor affecting it. A second factor affecting this is the type of surface provided by the ceiling, the walls, the floor and seating, as to whether they reflect or absorb sound waves.

The older type of 'music hall' design of Salvation Army halls usually had large volumes and reflective ceilings and walls. Consequently the long reverberation of sound in the singing, often boisterous, gave Army meetings a special quality. As pressures came to economise on the capital cost, the heights of halls were gradually reduced and at the same time absorbent acoustic tiles were often used for ceilings. The result was an apparent 'deadening' of the music, with suggestions that the spirit had gone out of Army meetings. Even in existing halls suspended ceilings were sometimes introduced to reduce heating costs, which in turn reduced the reverberation time and the acoustic qualities of the halls.

In the light of the above experience, by the mid 1970s the design of new larger halls had to include an acoustic analysis. One of the first halls where this was done was the new main hall at Wood Green in London seating 500 people, which was officially opened on 14 March 1976. The volume of the hall had to relate to the seating capacity, so that the initial criterion to be established was its required volume. The surfaces which might reflect sound waves received special treatment with the balcony front and down-stand beams being treated with perforated and moulded timber with absorbent backing. The projecting columns were treated with absorbent acoustic plaster. The ceiling had pine structural decking exposed as a sounding board and the floor was hardwood block. As special acoustic seating (which has sound absorbent qualities similar to those of a person) could not be afforded the correct reverberation period for music could only be achieved when the hall was full of people. An initial band practice held in the empty hall produced radically different results from the opening festival when the hall was full of people. Later halls, particularly those designed in-house benefitted from these experiences.

In contrast to such large halls, the corps at Driffield in Yorkshire converted a bungalow into its new hall, which was opened in May 2004. Many churches and Army corps commence as a 'house church' but that description

68. Driffield Corps hall.

69, 70 & 71. Chelmsford Corps hall 2009 building, interior and reflective tower. (Opposite)

may continue as an appropriate description for this corps for some time.

The new halls opened in Chelmsford in 2009 illustrate the latest development in the design of a large Salvation Army church and community building. Designed by Hudson Architects, the building has already received two awards in the Royal Institute of British Architects (RIBA) East Region Spirit of Ingenuity Awards 2009 as well as the ACE/RIBA Religious Architecture of the Year Award 2009. The building has won the Community Architecture Award as well as receiving the top accolade in the East of England Building of the Year Award, 2009. The building provides an assembly hall for worship and recreational facilities for a wide range of community outreach activities. It also used pioneering modern methods of construction in a cross laminated timber panel system, which allowed the building frame to be erected in just 24 days! Constructed entirely of timber and cloaked in an undulating zinc sheets, the new £2 million hall for Chelmsford Corps provides 900 square metres of new accommodation on the site of its former premises, which it had occupied since 1974. The recreational facilities provide for a wide range of community outreach activities, such as an elderly persons day centre, youth activities and toddler care. An indoor sports hall, outdoor play area, lounge, kitchen and foyer with reception café facilities are arranged around the 310-seater worship hall with administration offices located on the first floor.

Comments on Corps Halls

The initial requirement for corps halls was to build as cheaply as possible to seat as many people as possible. The cost of the first halls calculated at £1 per seat was initially thought to be too expensive. However, the latest corps building in 2009 cost a total of £2 million. As the variety of activity and programmes increased, the simple meeting hall concept developed into a building complex providing a wide range of different rooms and facilities. The development of the Army and its buildings was interrupted by two World Wars, thus preventing any progress during these periods. However, after a further short period of delay, the development of corps and the emergence of new design approaches for their buildings gradually gathered momentum.

During the 1960s, under the influence of Staff Architects David Blackwell and Ray Oakley, the establishment of a Client's Brief for all the requirements of new corps buildings instigated a process of extensive consultation with all the 'stake holders'. These included representatives of international, national and divisional headquarters, alongside the corps officer and representatives of the corps council. Inevitably there were strong personalities among these varied groups which sometimes led to long discussions. When disagreements arose, one of the principal questions in resolving matters was 'who is the 'client'? The Salvation Army Trustee Company, at that time part of IHQ, held the legal ownership of the property but the corps would be the building user. Internal funding often came from a variety of sources with the respective headquarters contributing funds. External sources such as local authorities or charitable donors were sometimes involved and they often had their own requirements. Blending all these views into a single set of requirements needed considerable skills of negotiation and 'arbitration'. This task was usually undertaken by the Salvation Army in-house architects. A concise, written 'Client's Brief' was essential before the building design could be carried out. At Wood Green a committee of all representatives previously mentioned met once a month for six months to establish the principles of the design for the buildings in Lymington Avenue. This suite of buildings was to replace the former halls, due to be demolished under a compulsory purchase order. One of the numerous issues to be resolved was whether community service rooms or the worship hall should take precedence in their location in being adjacent to the main pedestrian entrance. Another area of contention was whether corps sections, such as the band and songsters, should have rooms designated for their sole use or share them with other users, thus becoming multi-purpose rooms. The decisions taken there were to locate the community service areas nearest to the main entrance and to provide only multi-purpose rooms. These decisions at such an important corps set an example which other corps generally followed.

Even when the Client's Brief was established, it often took a large number of different feasibility studies, where time permitted, to agree the final design. For instance, at L'Islet in Guernsey, where new halls also opened in 1976, the first design was identified as 'A' and the final one built was 'J', so that ten different designs or variations were discussed before agreement was reached.

Sometimes the rapid changes taking place in the size and activities of a particular corps made it very difficult to decide on the requirements of a new hall, which was intended to provide future opportunities for both growth in numbers and flexibility in creating new programmes of activity. In order to provide for these possibilities, a different approach was tried by Neilsen Warren, an Australian architect working in the IHQ Architects Office, when he designed a new hall for Keighley, opened in 1968. His approach was to provide a variety of multi-purpose rooms of different sizes without defining or specifying the activities for which they were intended. The intention was that whatever size of group or type of activity was required, it could be accommodated in the most appropriate space. While this approach appears to have its advantages in flexibility of use, specific requirements are necessary for some activities, so that such general spaces are not always ideal for all purposes. The largest space, which would be used for worship, had therefore of necessity a moveable speaker's dais and a moveable penitents' form to maintain the availability of the space for other uses. A visit some 30 years later revealed that the various spaces had subsequently been adapted and modified to suit the requirements of specific uses. These had changed over the years with a major renovation scheme taking place in 1999. The building however had not been extended or modified structurally, so the initial design concept had indeed proved to be sufficiently flexible to meet the corps's changing needs over those 30 years.

Mention was made earlier of the difficulty of deciding upon the appropriate size for the main hall, as the Sunday congregation would usually be smaller than the numbers who attended on special occasions, such as Christmas carol services or festivals. A number of different solutions have been tried. For the new halls at Guildford it was decided to design a relatively small formal hall suitable for Sunday worship and a larger multi-purpose hall for all other occasions, which was a reversal of the usual priorities when the Client's Brief was established. This larger hall was provided with a fully retractable platform with a moveable mercy seat and rostrum for use in festivals, etc. It could also be used as the Community Hall where meals could be served or youth clubs could meet. This hall was designed to be of a suitable size and height to provide a badminton court and other active forms of recreational activity. The finishes to the respective halls were quite different, reflecting their different purposes.

In March 1982 the Leamington Spa Corps had to vacate its premises in Park Street, as the structure had

72. *Leamington Spa original Citadel. (Far left)*

73. *Leamington Spa main hall with screen open. (Left)*

74. *Leamington Spa new hall. (Left)*

75. *Staines new hall.*

76. *Staines double-sided mercy seat.*

become unsafe. After using other church buildings for over four years it was eventually able to move into its new premises in Chapel Street in October 1986. The new site and new building were funded by the sale of the old site to make way for a major redevelopment in the town centre. The problem of occasionally accommodating larger congregations for festivals, etc was solved in a slightly different way. A moveable sliding screen was provided between the worship and community halls, both of similar sizes, so that either hall could be enlarged as the need arose. The only problem with this solution is that the sound reduction qualities of the screen are poor, so that the two halls could not be used simultaneously if one activity required a quiet environment while the other was more boisterous.

With the development of acoustic moveable walls, consisting of large, sliding, interlocking panels, this type of arrangement became much more useful. It enabled the flexibility described above but did not limit the type of simultaneous activity possible in each space. This arrangement was first tried in the refurbishment of Catford Hall between the front lounge and main hall. It was later used to good effect in the new halls at Staines and Hadleigh where it allowed the main hall seating capacity to be greatly increased by opening up the adjacent community halls. One unusual feature in the Staines hall was the design of double sided moveable mercy seats where the penitent seeker could kneel on one side and the counsellor kneel on the other side.

The most unusual use of the moveable walls was in the design of the new hall for Lower Early Corps. A relatively small, octagonal-shaped worship hall, commensurate with the Sunday congregations, was positioned in the centre of the building with moveable walls on four sides, so that when required for festivals, etc the seating capacity of the hall could be virtually doubled in size

77. *Hadleigh hall with screens open.*

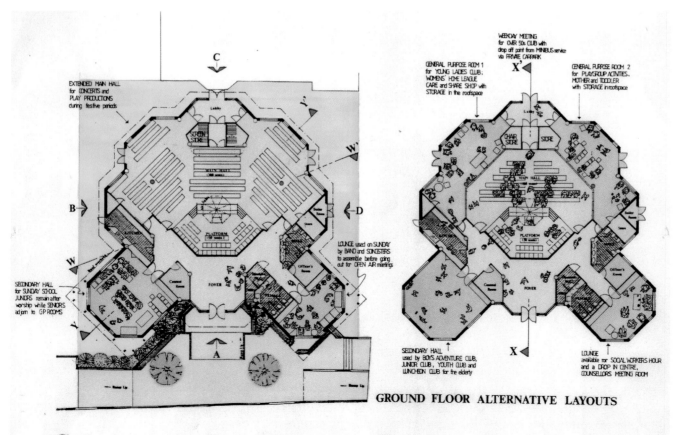

EXTENDED MAIN HALL for CONCERTS and PLAY PRODUCTIONS during festive periods

SECONDARY HALL for SUNDAY SCHOOL JUNIORS remain after worship while SENIORS adjourn to GP ROOMS

LOUNGE used on SUNDAY by BAND and SONGSTERS to assemble before going out for OPEN AIR meetings.

WEEKDAY MEETING for OVER 50s CLUB with drop off point from MINIBUS service via PRIVATE CARPARK

GENERAL PURPOSE ROOM 1 for YOUNG LADIES CLUB; WOMENS' HOME LEAGUE CARE and SHARE SHOP with STORAGE in the roofspace

GENERAL PURPOSE ROOM 2 for PLAYGROUP ACTIVITIES, MOTHER and TODDLER with STORAGE in roofspace

SECONDARY HALL used by BOYS ADVENTURE CLUB, JUNIOR CLUB, YOUTH CLUB and LUNCHEON CLUB for the elderly

LOUNGE available for SOCIAL WORKERS HOUR and a DROP IN CENTRE, COUNSELLORS MEETING ROOM

GROUND FLOOR ALTERNATIVE LAYOUTS

78. Lower Earley (formerly Reading East) Corps hall – interior and exterior views. Drawing shows alternative layouts possible with moveable screens. (Bottom far left)

while maintaining the minimum distance from the furthest seat to the platform.

Changes in legislation continued to play their part in influencing both new and existing corps halls. The Disability Discrimination Act 1995 included sections on facilities and services required in public buildings. It was implemented in gradual stages over a number of years, though regulations to cater for disabled people in *new-build* premises had already been introduced in 1987. Then, from October 2004, new responsibilities were placed on owners of all existing public buildings, including Salvation Army halls, to ensure that disabled people could gain access without obstruction and be provided with suitable toilet facilities. While the Army was keen to ensure that all of its facilities were available to people with physical disabilities, the difficulties and costs involved in adapting so many of its older premises in so short a time proved to be a challenge. The existing hall at Catford built in 1925 is an example of the type of alterations which proved necessary. Ramped access and exits without hindrances were provided to all of the ground floor rooms. A new entrance lobby to the Community Hall and internal link with wide corridors was provided between both halls together with toilets designed for both ambulant disabled people and wheelchair users. The renovated premises which included these improvements were opened in February 2005.

Since the separation of international and territorial headquarters administrations in 1990, there has been a gradual delegation of authority for corps building schemes from headquarters to the individual corps. Undoubtedly the more the corps members are involved in the process of deciding the building's requirements and its design, the greater will be their immediate satisfaction in the result. However, the gradual withdrawal of Salvation Army staff architects from this process has deprived corps of the benefit of their accumulated knowledge, not only of Salvation Army corps buildings, but of their experience and creative skills in assisting corps to think through the opportunities afforded when a new building is planned. Buildings designed for previous generations may have restricted growth and restricted the changes that corps need to make in their activities in order to meet fresh needs. Relocation or rebuilding is more than a building opportunity; it is a chance to remodel the nature and focus of each corps, freed from the previous physical restrictions of a building they have 'outgrown'. In presenting such opportunities as afforded by a new building, Salvation Army architects have sometimes presented blank sheets to corps, expressing their excitement about what possibilities it offers, not only for the design of a building but more importantly for the creation of a new concept for the corps, if this is then felt necessary.

When the Reverend Lesley Griffiths was invited to address Salvation Army leaders at THQ on what issues they should consider as part of their future strategic plans, the first suggestion that he made was *'a willingness to die'*. Subsequent discussion suggested this was both a scriptural requirement involved in personal salvation and also a principle evident in the natural world. New life and new growth can only take place after the old has 'died'. If churches or organisations are to stay relevant to each new generation and culture then it is essential that they are willing to sacrifice some long-held practices and customs. The story of the development of some corps, illustrated in and symbolised by their new buildings, is a clear example of this principle.

The Salvation Army does not have a set litany or prescribed liturgy for its services, so meeting leaders are free to choose and arrange the form and contents of the service in any way they wish; the only essentials are that they include a Bible reading and prayer. However, for many years a lot of corps have followed a fairly predictable pattern of worship, so the meeting format has become rather stereotyped. It is not until the last decade that this freedom has once again been fully exploited. In recent years there has developed a great variety in the form of worship with some corps using only modern songs, often projected onto a large screen, some keeping to the traditional songs from The Salvation Army Song Book, while others provide a combination of these. Some corps keep a very formal layout both in their seating arrangement and in the atmosphere of worship, while others have a much greater freedom of expression. A visitor from Australia visited several London corps in the year 2,000 and described the extremes of these approaches found in two very different corps; he described one meeting being like a 'mausoleum' and the other as 'bedlam'. While such comments are undoubtedly exaggerations, they do illustrate the very different forms of worship that can now be found within Army corps. The wide cultural and spiritual background of people now attending Army meetings is reflected in the variety of their preferred style of worship. A recent influx of Salvationists from Africa has also had a dramatic effect on the forms of worship in some corps, with spontaneous singing and dancing becoming a regular feature, as they seek to express the joy of their Christian experience in a way relevant to their own cultural background.

The location of corps has of course a bearing on the type of activities developed. Corps situated within deprived urban areas are often called upon to meet a range of community care needs, and the corps programme will be focused upon activities to meet those needs. This type of centre was originally designated as a Goodwill Centre where the Christian gospel was proclaimed more as 'love in action' rather than in preaching, such as the centre at Deptford.

Corps located in outer urban areas, among more affluent communities, tend to give priority to typical church-type activities. Their priorities would concentrate on worship for different age groups, Bible studies and prayer meetings, Alpha courses, other social activities as well as a comprehensive range of musical groups such as brass bands and singing groups for both children and adults.

Since the 1970s, the external walls of new Salvation Army halls have become more transparent with a greater percentage of clear glass windows, even to the main worship halls. Although not intended, the image created by the original external treatment of Salvation Army halls was one of 'protection against the world'. The main halls, where they had windows, were generally at high level and glazed with obscured glass, either to prevent people seeing in or to limit any distraction to the worshippers inside. Halls erected during the last 40 years generally provide more windows and have clear glazing to allow views in or out of the building. Some corps, however, use window blinds permanently drawn to the windows of the worship hall.

In his illustrated book *Doors* Val Clery states: '*History, belief and custom impose character on doors as heredity imposes it on faces*'. If this is true of doors it is similarly true of buildings as a whole and, I believe, of Salvation Army buildings in particular.

When The Salvation Army commenced it had a very clear mission focus, summed up in how William Booth described the purpose of Salvationists, which was '*getting saved, keeping saved and getting others saved*'. Even the early development of Salvation Army social work was questioned by William Booth as he considered that it might divert attention away from 'soul saving'. This mission focus was directed towards the 'downtrodden' poor but The Salvation Army's vision was huge; 'the world for God'. Because of this and other factors, such as the military organisation of the movement, it had tremendous success and its work spread rapidly.

Commentators in the present century have suggested that The Salvation Army was 'good at mission', presumably the result of Booth's prime directive but 'not good at building a church'. This is not of course intended to refer to the architecture, as the church is the people not the building. As mentioned earlier, Booth originally intended to send his converts to existing churches. When this proved impractical he commenced his own denomination, described firstly as a mission, then as an army, which provided places to which his converts could go for worship and to assist in saving the unconverted. William and Catherine believed in holiness of life for Christian people, so the Army gave equal weight to the preaching of the Gospel and to the standards required of Salvationists which focused on holiness through the indwelling of God's Holy Spirit. As regular patterns for Sunday worship gradually evolved, each of the Sunday meetings had a different focus, with the Sunday morning meeting generally called the holiness meeting and the Sunday evening meeting called the salvation meeting. These labels reflected the prime focus of all that took place, especially in the preaching. Other meetings had other emphases, such as the praise and testimony meetings. Salvation Army preaching and teaching is related to the individual development of a personal experience and a close relationship with God. General Frederick Coutts ensured that The Salvation Army Social Work was seen as of equal importance to preaching by stating that they were opposite sides of the same coin, revealing God's love by word and by action. The holistic purpose of The Salvation Army was encapsulated in General John Gowan's words describing the Salvation Army mission as *'saving sinners, growing saints and serving suffering humanity'*.

The Salvation Army was initially very efficient and highly effective as a mission. In order to achieve this, the average corps activity on a Sunday was extremely hectic for the majority of the soldiership. Band members for instance would attend three or perhaps four open-air meetings on a Sunday in addition to a similar number of indoor meetings. This demanding activity would often involve members of the band and songster brigade entering and leaving the hall by different entrances to the rest of the congregation, leaving little time for socialising. Other people would be involved in young people's activities, such as the Sunday Schools. This hectic Sunday programme sometimes led to the fragmentation of the corps membership with individuals and groups focusing solely upon their own area of responsibility. The buildings of that time reflected this separation in their layout, especially in the provision of separate entrance doors for different sections and even separate buildings for the young people's activity.

Comments about The Salvation Army at some periods of its history 'not being good at building a church' might have some relation to experiences of fragmented corps fellowships, where the hectic Sunday activity and other factors played their part. In recent years, where concerns of this nature have been expressed, some corps have developed activity specifically aimed at developing a united corps fellowship to combat this tendency. The labelling of Sunday meetings has also changed to titles such as 'family service' or 'fellowship meeting', suggesting an increased desire to build Salvation Army corps into church fellowships. The design of more recent halls has reflected the desire for a unified corps by the provision of a single large entrance foyer into which all entrance doors and the circulation routes lead. This

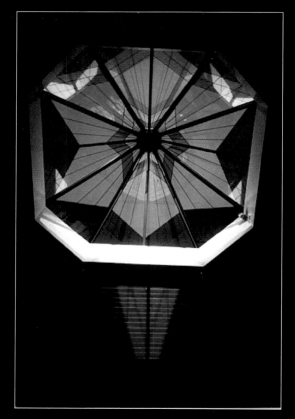

79. Coloured glass used symbolically in halls including
Aberdeen Citadel, Staines, Hadleigh, Brighton and Maidstone

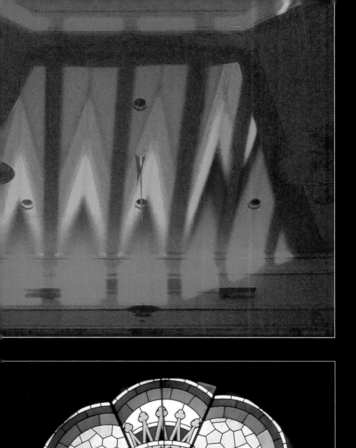
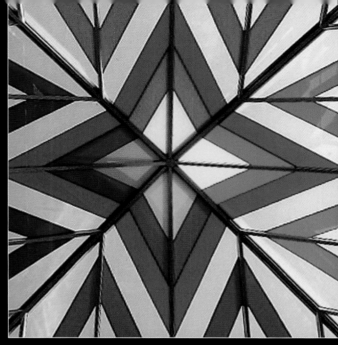

arrangement thus ensures that all members of the corps fellowship have an opportunity to meet at some time during their visit to the hall.

The evolution of The Salvation Army's corps activity, as it has tried to respond to changes in society over the 145 years included in this book, has been reflected in these changes in Army corps buildings. Each period has sought to reflect and cater better for the full gamut of the purposes of The Salvation Army encapsulated in John Gowans's description. As suggested at the start of this book, the human values and priorities set by any group of people tend to be symbolised in the artefacts created, especially in buildings, even where done subconsciously. Of course, there have been some conscious efforts to reflect spiritual symbolism, for instance in the use of coloured glass, in the same way that stained glass windows in churches have done for hundreds of years. The primary colours of red, yellow and blue to symbolise the Trinity have been used in Army buildings in windows, as in Aberdeen Citadel, and in the roof-lights and cupolas of modern Army buildings.

The buildings acquired or built for Salvation Army corps purposes have reflected changes in emphasis in their form and image as well as in the symbols attached to them. The original mission halls were secular buildings, such as music halls or skating rinks. Army halls had fortress-like castellations and turrets etc, added to show they were the base for the activity of an Army corps. Present halls are becoming more church-like both in appearance and style. The original symbols used on Salvation Army buildings were The Salvation Army crest, flag and the wording 'The Salvation Army', sometimes with additional words such as Barracks, Fort, Fortress, Citadel or just Corps Hall. Recent halls often have a cross on the outside or on the inside or both. The word Church is sometimes added to 'The Salvation Army' lettering. Some new corps halls have abandoned the crest, which traditionally was associated with Salvation Army places of worship, and substituted The Salvation Army shield, which was traditionally the symbol of Salvation Army service in centres such as the Red Shield canteens on British military camps. All these different styles and symbols can now be found on Salvation Army corps buildings, confirming the variety of views as to the nature of an Army corps and the freedom afforded in the style of worship and service provided. Some might suggest that Salvation Army corps in the UK are currently searching for an identity, but there seems no desire among the leadership to enforce any conformity in the style of worship, specific activity or style of building used by corps. This freedom should give each local corps a true sense of ownership of its corps expression and encourage it to freely respond to the needs of its own community and the leading of God's Holy Spirit.

The photographs of new halls at Hereford, Staines, Boscombe, L'Islet, Reading, Hadleigh, Deptford, Chester-le-Street, Maidstone, Sholing and Chelmsford and the renovated Norwich Citadel illustrate the wide variety of these buildings as expressions of this freedom, both in their exterior and interior design.

Clockwise from top left:

80. Architects perspective drawing of Hereford hall.

83. Chester-le-Street hall.

84. Maidstone hall.

85. Sholing hall.

86. Deptford hall.

82. Reading Central halls.

81. Norwich Citadel hall (after renovations).

87a. Ground floor plans showing alternative ways of enlarging the seating capacity of the main hall for festivals etc.

Horsham halls

Maidstone halls

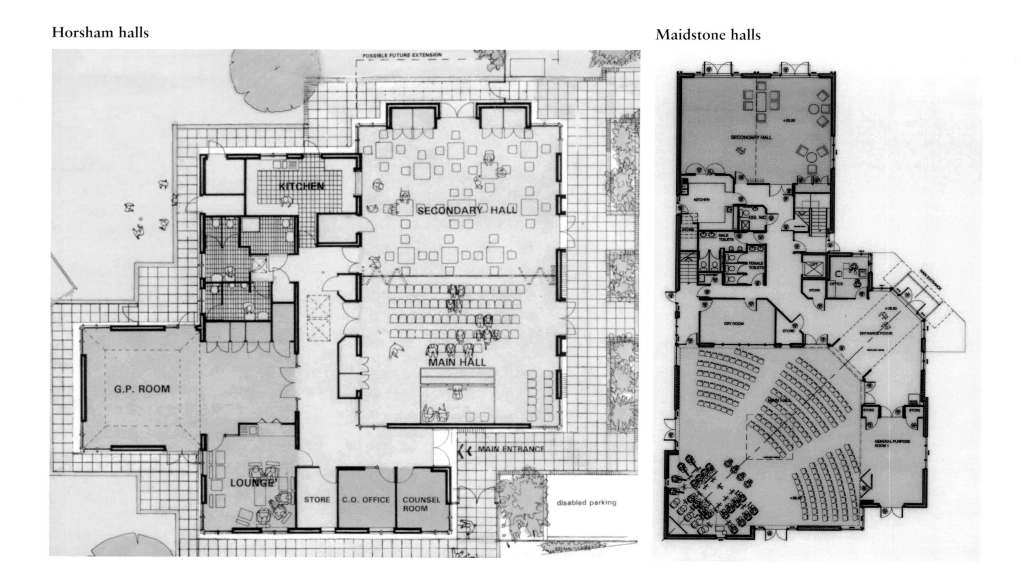

87b. Ground floor plans showing alternative ways of enlarging the seating capacity of the main hall for festivals etc.

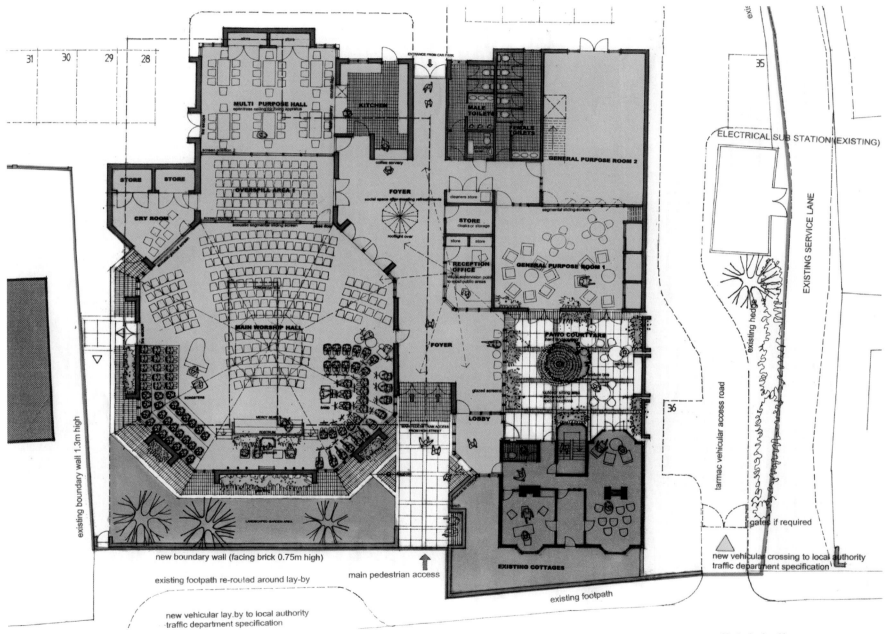

Hadleigh halls

88. *Brighton Congress hall – aerial view drawing*

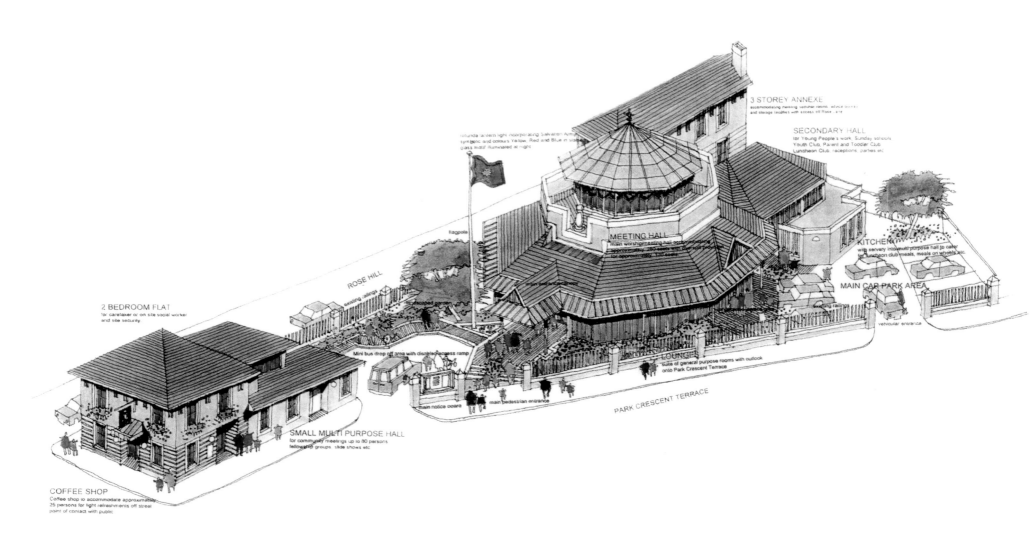

3 STOREY ANNEXE
accommodating meeting, seminar rooms, advice bureau
and storage facilities with access off Rose Hill

SECONDARY HALL
for Young People's work, Sunday schools,
Youth Club, Parent and Toddler Club,
Luncheon Club, receptions, parties etc.

rotunda lantern light incorporating Salvation Army
symbolic colours Yellow, Red and Blue in stained
glass motif illuminated at night

MEETING HALL
main worship/meeting hall accommodating
approximately 280 people with balcony provision
for approximately 120 seats

KITCHEN
with servery into main purpose hall to cater
for luncheon club meals, meals on wheels etc.

flagpole

ROSE HILL

existing railings

landscaped garden

MAIN CAR PARK AREA

2 BEDROOM FLAT
for caretaker or on site social worker
and site security.

vehicular entrance

Mini bus drop off area with disabled access ramp

LOUNGE
suite of general purpose rooms with outlook
onto Park Crescent Terrace

main notice board

main pedestrian entrance

PARK CRESCENT TERRACE

SMALL MULTI PURPOSE HALL
for community meetings up to 80 persons,
fellowship groups, slide shows etc

COFFEE SHOP
Coffee shop to accommodate approximately
25 persons for light refreshments off street
point of contact with public

SALVATION ARMY SOCIAL WORK

89. Architect's perspective drawing of Edward Alsop Court, Westminster

Introduction

As early as 1869 William Booth was aware that *'no one gets a blessing if they have cold feet and nobody ever got saved while they had a toothache!'* The need to link the spiritual challenges with practical assistance for people's welfare was therefore apparent at a very early stage of Salvation Army development. In 1881, a midnight meeting was held in Whitechapel. One of the Salvationists, Mrs Elizabeth Cottrill, knelt at the mercy seat with a girl who had no other home than a brothel. Recognizing that it would be impossible for the girl to grow in her Christian faith in such a setting and failing to find any place of lodging that would take the girl in, Mrs Cottrill took her into her own home. She was the first of many girls cared for by Mrs Cottrill, whose back kitchen in essence constituted the Salvation Army's first social home. As she patrolled the streets of Whitechapel to find these girls, she often suffered violence from men seeking the girls for prostitution. Her prayers for a larger house, which could be set aside for its purpose as a rescue home, found an answer in the availability of a house in Hanbury Street, Whitechapel.

Bramwell Booth was challenged as to whether The Salvation Army should take up rescue work officially, or confine its activities to evangelism, a dilemma that has engaged *some* within the Army ever since. When William Booth was asked if 'The Salvation Army proper' had suffered from the competition of the Social Work, he replied, *'It is The Salvation Army proper. We want to abolish these distinctions and make it as religious to sell a guernsey or feed a hungry man as it is to take up a collection in the barracks. It is all part of our business, which is to save the world, body and soul, for time and eternity'.* Mrs Cotterill set a lead by having her girls embroider 'The Salvation Army' in yellow cross-stitch on the red jerseys which constituted early day uniform (at 3s.6d per dozen).

By the time the twelfth rescue home was opened in Middlesbrough, this need to train the girls in work which would make them an honest living was also being addressed. Soon, the work extended from rescue and work training to campaigning on social issues. Ordinarily, the girls helped were young, but an older converted former brothel keeper, Rebecca Jarrett, played an important part with many others in the Salvation Army's successful campaign to raise the age of consent, incorporated into the Criminal Law Amendment Act 1885.

It was from this practical concern that The Salvation Army Social Services commenced and continued to develop. Booth's conviction that it was useless to preach about a God of love without trying to improve the living conditions of his listeners, grew stronger as the years passed. Having carefully considered what he should do, one night in 1886 he sent his son Bramwell to talk to Mrs Harriet Webb, a sergeant of The Salvation Army Corps in Battersea, London. Bramwell Booth asked her if she would be willing to work and live in the slums. In spite of the initial shock, Harriet and her builder husband agreed, so they moved into the Walworth area of London. Her days were spent visiting the poor and taking food to the starving and clothing to those in rags. A natural part of this ministry was praying with the sick.

Returning home late on a cold December night in 1887, William Booth saw men sleeping out on the London bridges. The next morning he challenged his son, Bramwell, to do something. Within a month, four centres were opened in London, located in West India Dock Road, Whitechapel, Clerkenwell and Burne Street. These premises gave shelter, food and work to homeless men. The need for this type of accommodation was so great that other centres soon followed in many other parts of the

90. Egg-box 'coffin' beds.

country. Some people starved to death on the streets of London, and many women and girls turned to prostitution as their only way of surviving. The first shelter for women, as mentioned earlier, was in Hanbury Street, London.

By 1890 The Salvation Army had established 33 homes for prostitutes, five shelters for homeless people and one for alcoholics. It was in that year that William Booth wrote his treatise *In Darkest England and the Way Out.* This book highlighted the tragic situation in the lives of 'the submerged tenth of the population' and gave a blueprint for more effective ways to help the poor and needy. It ran into five editions within twelve months and became recognised in many countries as a major social treatise making a significant contribution to social work thinking. William Booth had used the research findings from East London collated by Mr. Charles Booth (not a relative) to calculate the number of people in London who were paupers, homeless, starving or just very poor. The book was a call to action, as William Booth challenged his readers by 'The Cab Horse Charter', mentioned earlier. This 'prophet of the poor' reminded his British readers that this humble standard was at that time unobtainable by millions of men and women in this country, estimated as one tenth of the population. General Booth set out to change this situation in his 'Darkest England' scheme. In order to safeguard the money collected and the donations made for these social purposes The Salvation Army set up the Darkest England Trust by a Deed completed on 1 January 1891. In later years the name was changed to The Salvation Army Social Trust, but it has always been kept separate from The Salvation Army Evangelical or General Trust.

Some Victorians sought to divide the poor into those deserving assistance, being poor through no fault of their own and those undeserving of help, who were deemed to have caused their own problems. William Booth did not make any such distinctions but insisted that those receiving help should contribute by work and co-operation to their own rehabilitation. His plans included spiritual conversion as he believed that changed hearts led to changed lives.

In the nine years after the publication of his book, The Salvation Army supplied 27 million cheap meals, gave lodgings to 11 million homeless people, traced 18,000 missing persons and found work for 90,000 jobless people, in the British Isles alone. The provision of the lodgings was very basic as are shown in the illustrations, with wooden egg boxes for sleeping, which became known as 'coffins'. Leather covers were made in the Army workshops, which were easy to 'wipe down'. Photographs of the Burne Street shelter, on the next page, show some of these boxes and later improvements by the provision of metal beds with sheets and blankets, but even then, they were still tightly packed into the dormitories to provide the maximum number of beds.

The illustration of the exterior of an early shelter

The purpose of this colony was to train unemployed men in agriculture. The scheme was so successful that similar farms were set up in California, Colorado and Ohio in the United States and an 'overseas colony' was also set up in Rhodesia, now Zimbabwe, in central Africa. A 'City Colony' was set up in 1896 housing 600 men at Spa Road in the Bermondsey area of London as a first step out of poverty. These 'colonies' were part of Booth's elevator plan to help people lift themselves out of a life of despair. Food, accommodation and work were provided as well as training in a variety of crafts and trades. Many men moved from the city colony onto the farm colony and then overseas to Canada, New Zealand and Australia as well as Rhodesia, where labour was in demand. They thus were given a chance to commence a new life full of purpose and promise in a new environment.

91. Burne Street shelter dormitories (first and second class accommodation?) (Left)

92. Early shelter and labour exchange. (Below)

shows the first Salvation Army Labour Exchange, opened on 16 June 1890, which was combined with the first head-quarters for the Men's Social Work. This was 20 years before Winston Churchill instituted government labour exchanges on 1 February 1910 and 26 years before the creation of the Ministry of Labour in Britain. An example of the type of employment created by the Army is shown in the tin factory workshop on Battersea Wharf.

Within seven months of launching his 'Darkest England Scheme', William Booth took possession of an 800-acre estate at Hadleigh, Essex to set up a farm colony.

Services to Homeless Men

Following the publication of Booth's book, The Salvation Army rapidly expanded its social work and especially its provision for homeless men. Empty buildings of all descriptions were acquired to provide food, shelter, work and exposure to the Gospel message. These buildings included empty factories, warehouses, redundant workhouses, former asylums and orphanages. They were filled with as many beds as they could hold, with dormitories often containing between 80 to 100 beds with each building housing between 400 and 900 men. These hostels were opened as an immediate response to a desperate situation. The conditions were very basic but were considered preferable to living on the street. One of the buildings was a former music hall and theatre and was used initially to house the West End Corps in London. It was later used as a hostel known as the Great Western with only the minimum of alteration. The main theatre was used as a dormitory, and many of the beds positioned on the narrow tiers of the balcony. Many other existing buildings were acquired and brought into use as social centres but some later closed or were replaced. The interior walls of these buildings often had scriptural texts or other practical messages of hope such as 'No man need beg, steal, starve, sleep out at night, be a pauper or commit suicide. We will help you'.

In 1965, a century after the commencement of the Christian Mission by William Booth, his successor General Frederick Coutts published a review of The Salvation Army Social Work entitled *Tragedies of Affluence*. The findings of this review included a re-appraisal of The Salvation Army's work among homeless single men. It showed that at that time The Salvation Army:

93. Battersea Tin factory

Faith House

A midnight post was set up in Kings Cross in 1899 which became known as Faith House. Built as a show house for a building firm and erected in the forecourt of Kings Cross Station, it was later made available to The Salvation Army. Its strategic position facilitated work among prostitutes and those in danger of being drawn into prostitution. Faith House was relocated in 1965 to the present premises in Argyle Street. Midnight patrols were organised to make contact with vulnerable young people arriving on their own at the London Stations as well as continuing to make contact with street workers in the sex trade, until legislation made 'walking the streets' to tout for such 'work' illegal. A work of chaplaincy and befriending continues there with women officers still living among the people they serve.

Provided 60 hostels housing about 7,000 single men every night, more than the total number of men housed in all local authority hostels and in all other voluntary agency hostels. There were separate hostels for single women and families but the main provision was for single men.

The conditions within which those homeless men were housed were little better than those existing in the previous century, with beds set eighteen inches apart in dormitories still housing between 80 to 100 men each.

There were few facilities provided, with one London hostel having no showers and only three baths for 400 men.

There was only one purpose-built Salvation Army hostel at that time, located in Sheffield, with a few hostel buildings acquired from other organisations. Most of the remainder were converted workhouses or warehouses, designed more to store goods than to house people.

In spite of these dreadful conditions all the hostels were virtually full every night, with some men being turned away.

General Coutts was of the opinion that when William Booth commenced housing homeless people in the last century, he perceived it to be an emergency measure and would not have expected The Salvation Army still to be a major provider of hostel accommodation in 1965. It was also his view that no one would relieve The Salvation Army of this legacy of caring for so many homeless men. He stated that urgent action was needed to replace all of

94. Blackfriars Hostel. (Top left)

95. Riverside House. (Above)

96. Middlesex Street Hostel. (Far left)

97. Victoria Homes. (Left)

these inappropriate buildings. A selection of these hostel buildings in London is illustrated with pictures of Blackfriars, Middlesex Street, Riverside House and Victoria Homes, where, between them 2,000 homeless men were still housed every night in the capital city. Some plans had already been drawn up for new hostels to provide a further 1,000 beds nationally because of the heavy demand on the existing hostels. Following this review a challenging appeal, entitled *For God's Sake Care*, was launched. This appeal provided the necessary momentum to commence the replacement of these old hostel buildings, the first of which was Booth House in

Whitechapel. However, it has taken almost 40 years for this policy to be fully implemented. By 2010 all of those original buildings had been or were in the process of being replaced or adapted and significantly improved.

When The Salvation Army started to replace these old hostels, little guidance was available concerning the standards of accommodation appropriate for such buildings. Sections of the Housing Acts 1936 and 1949 and the Public Health Act 1936 provided the basis for a publication by the government's Department of the Environment entitled *The Interim Lodging House Standards*. This set out minimum standards for the space required for each bed in dormitories, the minimum size of single bedrooms as well as the minimum number and size of common rooms, such as dining and lounge areas. These minimum sizes were very small, such as 50 square feet for each bed in a dormitory and 70 square feet for a single bedroom. However, because the demand for hostels beds was still so great and the new hostels had to be funded by charitable giving, these had to be accepted as the design standards used for the time being.

Following its review of hostels in 1965, The Salvation Army both encouraged and sponsored a series of academic research projects and strategic reviews on homelessness because of the paucity of relevant information. This information has been used to help guide the policies and processes for the replacement of hostels. The following list shows the variety of documents and the wide range of issues which were explored:

- 1973 *A Study of the Environmental Conditions for Housing Homeless Men* carried out by Ray Oakley as part of his studies for RIBA membership.
- 1980 *Profiles and Perspectives of Hostel Residents* completed by Ray Oakley as the thesis for an M.Sc

degree in Environmental Psychology
- 1984 *Old and New Hostels,* a dissertation by Paul Oakley as part of his RIBA studies
- 1989 *Designing for Therapy,* a thesis by Jean Moore for an M.Sc degree in Environmental Psychology as a follow-up study to the above 1980 thesis.
- 1991 *Faces of Homelessness* – a major review of homelessness across London by the University of Surrey under the direction of Professor David Canter
- 1991 *Seeking Excellence* by Madeline Drake – research into Salvation Army views on the way forward.
- 1991 *Strategy for Change* by Ray Oakley – the response of The Salvation Army to the above research findings
- 1993 *Corporate Plan for the Salvation Army Social Services* setting out the manner in which The Salvation Army would implement its action outlined in the above documents.
- 1999 *The Paradox of Prosperity* by the Henley Centre
- 2001 *Window of Hope for Homeless People,* a dissertation by Loukia Lingi as part of her RIBA studies
- 2001 *The Burden of Youth* by the Henley Centre
- 2004 *The Responsibility Gap* by the Henley Centre
- 2009 *The Seeds of Exclusion* by Dr Adrian Bonner and Claire Luscombe.

The above Salvation Army sponsored research documents have also been used to challenge both government policies and public perceptions of homeless people, in addition to helping guide Salvation Army social programmes.

On 25 January 1986 Ray Oakley had the following article published in the periodical *Building Design* as part of this process. It described the situation at that time in The Salvation Army's programme of replacing the old type of hostels:

A HOSTEL? What kind an environment is that to live in? And in any case, who needs them? I would suggest that many people who live in their family home in a semi-detached house rightly question the need and role of hostels. Even if the need is accepted, the term hostel is often interchangeable with other expressions, such as 'doss house', which is indicative of the stigma associated with living in a hostel. Anyone involved in the design of hostel accommodation for the single homeless needs to understand the variety of roles which hostels fulfil and have knowledge of the range of people using them. Some homeless single people merely require emergency accommodation to help them over a temporary crisis, while others require long-term housing in a supportive environment to minimise a physical, mental or social handicap. To some people a hostel is a springboard back into society, while for others it is a necessary refuge from the problems and responsibilities of society.

The Salvation Army has been providing hostel accommodation for 101 years. Having observed homeless men and women sleeping on the Thames Embankment in 1884, William Booth, its founder, acquired redundant warehouses and workhouses to provide food and shelter for them. The concept of hostels as temporary emergency lodgings was developed with the criteria of minimum provision for the maximum number of homeless people.

While the coming of the welfare state has resulted in some voluntary social services becoming unnecessary, the shortage of suitable accommodation has resulted in many of these old hostels continuing in use until the present day. During the last 20 years, as the largest single provider of hostel accommodation, The Salvation

Army has replaced approximately 50 per cent of its hostels with new purpose-built premises. During the last five of these years, this has been made possible by funds channelled through The Salvation Army Housing Association from local authorities and the Housing Corporation. David Blackwell, the chief architect to the Army and myself have been involved in establishing the client's brief and in controlling the design for all of these new hostels, erected during that 20 year period.

In order to understand our 'clients', the hostel residents, a number of research projects have been carried out to gather data on what they require for both their immediate and future needs. Each new project has benefited from this research and also from further feedback from those schemes completed to date. The general 'open door' policy of referral has resulted in a wide range of clients with a variety of needs and preferences using these hostels. The concept of the new hostels is to create a therapeutic environment and to allow residents a variety of options in the type of accommodation available. The term therapeutic implies a change or improvement of behaviour, and one of the socio-psychological models on which the concept is based is one which allows personal growth at a rate, and directed to achievable goals, suited to the individual.

In some of the latest hostels at Bolton, Blackburn and Liverpool, the range of accomodation includes four-bed dormitories, single rooms, bed-sitting rooms and self-contained flats. Accommodation is arranged in groups of various sizes with a maximum of 10 beds within each group. A varying degree of independence and self-

reliance is therefore possible within these groups. These schemes have been designed to meet particular local criteria, but they seek to reflect the character of traditional housing in the north-west of England with red brick walls and dark grey slated roofs. The quality of design, construction and materials is intended to provide an image externally and an environment internally, which will counteract the usual stigma of hostel buildings, both for the benefit of the hostel residents and the local community.

The experience of being made homeless is traumatic, often accompanied by other problems, such as loss of parents or family. Entering a hostel may compound the problem with a feeling of lost individuality and the associated problems of living in an 'institution'. One of the design concepts of these new centres is, therefore, to provide an environment which is enhanced from the norm. As the role of the centre is a therapeutic one, the environment needs to stimulate hope for the future and restore a sense of pride in oneself. These goals are the very opposite of most hostel environments. In the new centres, the standard provided may appear closer to that of a high-class hotel than a hostel for the homeless. However, given the specific goals associated with a therapeutic environment, it is essential that the experience of entering a hostel can be part of a rehabilitation process and not a 'downward spiral'. Those residents capable of living independently are encouraged to do so.

Where necessary, social and domestic skills are taught before resettlement and independent living can be experienced in 'training flats', sometimes provided within the hostel, as at Bolton. Those

unable to sustain independent living may remain at the hostel, making it their home for as long as needed.

The new hostels provide facilities for housing physically disabled residents, including wheelchair users, although only in limited numbers. Special care units for elderly and long-term residents give greater independence, each person having a bed-sitting room and the group a separate lounge and kitchen.

The other units of accommodation have been used for other groups, such as women residents, or young people, or groups who require complete separation from the main hostel, due to behavioural or medical problems such as drug abuse or perhaps alcohol addiction.

Further research is now proceeding on the use of these latest hostels and it is hoped that future schemes will benefit from this feedback. The Salvation Army hopes that the remainder of the older hostels will soon be replaced by similar or better centres to those shown.

As described in this article, one of the key recommendations arising from the research reports was that the facilities for homeless people should be designed and managed as therapeutic environments, places of healing and support. Six different socio-psychological models of therapeutic environments were outlined in the reports, which described them as individual growth, enhancement, medical, custodial, prosthetic and normalisation models. However, a hostel environment does not fit neatly into any one model, so the recommendations included elements of a number of these models which were considered the most appropriate to hostel settings and the profiles of their residents. All the above information was fed into the design processes of new hostels as it came to light, so for the next two decades architects and policy makers had a wealth of information and directives to guide them as the replacement of old hostel buildings continued.

During the 1970s, new buildings replaced many of the old hostels in all areas of the country. In Birmingham a new hostel was built in Shadwell Street, opposite St Chad's Roman Catholic Cathedral, initially to replace two old hostels in the city. The policy at that time was to provide for the same number of hostel residents as were housed in the old hostels that they replaced, but housed mainly in single rooms. In Birmingham an additional floor was added after the third existing hostel closed. There was uncertainty as to whether this large number of beds would be needed in the future, so there was a need to allow for future alterations in the layout. The architect's solution here was to allow for this flexibility by designing the floor and roof structure to span across the whole width of the building, without any intermediate structural walls except around the lift shaft and staircases. The partitions between rooms were all designed to be demountable, with a modular layout to the lighting and power system to allow any future remodelling. The main problem with this approach was that the partitions between rooms provided very little sound insulation, so that it was alleged that if someone coughed in the night, it would wake up those sleeping in several adjacent rooms on either side. In spite of this provision very few of those partitions were altered in the next 25 years until a major refurbishment was carried out in 2002. Because of the sound-proofing problem, this approach to future flexibility of layout was not repeated.

Another similar project was Lawley House in Leeds Road, Bradford where the new hostel opened in 1976 by General Clarence D. Wiseman replaced two former hostels in Richard Street and Peel Street. The architect

98. *Birmingham Hostel (Shadwell Street)*

99. *Lawley House, Bradford. (Right)*

described it as a large home for a rather special family of people. This was the last hostel for the next 25 years to be funded solely by the Army's own resources.

Following the 1970s expansion of The Salvation Army Housing Association in England and its sister organisation in Scotland, the replacement of existing hostels accelerated but it was carried out with the help of SAHA mainly using government funding. Even some of the relatively modern hostels were completely refurbished through SAHA, including Lawley House which was refurbished in 1998 with much improved facilities.

The new building in Blackburn, by then called a Social Service Centre, which accommodated 80 single men or women principally in single rooms, was one of the new brand of Salvation Army/SAHA hostels. It was

opened in 1981 by S. Roy Fisher, the High Sheriff of Lancashire and a partner in the architectural firm which supervised its construction. A similar hostel opened in Duke Street, Bolton, included a central landscaped garden area. This not only provided a pleasant outlook from the dining room, small lounge and other day rooms but also a sheltered and restful private external environment where the residents could sit and relax, possibly watching the gold fish in the garden pond.

London was the exception to this rapid progress where, except for Booth House and Hopetown in Whitechapel, little progress could be made in replacing a number of out-dated hostels. There were a number of reasons for this, but after the demise of the Greater London Council which had assisted with the funding for both Booth House and Hopetown, there was no London-wide strategic planning or housing authority. Individual London boroughs tended to have a rather parochial attitude, being reluctant to tackle on their own what they deemed to be a London-wide homelessness problem.

100. Gilead House, Bolton, showing inner courtyard garden. (Above and right)

It was only after the publication of *The Faces of Homelessness* report and some embarrassing publicity that Central Government decided to provide additional funding to alleviate the London situation. These two factors were part of the pressure that produced the Government's new 'Rough Sleepers Initiative' focusing on the London homelessness problem. By then The Salvation Army had its own strategy in place and thus was able to benefit from this central government support and funding. New outreach teams were formed to contact the 'rough sleepers' and a redundant corps building in Rochester Row in the Victoria area of London was remodelled and adapted as a base for this work. It was funded with help from the Rotary Clubs of Greater London and opened on 5 June 1992. The centre is described by the then Captain Christine MacMillan as follows:

The newly furnished multi-purpose London Outreach Centre reflects a casual approach, with a central café area providing a venue for relaxed conversation, light refreshment and table games. Shower facilities and fresh clothing are available with offices providing a base for assessment and counselling. The new centre has widened the facilities open to The Salvation Army's London Outreach Team, established in the summer of 1991. The team endeavours to make contact with the city's street homeless through a planned, professional approach and offers a variety of vital follow-through services. Park benches, pavements, squats and railway stations are the usual backdrop of initial contacts. The new centre provides a non-threatening community base, and offers a wide-ranging assistance programme in a confidential and home-like atmosphere.

101. *Edward Alsop Court*

The first of the hostels to benefit from funding under this initiative was the new Westminster hostel for men, named Edward Alsop Court, after the late chief executive of SAHA who was instrumental in helping to achieve its

102. *Edward Alsop Court – views of dining hall, interior and exterior.*

103. Great Peter Street Hostel with dormitory and entrance shown below. (Below)

104. Aerial view of Edward Alsop Court, Westminster Abbey and Houses of Parliament. (Far right)

funding. It was opened on 12 December 1996 by Her Majesty the Queen. The new building is on the site of the former Great Peter Street Hostel, which had been opened by William Booth in 1911. That building, a former billiard table factory, had large dormitories accommodating 650 men in 14 rooms. Every man coming into the hostel had to enter via the small narrow doorway in the side street, as shown on the photograph. This was a common

feature of these old hostels, presumably to provide some control over the large numbers of homeless men entering the hostel each day, but it gave the appearance of a prison. However, during the First World War, the hostel with its staff and 650 beds was lent to the Imperial Office to house the Australian Expeditionary Force. This large Victorian type hostel, reminiscent of the previous century, was only a stone's throw from the Houses of Parliament and just across the road from the multi-storey Department of the Environment building – completed in 1971 – where the office of the Minister of Housing was situated. The tower of the Palace of Westminster could be seen from the windows of one of the large dormitories in the hostel.

The new building provided individual rooms or flats

for 125 residents. This building provided a variety of accommodation options with an initial direct access reception and assessment unit as well as some self-contained flats. These flats and the training facilities are designed to help men live on the site independently for a trial period while still receiving training in life and domestic skills. A ground floor restaurant, open to members of the public, was provided to help assist the greater social integration of residents into the local community. This was the first new Salvation Army hostel in London since Booth House and Hopetown hostels had been opened some 25 to 30 years earlier. During the next decade all the remaining hostels in London, including Hopetown, were replaced and Booth House completely refurbished. Her Majesty the Queen again opened the renovated Booth House. In the dining room of the refurbished Booth House is another of Rosa Branson's oil paintings depicting the history and current work of The Salvation Army among the homeless people of London.

An example of another new hostel is Lyndon House next to the docks in Ipswich, where locally it was suggested that the new building looked more like a high class hotel than a hostel, and a new hotel nearby looked more like a hostel. The high quality of the kitchen and dining room, as well as that of other facilities, reinforced this view. At the rear of the hostel are some training flats, where residents learn to live independently. Tom Raine Court in Darlington is a hostel which similarly has a variety of accommodation options including single rooms and self-contained flats, some of which were used for training in social and domestic skills.

Initially the 'new breed' of hostels aimed to provide the same number of beds as the hostels they were replacing. They also aimed to give each individual their own bedroom. However, it was found that contrary to Booth's intention, some men who had spent many years in hostel accommodation sleeping in communal dormitories, were by then unable to cope with the sense of isolation felt when sleeping in a room on their own. While the bulk of sleeping accommodation was provided in single rooms, the design requirements for the first phase of new hostels were changed to provide some shared bedrooms to sleep about four or five men. This was in the hope that when the requirement for this type of accommodation diminished, these rooms could be converted to single bedrooms or merely used as small group lounges, where the demand to maximise the numbers of beds had reduced.

At this initial stage the single bedrooms and small dormitories were seen as exclusively for sleeping and the residents were expected to spend the day-time in the communal dining room, in one of the communal lounges or outside. It was only later that the single rooms were re-designated as bed-sitting rooms, with day-time access allowed. This simple change had major implications in

106. Rosa Branson painting depicting SA work with homeless people. (Oppostie top left)

107. Lyndon house, Ipswich. (Opposite below left)

108. Self-contained training flats – Ipswich. (Opposite top right)

109. Tom Raine Court, Darlington. (Opposite below right

105. Booth House after renovations. (Left)

the requirements for space and other amenities, as well as affecting management policies and staffing levels.

The next significant step in the evolution of hostel design came with the decision to organise these bed-sitting rooms into small units. Initially the group sizes were for 10 or 12 residents, but later were reduced to groups of four or five. Each unit was provided with its own lounge containing facilities for making tea or coffee. Later, some units were provided with complete self-catering facilities. This cluster arrangement allowed the management to use the accommodation to house different affinity groups. The designation of each specific group was at the manager's discretion but might be because of age, thus allowing either the young or elderly to be housed in separate groups, or the grouping be related to their expected length of stay in the hostel. Most hostel managers used some of the group accommodation for the reception and assessment of new arrivals, while other groups were designated for people recovering from addictions, such as alcohol or drugs. The division of the hostel into small groups allowed a large variety of residents to be housed at a single location within a single building envelope. This further allowed specific services and facilities to be provided within the same building for the range of needs experienced by different homeless people.

If the small group concept was to be successful, however, it was essential that each unit of accommodation was private to that group, with no other residents entering or passing through that area, except in an emergency, such as a fire. This specific requirement had major implications for the layout of each new hostel and made the successful adaptation of existing hostel buildings more difficult. However, one of the benefits of this approach was that it meant the end of long hostel corridors and thus reduced the institutional feel of the hostels designed on this basis. It was a partial answer to the 'small is beautiful' approach to hostel design, as it allowed all the benefits of small group living to be combined with the benefits in resources and funding obtained by having a single large hostel on one site. This solution also provided an answer for those who wished to obtain accommodation for a homeless person with multiple needs. Numerous small, specialised units for homeless people with particular needs already existed but referral of new individuals into them was difficult, partly because they were dispersed but also because of a variety of entry criteria. This was especially true where existing residents in some small facilities had a veto over new

entrants. The ability to make a referral to a single location able to accept homeless people with a large variety of needs was clearly beneficial to the client and to the referral agencies.

The next step in hostel design was to provide each resident with a bed-sitting room with its own toilet and shower. The provision of some separate bathrooms was still necessary, as certain residents preferred or needed a bath in lieu of a shower. Some bed-sitting rooms were later provided with kitchen and dining facilities to allow self-catering. This type of provision was not considered appropriate for all residents, especially on initial arrival and prior to assessment of their social and domestic skills. Finally, some hostels were designed to provide self-contained flats, either for training in independent living or as 'follow-on' units for former homeless people, after a period of assessment or training. The former Victoria Homes hostel, next door to Booth House in Whitechapel, was replaced by SAHA with 43 self-contained one bedroom flats known as Victoria Court to provide follow-on accommodation for former hostel residents.

The bulk of The Salvation Army's residential provision for homeless people is still for single men, many of whom have never married or are separated or divorced from their wives or partners. One reason for this is that the vast majority of homeless people are single men and the other reason is that there is no statutory duty on local authorities to house single people unless they are classified as being vulnerable, due to age or illness. However, a number of centres do cater for women and families as well as men in the same hostel but in different sections of the building, for example Davis House in Swindon and William Booth House in Hull. The Salvation Army and SAHA together provide a variety of resettlement services and centres for former homeless people seeking to move to a permanent home and establish themselves in society. The

Army aims to provide an integrated 'seamless' service for homeless people from first contact, either on the streets or via a night shelter, through to resettlement – although the services or accommodation may sometimes be provided by other organisations.

In 2010 the Army still provides an extensive range of facilities and services for homeless men throughout the British Isles, continuing the service commenced over 100 years ago. Centres are located in most major towns and

110. Davis House, Swindon

cities in England as well as in Dundee, Inverness, Perth, Glasgow and Edinburgh in Scotland and Belfast and Dublin in Ireland. Most of these centres have been built or up-graded in the last twenty-five years and include night shelters, hostels, supported self-contained flats, resettlement and outreach centres as well as employment workshops, mainly collecting and renovating furniture.

Hostels for Homeless Women

The Army also provides hostel accommodation for single women, but traditionally this is in separate buildings and at different locations from the men's hostels. This is because some of the women have had difficult or abusive relationships with men and thus require a safe and secure environment, staffed mainly by women. The variety of women needing this temporary accommodation includes those made homeless by adverse circumstances as well as young people unable to find any suitable and affordable accommodation.

The first women's hostel or shelter, as it was then called, was the building opened in 1884 in Hanbury Street, London as mentioned earlier. Some five years later it provided accommodation for 60 women in dormitories. A derelict school in Finch Street, Whitechapel was purchased by The Salvation Army in 1929 and transformed into a home for the women previously housed at the Hanbury Street shelter. The cost of purchase and renovation totalled £32,000 with funding coming from a variety of city banks and companies. Lord Rothermere provided £5,000 and Her Majesty Queen Mary funded one of the cubicles. Queen Mary opened the centre on 16 December 1931 which was aptly named Hopetown. Some eight years later the street was renamed Hopetown Street by order of the London County Council. Hopetown provided accommodation for 300 women and a number of children too. The building was extensively damaged by enemy bombing in 1940 and remained closed until 1948 when it was re-opened following extensive repairs and renovations.

A new Salvation Army/SAHA building also named Hopetown, in Old Montague Street, replaced it and was opened by Her Majesty the Queen in 1980. This purpose-designed building accommodated over 100 women, all in single rooms, with two wings for those needing long-term help, one registered for the care of the elderly and the other for those who were suffering from mental illness. Other women needing long term help included those suffering from alcoholism or drug misuse and those suffering from the breakdown of marriage or other family relationships. As in the hostels for men, long stays became common, since life in a supportive environment, with caring officers on hand, provided the best way for

111. Hope Town Hostel – 2006 building.

many women to hold their lives together. The 1980 Hopetown building in Montague Street, Whitechapel has also recently been replaced with another purpose-built hostel on the same site which was opened in 2006. It still accommodates over 100 single women in single rooms, arranged in cluster groups, all with self-catering facilities. This change of catering policy was instituted as a result of a preference survey of women residents in the previous hostel, which included women from different ethnic and cultural backgrounds, who naturally had a variety of different food preferences and requirements. When Queen Mary opened the first Hopetown in 1931 she expressed the earnest hope that 'sunshine and blessing' would be brought into the lives of the homeless women who came through the doors. That hope continues in Hopetown Mark Three.

Hostels solely for women were also opened in other parts of the country. A former Baptist chapel in Liverpool was opened as a women's hostel in 1906. It accommodated 86 women and was named Ann Fowler Hostel, after a generous benefactor. This was replaced with a new hostel accommodating 40 women on a different site nearer the city centre in 1980. It is worth noting from the photograph the high protective brick wall around the building, necessary for the protection of the women residents and staff in this area of the city. Other such provision was made

at Hopedene in Newcastle, and Warrington in Lancashire, but both these have now closed.

As previously mentioned, the newer hostel designs made it possible for women to be accommodated in the same buildings as men, but in separate cluster groups. These hostels include Davis House in Swindon, Fewster House in Greenock, Huntley House in Inverness, Strathmore Lodge in Dundee, and Wallace of Campsie House in Glasgow. However, even with this arrangement some women are unwilling to stay in such hostels where the vast majority of residents are men. Social work policy aimed at rehabilitation has led to the provision of training programmes for independence and the availability of other types of accommodation, such as training flats with 'after care' to help women move out into the community.

112. Ann Fowler hostel – 1980 building.

Young Women and Students

After the Second World War it was established that there was a need for young women's residences for girls working away from home. In 1952 a building called St Ola in Edinburgh was adapted for this purpose and in 1966 Concord House in London was opened as an international student hostel for young women from across the world. Lefroy House in Dublin is in a strategic position on the banks of the River Liffey and The Salvation Army opened this centre to respond to a wide diversity of needs among teenage girls. It gives shelter to the vulnerable and gives training in independent living within a city which has few such resources.

Mother and Baby Homes

The special needs of women with babies were early recognised by the remarkable women who shared in the provision of shelters and rescue homes, under their inspirational leader, Mrs Bramwell Booth. One of the girls in the Hanbury Street shelter was devoted to her baby and fearful of being separated from it. The Army helped her to find work and a crèche for her baby's care and she was provided with a small room of her own. In 1884 Alpha Cottage in Chelsea was opened as the first Army place which provided help specifically for mothers with babies. Mrs Bramwell Booth saw redemptive forces in motherhood and helped girls keep their babies, persuading well-to-do women to take girls with their babies into their domestic service. An alternative arrangement was to place the baby in a foster home with encouragement to the mother to keep in contact with her baby. A 'cradle fund' was set up to interest wealthy women in donating funds to provide for the needs of these mothers and children. An Affiliation Department was a later off-shoot, whereby fathers pledged financial support and through work with a caseworker were encouraged to make regular payments. Still later, this became known as the Children's Aid Department, operating from 280 Mare Street in Hackney, London. This was, of course, more than 50 years before the British government introduced the Child Support Agency to ensure fathers provided financial support for their children.

Through the first half of the twentieth century a network of Mother and Baby Homes served the needs of unmarried mothers. This was especially important in times of war and where families refused to support their daughter or wished the pregnancy to remain a secret.

When a mother had no means of financial support or was of school age, parental support was essential if mother and child were to stay together. Some women were thus able, with such help and encouragement, to become independent and support their babies. For example at a Mother and Baby Home in Belfast, a 13 year old child was admitted with her baby. Both continued living there until the mother was 18, with help given to care for her little son during those early years. For others, many heartbreaking separations took place as girls reluctantly gave up their babies for adoption. As adoption law has changed in later years, it has required the former Salvation Army Social Services Headquarters to give information about natural parents to those seeking knowledge of their birth and parentage.

For the first six decades of the twentieth century, places of safety were provided for these girls, together with training in basic child care. The mothers received counselling and guidance as to the baby's future. Many parents of these young girls became reconciled to their daughters and were happy to receive both the young mother and child back home. The work of the Mother and Baby Homes declined as society's attitudes towards unmarried parenthood changed and became less judgmental. Local authorities then developed a policy of housing single parents, providing day nurseries and social security schemes to give financial assistance. Hence the Mother and Baby Homes closed and some buildings were adapted for other social work.

The Mothers' Hospital

As rescue work expanded into work with mothers with babies, new skills were needed and new aspirations were born in the minds of Mrs Bramwell Booth and the dedicated women who worked with her. The redoubtable Captain Mrs Carrie Frost became known as 'our Salvation accoucheuse' (midwife). The safe delivery of babies called for trained nurses and 'a properly qualified medical person'. As early as 1887 Mrs Booth had plans for setting up a maternity hospital. However, the opportunity to buy one of 15 beds, complete with all necessaries, for £400, had unfortunately to be passed over at that time. An efficient lady doctor was found for the rescue homes however and it was soon apparent that many women in the neighbourhood wanted to benefit from the service of a Christian lady doctor. In 1891 Mrs Booth advertised for young Christian women to train as Salvation Army nurses. Within a few weeks 170 women had applied for these posts. Ivy House in Clapton began to concentrate upon training nurses for midwifery rather than just giving charitable relief. The scheme attracted outstanding women, such as Elizabeth Sapsworth and Mrs Annie Sowden, who were able to steer it through the requirements of the London Obstetrical Society and later the Central Midwives Board. Mrs Carrie Frost was

therefore free to develop the Slum Maternity Work and later to branch out into District Nursing. This work took the benefits of improved midwifery care to a wider section of the poor of London. By 1918, the improvements in maternity and child welfare work earned a Treasury grant of £2,000. This was the first gesture by the British Government of state aid for Salvation Army social work.

To branch out into the provision of a voluntary maternity hospital was a bold step. The Mothers Hospital in Clapton was purchased at the cost of £50,000 and opened in 1913, serving the poor of East London, whether married or unmarried. It was soon in demand across a much wider section of women who wished to give birth in a Christian hospital. The demand was such that before long 2,000 babies were delivered there annually, a number which increased dramatically as years went by. For women whose men were fighting in the first and second world wars, the Mothers' Hospital was a

113. The Mothers' Hospital

place of safety and sanctuary. However,, during the Second World War, on 30 December 1940, the hospital was bombed. The building was only partly damaged, so it continued to operate and remarkably a total of 18,000 babies were born there during those war years. Some of the work and a number of staff were evacuated to Willersley Castle and Bragborough Hall, both in Derbyshire, presumably in case there was further bomb damage in the future.

The hospital's Midwifery Training School was held in high regard and became in standing second only to that of Queen Charlotte's Hospital. It attracted women with a sense of Christian vocation. In one intake, there were students from eleven different countries. Qualified midwives left the Mothers' Hospital to serve in every continent, in Third World clinics and hospitals, in pioneering health care and in preventative health ventures. They taught qualifying courses whereby indigenous women became qualified nurses, midwives and medical aides, who in turn could teach others. In total 3,119 nurses qualified in midwifery from the Mothers' Hospital. For many, it proved a first point of contact with The Salvation Army, and many women came to faith because of the Christian influence there. Some of these women entered full-time Christian service, with a total of 330 women entering the Salvation Army's International Training College to train as officers. They were generally appointed to medical work overseas or to the staff of the network of Salvation Army Mother and Baby Homes within Great Britain.

The Mothers' Hospital became the pride and jewel of The Salvation Army Women's Social Work. This was despite the enormous demands of growing professionalism, the demand for ever more skilled staff and the problems of funding a voluntary hospital. In 1948 it was transferred into the National Health Service, while retaining its distinctive Christian emphasis and spiritual ministry. It upheld the Salvation Army's stand against abortion, except in cases of medical necessity or rape. In 1986, as with other voluntary hospitals, it was absorbed into the NHS Regional Hospital Schemes, so the Mothers' Hospital eventually closed and its work was transferred to the Homerton Hospital.

To serve the local Mother and Baby Homes, The Salvation Army set up a few regional maternity hospitals, such as the Crossley Hospital in Ancoats, Manchester, established in 1919. They developed some wards to serve 'private patients' in response to demand and to help funding the service to those who could not pay. Eventually the Crossley Hospital suffered the same fate as the Mothers' Hospital and closed. The building was later used as an elderly care residential home before eventually closing completely.

District Work

From The Mothers' Hospital, teams of trained Salvation Army midwives carried out District Work in poor areas of London, delivering thousands of babies. In the 1920s and 30s poverty was such that in some people's homes which they visited, there was no food, fire, light or baby clothes. A new-born baby often needed to be wrapped in a nurse's apron and bathed in a cracked dish. Salvation Army District Posts later declined with the growing practice of hospital-based deliveries.

Children's Work

Work on behalf of abandoned and homeless children started slowly and grew from the private philanthropy of the Booths. On his mother's death, a child called Harry Andrews was taken into Booth's home in 1873 and cared for by William's daughter Emma. He was to abundantly repay the Booths, becoming The Salvation Army's first medical missionary in India, where he served for 30 years. He was posthumously awarded the Victoria Cross for his heroism when attached to the Indian Army on the North West frontier in 1919. The Booth family had concern for the orphaned children of Salvationist parents and put out appeals such as that worded 'for a home for the daughter of a saint in heaven' printed in the Salvation Army publication *The War Cry*. William Booth was unwilling to open children's homes, having a horror of Dickensian Victorian institutions. Because of this view he declined the gift of a freehold building large enough to accommodate 200 children.

However, in 1902 'The Nest' opened in London, a small home for children. Its flexibility of purpose was shown by the inclusion of a service girl's room. This was used as a club room by working girls whose children were in The Nest and thus kept them in touch with their children. This initial project was followed by The Haven in 1909 in Ramsgate and a number of subsequent openings in a variety of locations including Southend, Liverpool, Southport, Glasgow and Dundee. The first purpose-built home was opened in 1973 in the grounds of the original Strawberry Field home. It was a big step forward when boys as well as girls were admitted. The Haven, Sydenham, was the second purpose built home, opened in 1982. The kind of provision made in these new homes reflected changing child care practice, a growing knowledge of child psychology and the importance of keeping parents and children together wherever possible.

We now regard with a degree of horror the practice of placing the children of missionary officers at a children's home in Southend. With seven year terms of service for officers overseas, coinciding with the beginning of World War One, this meant that children were separated from their parents for more than ten years in some instances. However, the Army was not alone in requiring this sacrifice. The China Inland Mission literature included heart-breaking accounts both of parents seeing off little ones returning to England when they reached school age and also of many infant graves. The children of cadets in training were often separated from their parents during the training period. This practice eventually ended in the mid 1960s, after the introduction of a two-year training period and with the provision of family flats, a nursery and playrooms at the William Booth College.

Children's Homes attracted devoted staff, who were appointed for long stays and sought to give the children as normal a routine as possible. Originally children stayed in the Children's Home until they were of school leaving age and sometimes beyond that age. Later on admissions became more short-term while family problems were being resolved. Respite care was then introduced, giving relief to the stressed parents of disabled children or those with severe behaviour problems, for weekends or for longer periods. With the 1969 Children and Young Persons Act, social policy was concentrated more on non-residential forms of care and treatment. Demands on the homes became more staff-intensive and expensive, with local authorities using their own homes on grounds of economy rather than those of voluntary agencies. Despite The Salvation Army's excellent reputation in this field of care, only one children's home in the UK remained open by 2009. However, the number of children more recently adopted by serving Salvation Army officers, due to a change in Salvation Army policy, may well approximate to the population of one or two children's homes. William Booth had considered that accepting the parental care of

114. Strawberry Field original building

widow, Yoko Ono made a number of later visits and made donations to the home following John's death. On one occasion, the metal gates to 'Strawberry Field' were stolen, but they must have been 'too hot to handle' because they were back within a day. However, these homes have been gradually closed as local authorities assume responsibility for this work and the concepts of appropriate child care change, so it is unlikely that this work will continue in the future.

Training for Neglectful Mothers

The Army opened the Mayflower Training Home for mothers who were convicted of child neglect, as a pioneering venture in social work. There was widespread concern after the Second World War when about one thousand women each year were charged with neglecting their children. Half of them were sent to prison and the other half were fined. Neither of these responses helped the women nor their families. A study undertaken by the Women's Group on Public Welfare publicised the need for such mothers to be trained. The Prison Commissioners of Holloway Prison estimated in the 1940s that nine out of ten 'neglectful' mothers should not be in prison. The Salvation Army was therefore asked to set up a home where women, together with their children under the age of five, could be trained and helped. A Home in Plymouth was no longer needed for its previous use and so the Mayflower centre came into being. About eight or nine women initially came to this home with a total of 20 children between them. They were sent there either through the courts or by Welfare Officers. The purpose was to prevent disturbed situations in the families deteriorating to the point where court proceedings became necessary. Women came for a period

abandoned children by officers was 'injurious to the general interests of the salvation war'. This policy has only been relaxed in the last 40 years.

The Salvation Army had originally developed the children's homes in existing buildings around the country, including the Strawberry Field home in Liverpool which was opened in 1936. That existing building was replaced in 1973 by a smaller purpose-built home, called John Lennon Court, which provided three family units, each for 12 children. This was one of only two purpose-built centres erected by The Salvation Army, the other being The Haven in London. Both buildings were designed to reflect the concept of housing the children in family groups. The Liverpool home was of course made famous in John Lennon's song by the Beatles *Strawberry Field for Ever*. Lennon used to explore the grounds of the original children's home at Strawberry Field as a child and he later visited the home in 1970 on his last visit to Liverpool. His of four months with rehabilitation beginning from the moment they came in. In the homes an environment of warmth, acceptance and helpfulness was created. Each new arrival received a new outfit to lift their morale in the first week.

A simple and workable daily routine was established. This included rising early, having regular meals, cleaning rooms and washing clothes every day and putting children to bed early. Training was given in child care, cooking, cleaning, laundry, budgeting, shopping and making and mending clothes. Domestic appliances provided were only such as the woman was likely to be able to afford when she returned home. A visiting health visitor gave family planning education while children were cared for in a nursery.

With these regular routines, feeding difficulties, behavioural problems and temper tantrums lessened considerably. Children of three and four years of age became toilet trained for the first time. They ceased being listless, apathetic little beings and began to play. A second miracle happened when the mothers began to play with them. The women were fully involved in their children's progress, having them in their care from mid afternoon onwards, to take them out for walks, give them their tea, a bath and put them to bed. The children improved dramatically and the women within a few weeks lost their apathetic hopelessness and gained in health, energy and self confidence. Family flats enabled fathers to visit and they were enormously encouraged when they saw the progress of the women and their children.

Simple religious teaching was given in morning prayers and the women attended meetings at Plymouth Exeter Hall corps. Many sought God's help at the mercy seat and found a new source of strength in their lives. This also happened for visiting fathers as well.

The success of the Mayflower Home depended heavily upon the inspiration of the matron, Brigadier Gladys Newcombe. She was a humble lady of radiant faith who was justly honoured by Her Majesty the Queen by being awarded the MBE for the establishment and success of this pioneering venture. The work of the centre was studied by students from other countries and its model copied by other agencies. Women could come back to visit Mayflower and sometimes have a holiday there. The matron gave supportive and encouraging aftercare. Home Office follow-down statistics assessed that nine out of ten women managed adequately after their training at Mayflower. That interesting statistic equated to their earlier assessment that nine out of ten women on child neglect charges should not be in prison.

An increase in family support programmes and emphasis on care in the community and family casework became more available and this led to the closure of the work at the Mayflower Home. The importance of family work however continued within the Salvation Army Social Services in its developing network of Family Centres.

Family Centres

The diversity of social work, particularly relating to families, which developed from the early years of The Salvation Army reflected the inter-relatedness and complexity of needs they encountered. There was a growing conviction within William and Catherine Booth, helped by their daughters and others, that this was indeed work to which the Army was called. Hence rescue work led on to work training and placement, help for unmarried mothers, crèches for babies, and fostering which kept mothers in touch with their children. The Affiliation Department's work with putative fathers and an early, but soon to be discarded, adoption work also developed from those situations. Mother and baby work in East London showed the need for improved midwifery care and the establishment of nursing and midwifery training for those working in the mother and baby homes. The opening of The Mothers' Hospital and its later network of District Posts with its qualifying training courses in midwifery were impressive developments from small beginnings. The hospital came to serve both poor and rich, Jew and Gentile, married and unmarried. Its development called for ever increasing professionalism and cooperation with government departments, which entailed a strong learning curve for the growing Social Work Department, but laid the foundations for the strength and credibility of subsequent developments.

115. Thorndale House, Belfast

The results of the flexibility and adaptability practiced within Salvation Army service can be seen in the history of individual social homes. For example, Thorndale House in Belfast opened in 1920 to serve unmarried mothers and their children, women who had 'lost their way' and the little waif girlie (a quaint term for teenagers abandoned by their parents which would not be appreciated by teenagers

of today). Perhaps it was due to a growing need for the latter that in 1923 Thorndale House added a wing defining itself as a Girls Industrial Home and Hostel. In 1971 it was registered as a Children's Home and in 1984 it amalgamated with the adjoining Mayflower Training Home for Mothers and Children, which operated on the Plymouth Mayflower model. During the sectarian conflicts at the time of the troubles in Northern Ireland, many families suffered insecurities and needed to escape from threatening neighbourhoods. Thorndale was equipped with new build facilities in 1991 to provide a safe house for 20 families and four single women at a time, with its staff coming from and working across the political divide. A community centre running a playgroup for 24 children also operated within the grounds.

An important later expansion was the development of a half-way house in the form of independent family flats, with the resources of the main house available should a crisis arise. When the Glen Alva Eventide Home became assessed as no longer suitable for elderly residential care, the local authority requested that it be adapted for a further extension of family work, on the successful Thorndale House lines

Family Centres in Leeds, Birmingham, Portsmouth and Greenock working in cooperation with local authorities, served different needs. Housing authorities became less willing to evict families with chronic rent arrears because that meant the children going into care. These centres provided a placement for families who had been removed from areas where they may have had bad reputations and gave them supervision, training and help until they were assessed as ready for re-housing and a fresh start.

In the 1970s, high profile child abuse cases were accompanied by growing concern about another manifestation of violence in the home, the 'battered wife' syndrome. Lyncroft House in Birmingham and Mount

Cross in Leeds provided places of safety for mothers escaping from violent relationships, together with their children. If reconciliation with husbands or partners was feasible, then this formed part of the programme objectives. If an independent start was necessary for the safety and well-being of mother and children, training and support were given and with the local authority's involvement, the family was re-housed. A new nursery called Copper Beeches has been built in recent years to help integrate the children from Mount Cross with the local community.

The Salvation Army also initially provided accommodation for homeless families but generally did so in adapted existing buildings. The need for this type of provision reduced, as legislation was passed to require local authorities to house homeless families as a statutory duty, following the 'Cathy Come Home' TV programme. The Salvation Army has in recent years sought to fill gaps in family provision or where requested by the local authority to provide some specialist service. While the number of Salvation Army centres has reduced in recent years, new purpose-built centres have been developed in Belfast, Leeds, Birmingham and Portsmouth. This family accommodation is of a specialist nature providing a range of self-contained accommodation for families in crisis, with training, counselling and support services to help families move back into the community.

Shepherd's Green House in Birmingham is one such new purpose-built facility, which was provided with the help of The Salvation Army Housing Association and opened in 2006. The centre provides 18 family homes for women and children, some of whom are fleeing domestic violence. The accommodation is in a variety of two and three bedroom flats with two designed specifically for disabled residents. It has a separate resource centre which provides crèche and nursery facilities for those living on site and also for the local community. It provides 24-hour support and management for the whole complex as well as other practical facilities such as a laundry.

116. Copper Beeches Nursery, Leeds. (Left)

117. Shepherd's Green Family Centre, Birmingham. (Left)

118. Hyrstlands Approved School, Batley.
119. Hyrstlands new study centre. (Below)

120. Hyrstlands new classroom/main hall with security link to main house shown alongside. (Below right)

Approved Schools for Girls.

During the Second World War, the then Home Secretary approached The Salvation Army with the request that they open homes for the training of teenage girls. In response to this, the first of The Salvation Army's three Approved Schools was opened in 1942 at Woodlands, East Grinstead in Sussex, soon followed by Hyrstlands at Batley in Yorkshire which opened in 1944 and Avalon at Chislehurst in Kent, opened in 1949. Approved Schools operated within the correctional services of the courts. As a result of behaviour deemed delinquent and out of the control of parents and schools, girls were committed to a three-year period of training, although in practice the term was generally halved. Many had very disturbed family backgrounds. Their education included basic literacy and numeracy, catching up on lost schooling, as well as home management, cookery, dressmaking, baby care, domestic science and vocational skills such as typewriting and secretarial training. Their recreations included swimming, netball, square dancing, concerts and voluntary service. All of these centres had alterations and improvements over the years to cater for the developing programmes. Hyrstlands at Batley had a purpose-designed study centre added in 1978 which had a fully glazed secure link with the main house, as girls were not allowed out of the premises without supervision.

Approved Schools served many purposes; the girls were removed from unhelpful relationships and activities as well as from cycles of failure and discord. They learned, often for the first time, the laws of cause and effect through systems of privileges and sanctions. They also learned to relate to trusted adults. Standards like good regular meals, reasonable bedtimes, predictable daily routines and standards of cleanliness and comfort were established. They were treated individually and their personalities and potential were developed. The value of building a programme upon Christian principles, with Christian teaching and influence, was recognised and accepted by the Home Office. Morning prayers, a Sunday gospel service and attendance at Salvation Army meetings were part of school life. Many girls accepted Jesus as their Saviour, with changed lives coming from changed hearts.

The 1960s and 70s saw great changes in social work policy, philosophy and practice so that vocation and commitment were less valued. Delinquency was interpreted in terms of deprivation rather than personal responsibility. Society became less ready to commit young offenders for training with established boundaries, discipline, religious teaching and moral values. The 1969 Children and Young Persons Act shifted jurisdiction for children from the courts to the local authorities. Approved Schools were renamed Community Homes with Education. Social workers, under pressure for cheaper methods of child care and correctional services, developed systems of care in the community. Where residential placement was deemed essential, they used local authority homes before those of voluntary and religious agencies. This led to the decline and closure of The Salvation Army Approved Schools and also of The Salvation Army Approved Probation Hostels and Children's Homes.

The Salvation Army has, since its earliest days, been involved in seeking to aid the most disadvantaged people, especially children. The buildings which The Salvation Army used for the approved schools were former country mansions, often with extensions added for teaching facilities. The Avalon building was used, after its closure as an approved school, as a training centre for The Salvation Army Social Services, before being converted to provide residential flats for Salvation Army officers returning from overseas service. The Woodlands and Hyrstlands buildings were sold soon after the schools closed in 1986 and 1988 respectively.

Probation Hostels for Girls.

The Salvation Army also set up a number of Approved Probation Hostels for teenage girls, which became registered during the 1950s and the 1960s. They included St Margaret's in Sydenham and St Cuthbert's in West Norwood, both in the London area, as well as a number of others throughout the country. Similar to the Approved Schools, they came under the jurisdiction of the courts and the Home Office. They were used for the placement of girls on probation who needed to be removed from their home setting and who would benefit from the training provided. The training and routines were similar to that given in the Schools, but as they were for older girls they added training in preparation for work and independent living. While most centres served the 15-18 age group, St Cuthberts served the 18-21 age group and received women whose offences might otherwise have taken them to prison. It had a firm and disciplined environment, along with the care and love which were the hallmarks of Salvation Army social work. Similar to the approved schools, these centres had high success rates as women responded by turning their lives around. The Home Office assessed St Cuthberts as the most effective centre catering for the older age group within the country. Despite this success, changes in government polices resulted in their closure in 1979, thus suffering the same fate as the Approved Schools.

Residential Centres for Adolescents

The Salvation Army provided a variety of residential services for young men of adolescent age. These young men initially came to the hostels as homeless, but were in need of more specialised accommodation with training in life skills and equipping with skills to gain employment. Sections of some existing men's hostels were set aside as specialised provision for this purpose, such as the 259 Project at Blackfriars Hostel in London. As this work developed it was transferred to separate centres, such as

Springfield Lodge in Camberwell which was opened in 1992. This centre provides a programme for young men aged 18 to 25 years with training in 'life skills', job search and work training or help in seeking further educational opportunities. The accommodation is linked to residents' commitment to these programmes, intended to lead to independent living back in the community.

House o' the Trees

This farm was originally just 42 acres at Pen-y-Graig in Glamorgan, located in the Rhondda Valley in Wales. It was acquired in 1932 by Hugh Redwood for The Salvation Army and administered initially by The Salvation Army's Goodwill Department. This small farm was a centre which provided employment and accommodation for homeless young men. One feature of the centre was the provision of a Salvation Army hall with facilities, such as a band room, similar in many ways to corps buildings. Local people were invited to worship on Sundays and also to attend the Home League meetings during the week. The Second World War reduced the need for such a centre, so it then became a Probation Home for boys. The administration was then transferred to The Salvation Army Men's Social Services and following changes in Government policy, it became an approved probation home. The boys came originally from courts throughout the United Kingdom to live at the centre for a period of 12 months. They were occupied by working either at carpentry, in farming or market gardening. Subsequent Government policy dictated that such homes should only be used to meet local needs. As there were insufficient eligible boys in this locality to fill the home, it was no longer viable and therefore closed in 1989. The Sunday meetings and Home League continued all throughout the time the centre had been an approved

home, but sadly with the sale of the property this work ceased as well.

Redheugh Centre, Kilbirnie

This magnificent old property built in 1865 was given to The Salvation Army by the Knox family, local mill owners. From 1953 it was used as an approved home with education for boys in need of such a home. Not all who came were delinquents but they all needed somewhere to live because of family breakdowns. The centre developed as a good example of such work, particularly under the leadership of Captain Jack Henderson and later of George Steven. The varied programme of the home included sports, crafts and educational activities. Redheugh was one of the first Salvation Army centres to devote time and expertise to the professional training of staff. Later, the centre received girls as well as boy residents. Once again Central Government policy changed and with it a decrease in the amount of funding provided. This resulted in the centre being no longer financially viable and it closed in 1993. As its original purpose had ceased, part of the building became a Day Centre for local people with learning difficulties. The building was far too big for such a limited use but it continued in use for this purpose until the work was transferred in June 2003 to a new, purpose-built centre in Kilbirnie, now known as the George Steven Centre. The house and estate were then sold for redevelopment.

Raisdale, Glasgow

This building was formerly the residence of the Shanks family, who were the owners of the sanitary fittings manufacturing firm of the same name. The home and grounds passed to The Salvation Army in 1954 and became a residential care home for the elderly, under the management of the Women's Social Services. There were many magnificent elements of this building, especially the bathrooms and toilets as one would expect in this family's former home. However, as new government regulations were introduced for accommodating elderly people, the home did not meet those standards and it proved impractical to up-grade it.

Another home, the Mount Bruce Centre for boys in Glasgow, which worked closely in conjunction with the Redheugh centre, needed better facilities, so the work was transferred in 1980 to Raisdale.

In the 1970's Strathclyde Social Services had carried out research on work with young people in its area. The report was highly critical of residential work with young people in the region. Consequently they closed many of their own homes and eventually ceased funding work done by voluntary organizations including the Salvation Army. Raisdale was ultimately affected by this change of policy and eventually closed in 1998. Sadly, the building was completely destroyed by fire shortly after it closed.

121. David Gray House, Isle of Man.

Bail and Probation Hostels for Men

The Salvation Army pioneered the provision of bail hostels. A section of the Booth House hostel in Whitechapel, London, was first set aside as a 'Bail Wing' through the exhortation and financial support of philanthropist Mrs Xenia Field. who was the gardening correspondent of the *Daily Mirror* newspaper. She had been deeply concerned that men who were charged with a first offence were remanded in prison while awaiting trial, especially if they were homeless. She argued that they should be sent to a different environment where they

could be helped, not to a place that could encourage wrong-doing. This wing was opened in November 1971 by the Home Secretary, Reginald Maudling. In this new setting the men were also able to keep in touch with their families and to continue to work until their case came to court. One year after its opening, Mrs Field visited the wing again with the new Home Secretary Roy Jenkins.

The courts were initially reluctant to accept this new idea and the Salvation Army officer in charge of Booth House had to speak to magistrates on behalf of each man that came before them to convince them of the value of this alternative method of sentencing. The experiment became

122. Grenville, Godalming, Surrey. (Above)

123. Wickstead Hall, Whitchurch in Shropshire. (Below)

the subject of research by the Home Office which eventually led to changes in policy and the opening of more Bail Hostels by the Government's correctional services. Having shown the way, as with other pioneering projects, The Salvation Army then withdrew from this work.

Repeated requests in recent years from the probation department of the Isle of Man authorities led to the establishment in 1994 of a new Salvation Army Probation and Bail Hostel named David Gray House in Douglas. The building was a former guest house in the town centre of Douglas and may be replaced by a new development in the future. It is now the only Salvation Army hostel wholly classified for this purpose. However, some of the other general hostels still receive men and women on probation with some designating a specific wing or group area for these residents.

Elderly Care Centres and Sheltered Housing

The first Salvation Army care home for elderly persons, known as an eventide home, was opened at 128 The Avenue, Highams Park in Walthamstow in 1911. During the First World War it provided residential care for elderly women, whose sons had been killed in the war. The need was so great that 17 others had been opened by 1921. The first home to admit husbands and wives together was opened in 1923, at a time when elderly couples dreaded above all else being separated from each other and being put in the workhouse.

After the Second World War many large country mansions became available at low cost. Some of these were acquired by The Salvation Army and turned into residential homes for elderly people. The Salvation Army's growing reputation also led to the donation of

some other beautiful large country houses, such as the illustrated examples in Surrey and Shropshire. The large bedrooms in such existing buildings necessitated residents sharing. The buildings initially had no lifts but were successfully used for a number of decades for people able and willing to accept these difficulties. However, despite some improvements they were eventually deemed unsuitable unless major alterations and improvements were possible. The Salvation Army Housing Association assisted with funding to bring two of these homes up to the required standard, in Clapham, London and in Weston-super-Mare.

One of the first new purpose-built eventide homes,

funded by the 'For God's Sake Care' Appeal was Rookstone in Sydenham, London. As standards of required care rose and the levels of dependency of residents increased, so did government regulations. People entered residential homes at a greater age and with much higher dependency needs. The needs of the more able have to be balanced with the needs of those who have Alzheimer's disease or are mentally infirm. The dividing line between residential and nursing care is a very fine one. All homes aim to provide a warm, loving, Christian atmosphere with routines as interesting as residents' disabilities allow. Residents are generally allowed to remain in these homes as long as possible, including being nursed through terminal illness.

Further Salvation Army developments have included semi-independent housing and sheltered housing as at Alver Bank in Clapham, Charles Court in Tunbridge Wells and Sunnyside in Edinburgh. These were provided mainly with the help of The Salvation Army Housing Association, who also have numerous similar schemes elsewhere under their own direct management. Some residential homes and corps centres have also developed non-residential day care programmes, which enable people to remain in their own homes longer than would be possible without such help.

Some men, who came to the Salvation Army hostels initially homeless, stayed there a long time until they were elderly. It was felt that some of these men would not readily fit into the main residential homes for elderly people, so The Salvation Army began to provide elderly care facilities for them, initially as wings or sections of these hostels and later in separate buildings. One of the first centres for these men who were former hostel residents was Greig House. It is located in the grounds of Riverside House men's hostel in the Docklands area of London. However, this work was later transferred to

124. Bradbury Home, Southend-on-Sea – views from road and garden.

separate elderly care homes elsewhere, away from the hostels.

As the required standards for care homes increased further, The Salvation Army began to build purpose-designed homes and to adapt and improve their existing homes. Because of the very high cost of residential elderly care, each residential home has been comprehensively reviewed in recent years. Sadly not all have been capable of adaptation to the required standards while others could not be replaced due to lack of suitable sites or funding. In the last decade numerous Salvation Army care homes have been closed with a subsequent reduction in the total numbers of residents accommodated. To re-house elderly people from an eventide home creates great

125. Youell Court, Binley in Coventry, with aerial view shown below.

professional, loving, Christian service.

Some centres were rebuilt however, such as Bradbury Home in Southend with funds from the Bradbury Foundation, and Youell Court in Coventry, described below. All the new homes built during this period were designed to a very high standard, exceeding the standards required under recent legislation. These have included the new home in Southend and Smallcombe House in Bath, both opened in 1992, as well as those in Coventry and in Glasgow, completed in 2000. The Salvation Army Housing Association complemented these residential care homes by building sheltered housing schemes, sometimes on adjoining sites. The Salvation Army has also branched out in recent years to provide a community care service to people in their own homes, particularly in rural areas, such as the Angus area of Scotland.

Youell Court in Coventry was designed to meet nursing home standards as well as the current residential care standards for 40 elderly people. Opened by HRH the Princess Royal in March 2001, it was designed to provide five group homes, each for eight residents, clustered around an open internal court yard, thus providing an identifiable community group in a secure environment. Each resident has their own bed-sitting room with en-suite toilet and shower. Each cluster has its own lounge, dining room and tea kitchen. A general lounge, main dining room and other facilities located on the ground floor are used when all the residents gather together for special occasions. The clusters are located with two on each of the upper floors and one on the ground floor. This arrangement is provided in a three storey building with centrally located passenger lifts, thus minimising walking distance for residents and staff, as compared to the convention of placing all units on the ground floor. One of the lifts is designed as an evacuation lift, with special specification aspects incorporated in its

trauma for the residents and their families. Closures, especially in country areas, also affect staff who have benefited from work and suppliers who have benefited from their business dealings with the home. The visibility of The Salvation Army has thus diminished in those areas together with their witness as centres providing a construction, to allow it to be used in the event of fire. Each floor has a nursing station and one bedsitting room in each cluster is specifically designed for a resident who requires the use of a wheelchair. While categorised as an elderly care home it is designed to meet nursing home standards. Some of the cluster units were initially used as an interim care home for people entering or leaving hospital but are now available for elderly people who are dementia or Alzheimer's sufferers. This scheme was only possible by the generosity of a benefactor, Mr A. E. Youell, the son of E.K.Youell mentioned later, who donated the land and £1.5 million towards the cost.

Substance Abuse Treatment Centres

A large percentage of homeless single people have a substance abuse problem, so The Salvation Army has long been involved in providing holistic treatment for such addictions. Originally the problems were mainly associated with alcohol dependence but in more recent years drug addiction has also become a major problem. Originally this treatment took place in a wing or section of the hostels, but in more recent years specialist centres have been developed in Greenock, Newcastle and London providing both detoxification and rehabilitation services. A purpose-built residential centre incorporating the existing listed building of Greig House in the Docklands area of London, now provides detoxification services for people with multiple addictions. It has medical staff qualified to provide psychiatric as well as general medical treatment. A sophisticated monitoring and assessment system has been developed with the help of new technology, and a machine which is able to analyse blood or urine samples for any trace of drugs or alcohol as well as the ability to recommend dietary

changes. As with all Salvation Army social services the spiritual content of the programme remains an essential element of the treatment at this centre. Some follow-on accommodation with support has been provided on the same site in a new residential centre, as part of Riverside House, especially for those who have had these addictions. A separate building at the rear of David Barker House, a new hostel in the Blackfriars area of London also provides self contained flats, similarly for men recovering from drug or alcohol addictions.

126. Greig House Treatment Centre, Docklands, London.

127. David Barker House Annexe, Blackfriars.

Centres for Adults with Learning Difficulties.

Finding an alternative use for a building when the work it has previously housed is no longer needed or is no longer viable, sometimes means entering a new branch of work. Such a generic approach holds difficulties from the standpoint of practice and supervision. Most voluntary agencies confine their work to one particular client group but The Salvation Army has continued to meet a wide variety of needs, adapting programmes and buildings as necessary, as well as retraining its staff.

The Salvation Army has adapted two of its existing buildings to provide centres for work with adults with learning difficulties, as follows:

(a) The Mayflower Centre, in Plymouth, which provided a secure and loving residential home for moderate to severely handicapped adults, needing more support and care than the wider community could provide. This has now been replaced by a new building, Pilgrim House, which provides supported tenancies in association with Devon and Cornwall Housing Association.

(b) Redheugh in Kilbirnie, after a highly successful history as a training centre for adolescent boys and in latter years girls also, became a Day Training Centre for Adults with Learning Difficulties before the work was transferred in June 2003 to a new purpose-built centre, named the George Steven Day Centre.

Social Services Headquarters.

A building of primary importance to the fast-developing and ever-changing social work of The Salvation Army was the Headquarters of the Women's Social Work. This headquarters, opened in 1911 was until 1987 based at 280 Mare Street in Hackney, London and affectionately known as 'Two Eighty'. A separate building in Middlesex Street, within the City of London, operated as the Headquarters of the Men's Social Work until the amalgamation of the two services. The combined services then moved to 105 Judd Street, Kings Cross, before finally joining the remainder of Territorial Headquarters administration in the new building at 101 Newington Causeway, near the Elephant and Castle.

Stability and continuity in leadership and direction were crucial to the developing Salvation Army social work. As standards rose and government regulations increased, The Salvation Army needed to resource its social centres in all their diversity to meet these demands. Funding methods became ever more sophisticated with government funding crucial to the continuance of most kinds of social work. Hence The Salvation Army Social Headquarters became the depository of increasing professionalism. It needed to liaise with government departments and provide information for its officers to keep them informed of the latest policies. It also set up policies for staff development and training, for personnel management and effective employee relations, for subsequent supervision and monitoring, research and development and finally, operational reviews to guide future strategies.

128. George Steven Day Centre, Kilbirnie.

Other non-residential services based at headquarters included:

The Family Tracing Service.
The Prison Visitation Service.
The Counselling Department.
The AIDS Support Service.

Two further branches of work *driven* by this Headquarters are:

The Training and Development Centre, which was originally based at Avalon in Chislehurst, Kent and now at the William Booth College in Denmark Hill. This centre provides a programme of specialised short courses, material for in-house training courses and tutoring for officers and employees on qualifying courses.

The London Homelessness Project, which commenced in 1988 when The Salvation Army commissioned the University of Surrey Psychology Department to carry out research into the scale and causes of homelessness in London. After two years of work, the results of the research and a strategy to more effectively tackle the problem were presented to members of both Houses of Parliament and then to the public at large through the Press and Television News Programmes. The results of this research were published in the book *The Faces of Homelessness in London* and the Army's own action programme was published in the booklets *Strategy for Change* and *Seeking Excellence.*

Each of these functions still remains but some are now directed from various other departments of Territorial Headquarters.

Salvation Army Housing Association (SAHA)

SAHA is an independent body but is a mission partner with The Salvation Army. It is a national, charitable, registered social landlord specialising in the provision of supported affordable accommodation, education and employment opportunities for homeless single people and families. It works towards the empowerment of vulnerable groups in society to achieve positive, stable and independent living. This commitment is based on the belief that homeless people need a hand up and not a handout. As a partner in mission with The Salvation Army it shares the same ethos, history and Christian values. Working alongside the Army, SAHA helps more than 7,000 homeless people each year to find accommodation. The present chairman of the board is a Salvation Army officer as have been most previous chairmen, with a number of other officers also serving as board members.

In 1959 The Salvation Army set up an Association to help provide accommodation for retired Salvation Army officers as it did not possess sufficient housing for all officers who were retiring at that time. However, this did not materialise as originally envisioned and in 1962, with a very small cash balance, the department decided to find out exactly what government grants were available for housing needs.

By 1966 with property prices and mortgage costs increasing, SAHA suggested that the Army lend capital to the Association to enable it to start developing housing for homeless people. In the same year the needs of homeless people were highlighted in the BBC's production *Cathy Come Home* prompting the birth of the charity 'Shelter'.

The time was definitely right for something to be done

129. Youell Court Flats, Bournmouth.

and in April 1967, SAHA identified a Salvation Army building in Essex in need of much work. It developed this to provide ten single-bed units, eight two-bed maisonettes and three family homes. So began the long partnership between The Salvation Army and SAHA.

From the 1974 Housing Act emerged the formation of the Housing Corporation, the government funding agency and regulator of housing associations. For SAHA to secure funding and grants, it registered as an independent housing association in 1976 and at this time passed the responsibility for retired officers' housing back to the Army. It did, however, build some retirement accommodation for elderly people generally and offered some tenancies to retired officers who wished to live in the areas where those developments were located.

One interesting story associated with retired officers concerned a public relations officer, Brigadier Laurie Johnson. He was due to retire in a few months time when he visited one of his regular donors to The Salvation Army, namely Mr. E.K. Youell of Coventry. Mr. Youell's family were all devout Methodists and, with his son, he had built up a very successful building and civil engineering business. When Laurie informed Mr. Youell of his impending retirement, he was asked: *'Where will you retire to?'* His reply surprised Mr Youell as he said: *'Well I am hoping that the Army will find me a place.'* When he was told that Laurie had served as an officer for 40 years, Mr. Youell said: *'Don't worry, I will build you a place'*. Laurie thanked him for his offer but replied: *'I have trusted God all my life, so I will not doubt him now.'* He then thanked Mr. Youell for his generous offer but added that he could not accept it, as he was not allowed to benefit personally from his officership. Astounded but impressed with Laurie's faith and integrity, Mr Youell asked: *'If I build a block of flats for the Army would that be acceptable?'* Laurie said he

thought that it would be and the Army might then rent him one of them, so that was agreed. A block of 11 flats for retired officers and a family room for visiting relatives was later built in the grounds of Cliff House in Bournemouth with funding provided by the Youell Trust. While the flats were designed by The Salvation Army in-house architects, the development was carried out by the Youell's own building firm, organised and supervised by Alf Youell, the donor's son. Upon completion in 1980, the flats were handed over to SAHA to manage.

As SAHA was now an independent organisation, it was able to secure government funding and so it began to make the most of these new opportunities. The Salvation Army agreed to sell the leaseholds of its old Victorian hostels at peppercorn rents to the association in order to get them rebuilt or refurbished. The Army retained the freehold so that eventually the sites and properties would return to it. SAHA and The Salvation Army entered into management agreements which have allowed The Salvation Army to continue the management of these centres. This means that SAHA provides the fabric of these buildings, at present numbering 40, and has until recently acted as the main mechanism to access government funding to enable The Salvation Army to continue its work. To date this funding has amounted to more than £100 million.

So in 1976 began a major re-development programme of Salvation Army hostels which was eventually to encompass the whole of England. This programme of hostel replacement and the building of other self-contained accommodation for homeless people in the UK, which was undertaken over the next 30 years, would not have been possible without the help of the Salvation Army Housing Association. Initially SAHA concentrated on replacing existing Salvation Army hostels but subsequently broadened its aims to provide rented accommodation for single homeless people and couples, homeless families and foyers for young people. Sheltered housing for elderly

people has also been provided, such as the scheme in Sale, Manchester, named after another generous benefactor. A similar housing association was set up to aid the Salvation Army developments in Scotland but this role was eventually taken over by Lorretto, another housing association. A similar arrangement with The United Welsh housing association was used for the new hostel, named Ty Gobaith (meaning Hope House) in Cardiff, Wales.

SAHA employs staff with relevant housing qualifications and the Army provides the social services

130. *David Barker House, Blackfriars.* (Far left)

131. *Riverside House, Docklands.* (Left)

132. Ty Gobaith, Cardiff in Wales.

expertise. The Army appoints chaplains, as well as managers to these centres, to ensure that the spiritual element of this service is maintained. It is a partnership that works well for the benefit of homeless and vulnerable people.

In the year 2000 the publication of the Government's Strategy on Rough Sleeping, *Coming in From the Cold* recognised that people became homeless for many reasons, including relationship breakdown, mental health problems and substance abuse. It emphasised the need to provide not only accommodation but also a range of services to address issues such as training, mentoring, life skills, literacy, numeracy and confidence building.

The Salvation Army and SAHA had already been doing this for many years and welcomed the Government's endorsement of these services. Together SAHA and The Salvation Army provide a wide variety of these additional services in their Hostel Plus and Employment Plus services as well as in relationship management. The aim of all these services is to enable individuals to live independently in the wider community. This partnership is vitally important in the mission aims of The Salvation Army to allow it to continue with the work that it was initially called to do.

On 19 January 2011 SAHA became a wholly controlled subsidiary of The Salvation Army in a new group structure, thus returning to its original form when SAHA first commenced.

Hadleigh Colony

When in 1890 William Booth wrote a social treatise *In Darkest England and the Way Out*, he set out in detail his proposals for rescuing and training for work the poor and unemployed people of England. The plight of the poor and his vision to rescue them was illustrated in a dramatic picture provided at the start of that book. This vision was for the provision of a number of colonies commencing firstly with City colonies, then farm colonies and then overseas colonies to which men could be sent, trained and employed in a variety of jobs. His proposals and requirements for the farm colony were set out in detail in that book, so that within a year, despite opposition and prejudice, Booth had acquired a number of farms and properties in the area of Hadleigh in Essex. He thus commenced the setting up of the land and industrial colony which became known as Hadleigh Farm

Colony. The farm area was initially about 800 acres for which he paid £12,000 but quickly it was enlarged to 1,236 acres. The site of this colony encircled the ruins of Hadleigh castle, a relic of Plantagenet architecture, dating back to 1231 and sited to provide a commanding position overlooking the river Thames and surrounding countryside.

William Booth insisted that those who needed a revival of self respect and desired rehabilitation must lend a hand to help themselves; in other words, self help was a key to the purposes of the colony. Work was given to men consistent with their ability and physical fitness. The spiritual aims of the founder were always kept to the fore, with men required to attend the gospel meetings in the citadel building erected on the farm.

The colony eventually comprised 1,500 acres of drained marshes and saltings, meadows, slopes, hollows and highlands, orchards and gardens, arable and pasture lands. Dotted profusely over the site were a whole variety of buildings including cottages, dormitories, dining halls, stores, farm buildings, workshops, offices, industrial buildings and cattle sheds and of course the citadel meeting hall. All the accommodation buildings were located on the upper levels of the site, so that inhabitants could enjoy a healthy environment, bathed in sea breezes and with marvellous views across the Thames valley.

The farming activity between 1896 and 1904 covered a wide range including growing a variety of crops as well as dairy farming with a herd of 80 cows plus 200 beef cattle. Other farm activity included 800 sheep and lambs, 360 pedigree Middle-White Yorkshire pigs and pedigree Suffolk Punch shire horses as well as 2,000 chickens, rabbits, Persian cats, bulldogs and bee keeping. The animals won many prizes at local agricultural shows. Market gardening was also undertaken including 16,000 to 18,000 fruit trees providing a great variety of fruit in

an orchard covering over 70 acres. The market gardening covered 200 acres where vegetables were grown in great quantities including comparative luxuries of the time, such as asparagus and sea-kale. Thousands of square feet of glass provided a nursery where innumerable types of bedding plants and seedlings as well as tomatoes and cucumbers were grown. Flowers such as arums, chrysanthemums and geraniums were also produced in these greenhouses. All of this produce found a ready market and was in great demand. The population of the nearby village of Hadleigh increased from 525 to 1,300 in the 10 years after the Hadleigh Colony was established.

In setting out his detailed requirements for the farm colony, William Booth stated that the farm should have clay for brick making, be on a railway line and have access to the sea and river. Hadleigh colony met all of these requirements as well as another requirement of being a considerable distance from any town or village that might have a public house and so tempt the colonists to return to alcoholism. As a result of the availability of

133. Some of the original farm activities, including tending the orchard, making bricks, feeding the chickens and using the heavy work horses.

suitable clay and those potential transport links, the colony set up a brickfield. Besides the construction of the necessary kilns for making the bricks, a small railway with tracks and engine were provided to take the finished bricks to a new wharf constructed on the banks of the Thames and thence by barge on to London. The brick works produced about two million good quality wire-cut bricks annually, providing employment for men throughout the year. By the time of William Booth's death in 1912 almost 7,000 men had been trained there and the scheme had attracted many well-known visitors, including Cecil Rhodes and Rider Haggard, who commended its achievements.

The colony developed its own Salvation Army corps with brass band, songster brigade and home league activities. In addition to the importance given to the spiritual welfare of the colonists, the colony also developed a whole range of leisure and welfare activities with the provision of a library, separate reading and writing rooms and facilities for playing cricket, football, tennis and other recreational activities.

Special provision was made for youths aged 14 to 19 years to be trained during a six weeks course in a variety of crafts connected to life on the land. This was in order to equip them for life should they wish to settle elsewhere in the British Empire, in such countries as Canada, Australia, New Zealand and Rhodesia. In addition to the farming experience and training the youths received instruction in 'looking after themselves' in such skills as repairing their boots, rough carpentry, cooking, clothes washing and other domestic skills. Thousands of these youths passed through Hadleigh colony before emigrating to these countries. Those who did not wish to move abroad were offered the chance of working small holdings at Boxstead in Essex.

After the First World War, the nature of this social experiment began to change, with a number of the operations scaled down and some land sold off for housing. With the coming of the Welfare state after the Second World War, the aims of the colony seemed no longer relevant or necessary, although some boys on probation continued to be trained on the farm.

In 1968 the Colony closed and the farm was then run as a commercial undertaking with the profits supporting The Salvation Army Social Trust (previously the Darkest England Scheme). In 1990, the centenary of the publication of *In Darkest England and the Way Out*, an employment training centre was set up in the former dining hall building of Hadleigh farm. The training, offered to those with special educational needs or who were long-term unemployed, was in carpentry and joinery, catering and office skills including use of computers. Life and social skills training, for those who would benefit, ran alongside the other more technical training.

As the year 2000 approached, the Salvation Army adopted a document entitled 'Vision for the Millennium' in relation to the whole site of Hadleigh farm. This new approach for the farm and former colony, firstly set out its environmental responsibility, as follows:

The Salvation Army believes that as people are made in the image of God, we have a responsibility to use the resources of the earth in a way that ensures that people in this and future generations do not suffer poverty, injustice or harm. This is part of our stewardship of the land and our love for each other. Christian stewardship implies major and permanent changes towards God's creation, so that we begin 'to replenish the earth'.

This statement was the motivation behind the new vision for Hadleigh, which was:

To develop Hadleigh Farm and its buildings to reflect current social and environmental needs by increasing opportunities for employment training and work, by seeking to introduce greener farming policies and public access to the countryside, while respecting greenbelt planning policies.

These new priorities to provide employment training and 'back to work' opportunities and a move to 'greener' faming policies were then developed in detail. With a growing demand for organically-grown crops and the natural feeding of animals, it was planned to turn the farm fully organic in phases over a period of time. Field margins would be left where arable crops were grown to encourage wild-life in accordance with the Countryside Stewardship Schemes. With government policies encouraging access to the countryside as a recreational activity, new public foot-paths were planned to improve links to the adjoining Country Park and Hadleigh Castle. It was essential to have an integrated approach to the training and farming activities if these goals were to be met. This necessitated the farm manager and training centre manager working closely together to provide more training opportunities and restore something of the original vision of William Booth. This vision included viewing the land as being a sacred trust from God; so that The Salvation Army should set an example as Christian stewards in ensuring that it was restored to a 'green' environment, free from the poisons of artificial fertilisers and pesticides. A new farm manager was appointed who shared this vision.

A Hereford herd of cattle with the original herd name of Reliance was introduced as well as free-range chickens. Later, a rare-breeds centre was opened, which attracts a large number of visitors in the summer. The long term plan adopted was to gradually transform the whole farm

134. Hadleigh tea rooms. (Left)

to produce organic crops including the major crops of wheat and potatoes. The new herd of cattle needed to produce organic beef and of course free range chickens and eggs were included in this vision. Organic horticultural crops, which are sold in a vegetable box scheme and at the monthly farmers markets, are produced as part of the Training Centre programme.

In December 2001, new tea rooms were opened to the general public as part of the training centre programme in catering. A further extension to these tea rooms was opened in 2008, expanding these facilities and the workshop training facilities. The new vision and its link with that of William Booth is portrayed in a large oil painting by Rosa Branson, which now hangs in the entrance foyer of the Hadleigh Corps hall and the story is told in a recent publication *Hadleigh Salvation Army Farm – A Vision Reborn* by Gordon Parkhill and Graham Cook.

Comments on the Social Work

On 21 October 1966, after days of heavy rain, a National Coal Board tip of colliery waste above the Welsh village of Aberfan slipped down the mountain side destroying a farm and a number of houses before engulfing the Pantglas village school. Of the 144 people killed in this disaster 116 were children. A group of Salvation Army officers returning in a minibus from Officers Councils heard the news on the radio and immediately diverted to provide what help they could. After the disaster, the site was visited by Her Majesty the Queen, accompanied by George Thomas, the Minister at the Welsh Office and Member of Parliament for Cardiff. She expressed her concern and sympathy to all affected by the disaster and then she met with all the agencies and individuals who were involved in the attempted rescue and support for

families affected. After meeting all the main rescue services she was presented to the Salvation Army representatives. The Queen immediately said to George Thomas: '*Of course, The Salvation Army*'. George Thomas later told officers and staff gathered at IHQ's weekly prayer meeting that: '*Those two small words of course are an immense compliment to The Salvation Army, as it showed that the Queen took it for granted that where there was such need The Salvation Army would be there*', This coment reflects the saying '*where there is need there is The Salvation Army*' which was first coined by Sir Winston Churchill.

The history of The Salvation Army's social services shows that The Salvation Army has never confined itself to meeting just a single area of social need but has sought to respond to whatever social problems are presented to it. Even when it has enjoyed great success in meeting specific needs, as with its approved schools and probation hostels, the Army has been faced with circumstances where it could no longer continue. In spite of having invested significant resources of trained personnel and property in this and other specialised work, it has always sought both to re-assign its people and adapt its property to meet new areas of need.

The Salvation Army has shown itself to be extremely pragmatic in adapting to changes in government policies and cultural trends. The opening and closure of so many programmes and the adaptation or sale of many buildings are ample illustration of this willingness to respond to new challenges. Often these changes have come about as a result of external pressures, but in some cases The Salvation Army has been willing to vacate an area of social work after its pioneering work has shown others the way forward, as with bail hostels. Adaptations and change of use of some existing buildings for completely different programmes reflect a reluctance to

THE PLEASANCE APPEAL
An Opportunity to Invest in the Future

pull out of buildings which have had a proud Salvation Army history. Some of these buildings on prestigious sites also have facilities which new-build properties cannot match. Examples of such are Lefroy House on the River Liffey in Dublin adapted to help homeless teenage girls and The Pleasance on the Royal Mile in Edinburgh, which underwent a major adaptation scheme to provide modern residential facilities for its continuing role of helping homeless men.

In the field of campaigning for social justice, the Army has shown a willingness to get involved in specific issues, only to withdraw once a successful outcome is achieved. This was the case with the Army's 'Maiden Tribute' campaign against child prostitution when its actions resulted in Parliament passing the Criminal Law Amendment Act of 1885 which raised the age of consent to 16. Similarly the Army campaigned against the use of phosphorous in the manufacture of matches because it caused an illness called 'phossy jaw' in the factory workers. When the initial efforts were unsuccessful, Booth opened a Salvation Army match factory that

manufactured 'Salvation matches' without the use of phosphorus, thus proving it was both possible and practical. The use of phosphorus gradually declined and was eventually made illegal, so the Army closed its factory, having achieved its purpose.

The Army's fight for Social Justice, especially for the poor and oppressed, finds its expression today in the establishment of an International Social Justice Commission under the leadership of Commissioner Christine MacMillan. Its principal base is in New York, so that it can seek to influence world leaders, from its membership of the United Nations Economic and Social Council with other bases in Vienna, Geneva, Nairobi and Jakarta. It is very active in seeking ways to combat the evils of human trafficking, especially of children and women, for sexual and other types of exploitation.

As forecast by General Frederick Coutts, no one has relieved the Army of its huge legacy of caring for single homeless men and women throughout the country. The Salvation Army has therefore had to continue this work, while developing increased expertise and significantly improved facilities to meet many major changes among this population and the raised expectations of society as a whole. This is despite a large number of other charitable agencies also working in this particular field of housing and social work. However, the capital cost of providing a bed for a homeless person in a new hostel in 1965 was about £1,150 but as a result of ever increasing standards of provision required over the next 40 years combined with inflation, these costs have risen to between £60,000 and £80,000 per person, depending on a number of factors, such as the size and location of the hostel.

In recent years the Army has re-emphasised aspects of William Booth's vision by relabelling their services to homeless people as 'Hostel Plus' because these centres

135. Appeal brochure painting of the Pleasance men's hostel, Edinburgh.

provide much more than food and shelter. They seek to equip the residents or clients (as they are now called) with the skills to return to an independent way of life. Many of these centres are linked with the Army's 'Employment Plus' services, which provide opportunities for employment, some in Army businesses, as part of this process. Some centres are no longer called hostels but resettlement centres to reinforce the concept that their main objective is to provide a 'springboard' not just a 'refuge from society' for former homeless people. Hostel buildings have for a number of years been given names, such as Edward Alsop Court or David Barker House, as it was felt that a hostel address might prejudice the chances of a resident gaining employment. In recent years there has been a revised emphasis on linking residential centres to local corps, which provide additional support for homeless people especially, both while living in a hostel and later when re-housed. There is also currently a drive to create, inspire or animate new stimulating activities for hostel residents. Maff Potts, the previous Director of Salvation Army Homelessness Services, commented:

> *This project is young unemployed homeless people helping other homeless people and the community; it's a win for everybody. Residents may be eligible to be an animateur (i.e. one who animates, facilitating staff and residents to create activities that build relationship and developing a sense of purpose). For example, a service user in an Army centre, who was a youth worker before he became homeless, is set to become one of the first animateurs. This project will deliver the transformation we want in our centres by giving our residents so much more to do. We believe strongly in the transformation power of fun.*

The Salvation Army has replaced the term 'hostel' with LifeHouse as the new name for its residential centres for homeless people. More than a place to stay a LifeHouse focuses on purpose and relationships to help people rebuild confidence, learn and develop skills, improve their employment prospects and to move into a place of their own. William Booth would certainly have approved, as he believed in keeping everyone in Army centres engaged in useful activities. In some original centres like Spa Home, in addition to many options for employment training, this City Colony had its own football and cricket teams. Hadleigh Colony also had its own brass band in addition to similar sporting opportunities.

In some social areas, such as in the provision of residential care of the elderly, The Salvation Army is a 'relatively small player', currently having 20 homes. However, in its residential homes, it provides an excellent model of care and support for elderly people and their relatives within a Christian environment. With an ever increasing elderly population in a largely materialistic society, this is an important example of the Christian response to a specific need. As the numbers of Salvation Army residential homes have declined, Salvation Army day care programmes for the elderly have greatly increased.

Hadleigh Farm Colony was originally the flagship of William Booth's 'Darkest England Scheme'. The current 'green' policies of Hadleigh farm create an important model of Christian stewardship of the earth and show the essential respect necessary for all God's creation. The focus of the Training Centre in its employment and training priorities, especially for those with disabilities, reflects the importance afforded to every individual in God's plan for the world. It is therefore still a 'flagship' for the essential principles which motivated the Army's founder in establishing the original farm colony.

There are a number of relatively recent changes in the environment in which the Salvation Army social work operates that have made its operations more difficult. The monitoring by local authorities of the quality of service provided and the current climate of competitive tendering with reduced revenue funding available is a major source of concern. Revenue streams, such as 'Supporting People' for hostel work and other residential work were originally operated by central government but are now the responsibility of local authorities who are operating with reduced budgets and hence looking for ways to save money.

In the field of residential care for elderly people, the assessment of need for such services was initially carried out by local authorities with the funding previously provided by central government. Now that the need assessment and the funding of such care in England and Wales are both carried out by local authorities, the decision whether to make the appropriate referral may have more to do with whether the cost can be afforded, rather than whether the individual needs such a level of care.

The re-organisation of the Army administration with the demise of the Social Work headquarters resulted in the delegation of the authority for these specialised branches of this work being dispersed among the new 18 divisions. The elderly care work has now been brought back under the direct authority of THQ and acommodation for homeless people is now following a similar re-organisation while other residential centres remain under divisional control. In instances where major operational problems arise, the ability to intervene and take decisive action to remedy the problem is now more difficult without the accumulated knowledge, resources and direct line authority that the previous social headquarters possessed.

136. *Lyndon House Men's Hostel, Ipswich – floor plans.*

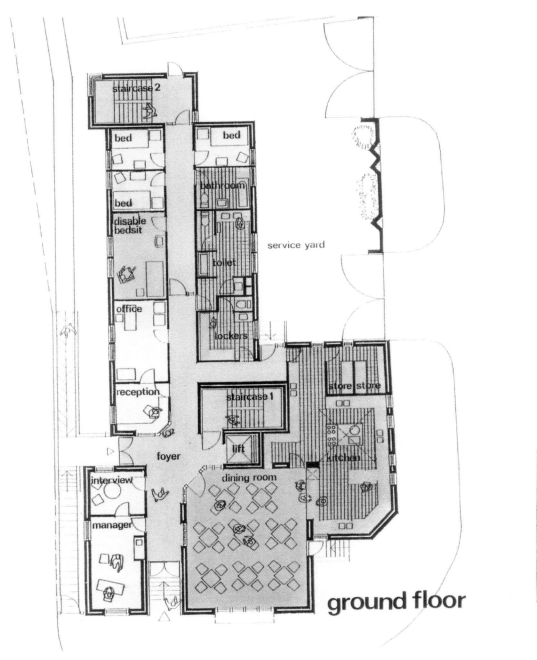

ground floor

levels 1 & 2

137. Edward Alsop Court – ground floor plan.   *138. E. A. Court – first floor plan.*

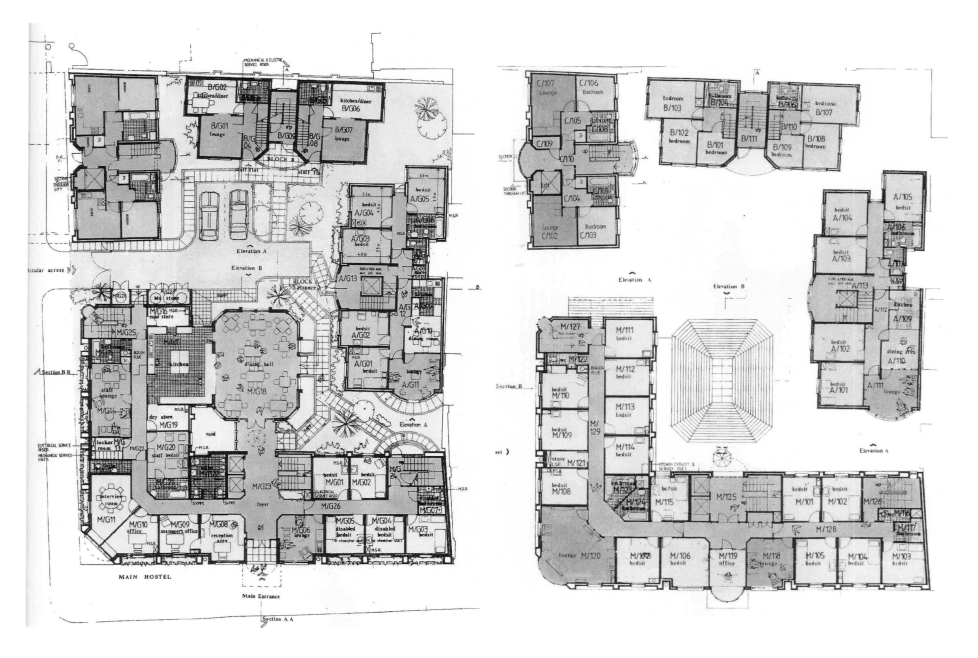

139. *Hope Town 2004 Women's Hostel, Whitechapel – upper floor plans*

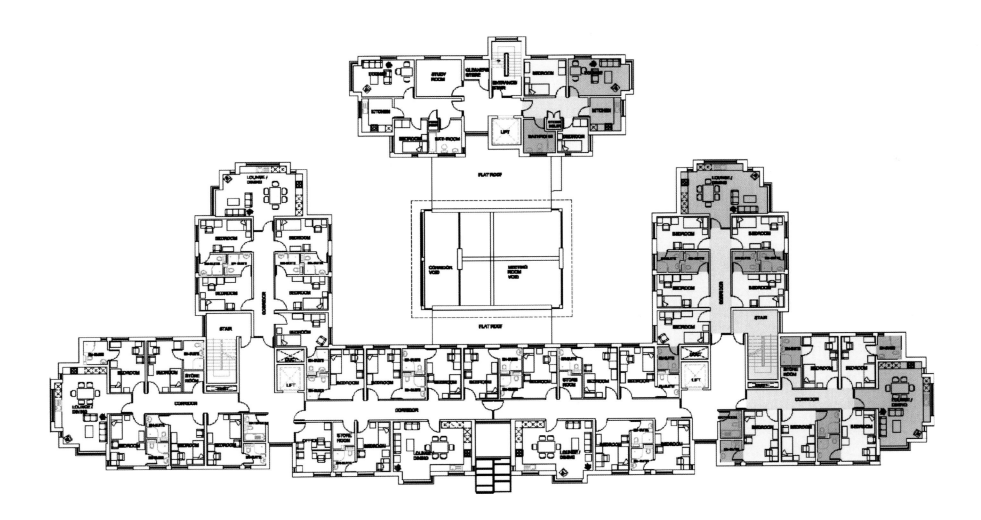

140. *Greig House Substance Treatment Centre, Docklands, London*

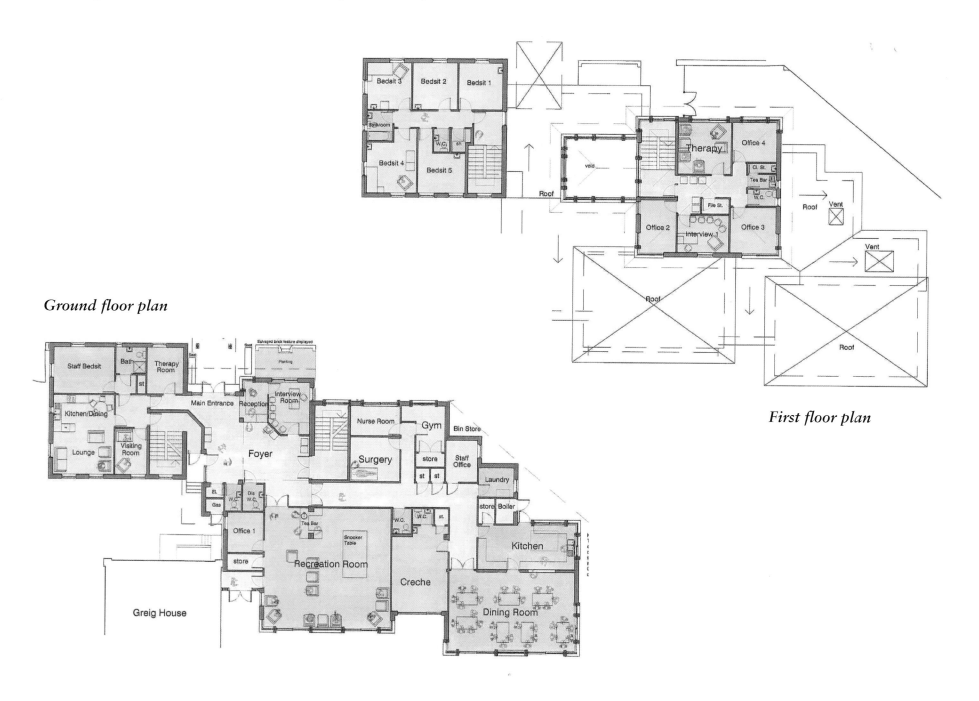

Ground floor plan

First floor plan

141. *Youell Court Residential Care Centre, Coventry – upper floor plan*

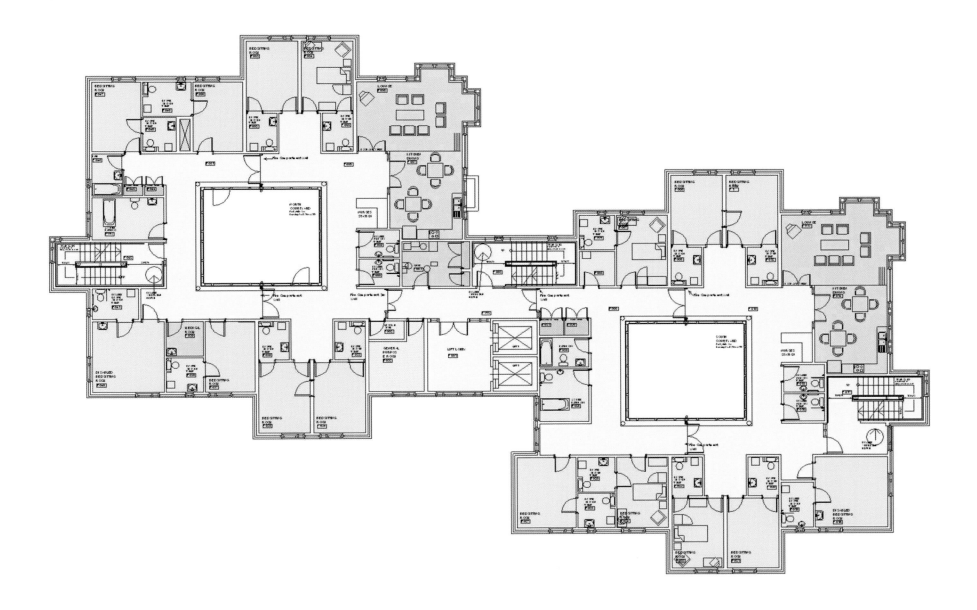

142. *Eva Burrows Residential and Day Centre, Glasgow – perspective drawing*

SPECIAL BUILDINGS

143. Sunbury Court

William Booth College

General William Booth, founder of The Salvation Army, was unable before his death in 1912 to achieve his ambition to found an 'International University of Humanity'. William Booth's often repeated and almost last recorded statement was:

My wish is the establishment of a great Training Institution, an International University for training men and women for dealing with sins and miseries of the submerged throughout the world. You have Schools of Art, Colleges of Music, Universities where men and women of wealthier classes are taught those things which will make them a help to the community and grace society. Now why not a University of Humanity? That is what I want to make our Training School – a University where consecrated men and women can learn how best to serve their fellow men and women.

The First World War further delayed plans by The Salvation Army to build one as his memorial. The *Daily Graphic* stated: '*No monument of cold stone is needed, but something that is warm and living which will help forward the work to which he consecrated his life.*'

The curriculum that William Booth envisaged was to include:

Women and child welfare work; study of moral and religious diseases; how to visit the poor in the slums, the aged, the sick and suffering and the despairing; the practice of public speaking; the study of principles underlying all sociological work; singing and its effective use among the masses, outdoors and in; also the application and use of constantly increasing skill and the latest experience in promotion of the best and most fruitful service for the rehabilitation of broken human earthenware.

In 1921 the Army was looking for a site in South London for this project. The present site at Denmark Hill near Camberwell was chosen because of its prominent position and they chose a leading architect, Sir Giles Gilbert Scott for its design. In July 1923 the architect wrote to William Booth's son, General Bramwell Booth, with a prospectus of his proposals explaining he had long experience of The Salvation Army. At the centre of Scott's design is the Assembly Hall, which originally seated 1,000 people. He explained that the design enabled the two sexes studying at the college to be able to attend assembly without co-mingling either when gathering or dispersing. The Assembly Hall remains virtually unchanged since it was built, with the flags of all the different sessions of cadets since 1929 hanging at the rear of the hall.

Gilbert Scott stressed the importance of greenery and undertook to preserve as many mature trees as possible. Scott proposed that for one per cent of the total cost he would be responsible for the layout but only for the external elevations and the interior of the entrance foyer and assembly hall. He insisted on control of the materials used for the exterior, stating: '*This is a very important matter as a design, which is fine on paper, may be ruined by using unsuitable materials.*'

The Salvation Army had very definite views about what it wanted. A memo of 1925 stated: '*The architectural character of the buildings fronting Champion Grove, however, was not approved and Sir Giles Gilbert Scott was asked to prepare a scheme of a more monumental character and semi-military-style as symbolic of The Salvation Army's work.'* It is suggested by some that this insistence is something of a lingering siege mentality which went back to the early days of The Salvation Army when it struggled against a hostile world. Its processions were sometimes beset by riots and sometimes by the more organised disruption of skeleton armies formed in opposition. This insistence is more likely to have been a desire to symbolically reflect the importance of the building and the semi-military style of the organisation. At this stage the proposed building was referred to as a garrison but by the time it was opened it was called a college.

Scott obliged as far as he could and responded: *'I am sending you herewith a pencil drawing of my suggestions showing the front more in fortress style. It is very difficult to produce this character in a building, which must necessarily have many windows. The windows in old fortified buildings were of course very few and very small. I have done what I can to attain the necessary effect.'* This amounted to giving it a more monolithic

look with thin buttresses protruding from the external walls presumably intended to give the necessary military air. The Salvation Army noted 'the adoption of the semi military character of the buildings has added £50,000 to the cost.' This was a significant proportion out of a budget of £250,000

The final building was, however, to be more austere than The Salvation Army had intended. In the original plan the windows were to have stonework surrounds but these were omitted to save costs. Their omission reinforced the strong resemblance to the Bankside power station, another building designed by the same architect and now known as Tate Modern. The Assembly Hall had been planned as an octagon, a shape John Wesley regarded as good for acoustics. It also had pinnacles and flying buttresses. It was decided to save £10,000 by building a simpler hall. The proposed towers for the men's and women's schools were also abandoned. The Army was determined however to keep the central tower which itself cost £25,000.

Scott was not very pleased, to judge from the somewhat caustic note he wrote to the General. It is clear that he thought the central tower should be cut before anything else. In 1927 Scott wrote: *'The upper portion of the tower is from a practical point of view a luxury and its omission would not affect the working of the college in any way'.* The Salvation Army, however was determined to have its tower which would rise as high as the cross on the top of St Paul's Cathedral. It was intended to be permanently illuminated and 'to shine over the slums of south London.' But it was many years later that an illuminated cross was eventually added.

Scott found himself involved in sorting out the problems caused by the sheer weight of the tower; problems for which he was not really responsible according to the original agreement. After calling in a

144. Gilbert Scott's axonometric drawing – William Booth Memorial Training College.

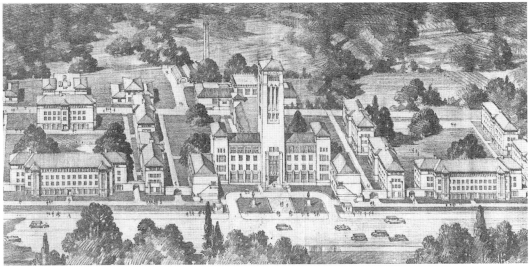

structural engineer, who waived most of his fee, it was decided to build 25 ft thick foundations of reinforced concrete. The tower was still not finished for the opening in July 1929, the centenary year of William Booth's birth. However, from the top of the tower there are magnificent views over London from Crystal Palace to St Paul's Cathedral and Canary Wharf.

Scott wanted the college to have an open façade to the world, with the lawns sweeping down to a low wall between the College and the street, with security achieved by walls and gates between the buildings. In August 1928 the supervising architects, Gordon and Viner, were clamouring for some instructions on the boundary fence and subsequently a high wall went up against the wishes of the principal architect. In more recent times when the college needed to replace these boundary walls, which were deteriorating due to structural defects, the in-house Salvation Army architects wanted to do something similar in presenting a more open aspect to the world. Their proposal was to build a low boundary wall with open metal railings above, similar to those in front of the two new blocks of family flats, known as Houses 11 and 12. Having overcome the problems of getting planning permission for those changes through a planning appeal, the Army then decided to ignore this recommendation and merely to replace the high wall with an identical one.

Scott, as originally agreed, was responsible for the interior of the entrance hall. On a modest budget he gave it a sense of dignity and style. On the floor is a marble mosaic of The Salvation Army crest. Two light brackets, in their shape recall the crown of glory that is part of The Salvation Army crest. The college interiors by Gordon and Viner were also carried out to a high standard, despite a tight budget. The original lift in the entrance hall of the administration block is still in place and is often used by film companies including the makers of

Agatha Christie films, where Hercules Poirot uses the lift supposedly in a smart mansion block where he lived in the 1920s or 1930s.

Now some limited stonework on the façade was included but the architect used Commanderie Traverton from France, much to the consternation of the English stone companies. Scott seems to have regarded the limited amount of stonework as rather incongruous in the vast areas of brickwork. A comment by Scott implies that it was Bramwell Booth who insisted on using some stone, being better than none to relieve the austerity of the façades. At the back of the Administration Block, Scott contrived some Gothic tracery in brickwork, which he considered to be more successful than the stone at the front.

Nobody seems to have tried to interfere with his choice of Dutch bricks. These are only two inches (50mm) deep as opposed to deeper English bricks. Scott apparently chose that size because the effect would resemble stone work in appearance and because they

145. William Booth College administration block and tower.

146. William Booth statue and entrance foyer to college. (Below)

147. College Assembly Hall. (Right)

were half the cost of the English equivalent. Many years later, when the tower and the Administration Block needed to be re-pointed, the successful contractor in estimating the cost failed to realise that these bricks were much smaller than normal and subsequently had to carry out the re-pointing work at a cost much below that estimated by others.

At the grand opening in July 1929, Scott was temporarily denied entrance because he did not have to hand his invitation to the ceremony. However, he was eventually allowed in to enjoy the triumphant occasion. King George V was to have opened the college but as he was ill, his son Prince George, later the Duke of Kent, performed the honours in front of a large and enthusiastic audience. It was an important moment and a stupendous achievement for The Salvation Army; a Royal Prince opening the College. There were ambassadors, High Commissioners, mayors, the high and the mighty paying homage to an organisation that some 60 years before had been little more than a few lonely figures preaching on the street corners and meeting in hired tents.

These new buildings replaced the Clapton Training Home and for those first cadets the change from their previous conditions in East London was considerable.

Each now had the luxury of a single room to themselves, each having a bed, washstand, cupboard and bookcase. These 'cells' were on the upper floors of nine individual houses with the ground floor providing a sitting room for all the cadets of each house. Laundry and storage for trunks, etc was provided in the basement of each house. Central kitchen and dining facilities, with separate dining rooms for men and women, were provided in another building off the 'top avenue'. A health lodge and an up-to-date hydro complete with Turkish baths for cadets were other facilities also provided off the 'top avenue'.

The William Booth Memorial Training College, as it was originally known, served the Army's training needs well until about 1960, having survived the bombing of the Second World War relatively unscathed. The College had been designed to accommodate large numbers of single men and women cadets in single rooms for the training period which was only nine months in duration. In 1960 the period of training was lengthened to a two-year period. As the numbers of cadets entering the college had greatly reduced by then, the accommodation was sufficient to house both the first and second year sessions of cadets at the same time. A further change in the pattern of training was that many more married cadet couples were entering the College. The only concession made to them initially was to make two of the small cell-like bedrooms into one double room. The double size rooms, however, were merely furnished with two single metal beds, two single wardrobes and two sets of drawers. The dividing partitions between bedrooms remained the original 50mm thick breeze block, which provided very little sound installation. No provision was made at that time for children, so that married couples with children had to leave them behind in their home town with friends or relatives before entering the training college.

The college buildings had received little attention, except for routine maintenance, since their completion in 1929. Virtually no improvements in the facilities had taken place during that period. In 1966 some improvement by the provision of a nursery was commenced. The following year, two of the residential blocks, namely houses number one and six were remodelled to provide small flatlets for married couples. House number seven was similarly remodelled the following year. During this period the replacement of the original central Lancashire boilers was carried out in the separate semi-basement boiler house. When the boilers were removed the concrete retaining wall around the boiler room collapsed and had to be replaced at the same time and before the cadets returned after their summer placements. The renewal of the heating and hot water mains, through underground ducts, followed as they had become extensively 'furred up' due to the lime-scale present in London water.

It was not until 1981, however, when Jarl Wahlström became the General that extensive improvements and renovations commenced and continued for the next decade. These improvements included the renewal of heating, hot water, plumbing and electrical services of all

nine of the residential houses, together with substantial improvements to the standards of accommodation. This work included improved facilities for the single cadets and self-contained flats for married couples and their families. In 1986 two complete new blocks of 16 self-contained flats for larger families were completed on vacant land fronting onto Champion Park. Each of these flats has three bedrooms and the standards provided were considered at the time to be luxurious. Planning permission proved to be difficult, due to the proximity of the grade two listed administration block and objections from local neighbours. After a public inquiry, planning permission was eventually granted and General Eva Burrows was able to open the completed new flats on 30 October 1986. The total cost of the 16 flats was £1,250,000. This compares with the original cost of a whole training college development of £400,000 in 1929.

148. New block of flats for cadet families.

All nine residential blocks were renovated and remodelled by 1990 with the complete renewal of all services and finishes. It was at this date that The Salvation Army administration of International and Territorial Headquarters were separated. The responsibility for the William Booth College then passed to the United Kingdom Territory. The major renovations and remodelling of the remainder of the buildings at the college then came to a halt. However, in the next decade the main kitchen block was rebuilt and the original dining rooms renovated. The boundary wall had to be completely rebuilt as it was in a dangerous condition due to structural movement. It was replaced in an identical manner to the original wall as previously described.

Since that time the William Booth College has incorporated a wide range of additional training roles, not only preparation of candidates for officership and ongoing training of commissioned officers, but also specialist courses for social services personnel – previously housed at Avalon in Chislehurst – are also now based there.

From October 2001 the college also provided, on a temporary basis, the offices for International Headquarters staff as well as the International Heritage Centre with its archives. Three years later IHQ personnel were able to return to 101 Queen Victoria Street to occupy their new building. This was the second time that the college had provided temporary accommodation for the IHQ administration. In 1941 the International Headquarters building at 101 Queen Victoria Street had been destroyed by fire following a German air raid. The William Booth College then housed International Headquarters administration for more than 20 years, from 1941 until 1963, when a new IHQ building had been completed.

The training of cadets for officership has recently undergone a review with changes which allow a variety of options in the methods of training, including long-distance learning. This means that it is no longer necessary for every cadet to be resident at the college for the full training period. These changes, together with reduced cadet numbers, may allow Houses 8, 9, 10 and 11 to be leased out to other organisations in future, bringing substantial revenue to the college and thus subsidizing the costs of maintaining the work there.

At the same time further improvements are planned to the college buildings including:

- A new energy-efficient boiler
- New roof coverings
- Some cleaning of brickwork
- Extensive refurbishment of offices and classrooms incorporating the latest technology to aid learning techniques
- Up-grading all of the residential accommodation in the remaining Houses numbered 1 to 7 to provide en-suite facilities
- A new fully equipped gym
- A new glass atrium to provide a meeting space and coffee area linking the Entrance Foyer in the Administration Block and the Assembly Hall.

International College for Officers

From the early days of The Salvation Army, its leaders saw the need for an International College for Officers. In 1905 the first Staff Training College was opened in the Lodge at Clapton. Then in 1909 some new premises were acquired at Clapham Common in London for the International Staff College, as it was then known. It closed in 1914 due to the outbreak of the First World

War and did not re-open until 1921. The courses by then included officer-training for missionary service including cultural understanding and the teaching of a variety of languages including Gujarati and Korean.

It was transferred in 1926 to Sunbury Court with the title of International Training Institute. Unfortunately in 1929 the economic situation resulted in its closure. It was eventually re-opened at a new location in Sydenham, South London where it was housed in a large country house acquired for £23,767.

This building called 'The Cedars', located on the highest hill in London, Sydenham Hill, is also known as *'the house on the hill with a world view'*. It was opened by General Albert Orsborn on 10 October 1950 when he reminded those present that *'The Founder saw the value of training his staff officers; men all over the world who were with him in principle'*. The role of this college was to provide education in leadership for officers from around the world and to aid in their understanding and commitment to the Army.

With the arrival in 1954 of a new principal, Commissioner Alfred Gilliard, the college name was changed to the International College for Officers. Any reference to it being a staff officers' college was dropped because he believed that no officer's training is completed at commissioning. Officers need to continue to develop a deeper understanding of their faith and the purposes of the Army in which they serve. The basic purpose of the college is officially stated as *'providing the Army of today and tomorrow with officers further equipped in mind and spirit for the tasks to which they are appointed'*. The rich international, inter-cultural experience of meeting officers from around the world is a fertile ground for nourishing the spirit of internationalism, which is so necessary for the continuing unity of The Salvation Army. Arrangements are made for translation sessions for those

149. The Cedars, Sydenham Hill – view from the front. (Below left)

150. The Cedars – view from the rear garden. (Below)

151. Rosa Branson's oil painting representing the essence of The Salvation Army's message.

not fluent in English. Commissioner Gilliard suggested that the ICO *'may yet prove to be one of the Army's most brilliant long-term investments'*.

Its accommodation, however, was rather limited resulting in crowded conditions for the initial sessions of 24 officers who attended the college. The sleeping arrangements necessitated 4 or 5 officers sharing a room. However, this situation was greatly improved in 1961 when a new motel-type annexe was built allowing each officer to have a room of their own. The building was described by General Eva Burrows as a gracious dwelling house. The lovely grounds of the Cedars provide an oasis of quiet beauty for officers needing a retreat from the pressures of their appointments. The building has been sensitively extended in recent years to provide greatly improved dining facilities and its role widened to become the Centre for Spiritual Life Development. Another recent addition is one of Rosa Branson's oil paintings depicting the centrality of Jesus in the world- wide message of love that Salvation Army officers take around the world.

Sunbury Court

The main house of Sunbury Court probably dates back to 1723, built by a John Witt, a master builder of the Parish of St James, Westminster and it was known until 1866 as Sunbury Place. It originally had stables, coach house, yards, gardens and orchards all enclosed by a brick wall. It was set in an estate of over 100 acres which extended to the banks of the Thames and included the two islands now covered by the adjacent park and private residences. It had earlier been part of an even larger estate, the Royal Manor of Kempton.

It was sold in 1735 and changed hands again in 1751 and in 1755, when it became the home of one of the country's great heiresses, Anna Maria Delegard. In 1764 she married George Fermor, second Earl of Pomfret, Lord of the Bedchamber and Ranger of the Little Park in Windsor. It was he who commissioned a young Swedish artist, Elias Martin, to execute the murals, which are still retained in the main dining room. These murals show decorative landscapes painted in oils directly onto the plaster of large panels. The room was decorated in typical neo-Palladian style with these panels framed with plaster mouldings surrounded by broken pediments.

In 1799, the estate was sold and underwent numerous changes of ownership resulting in many alterations and adaptations to the property. One of these owners was Jack Needham, the Lord Kilmorey, who bought the estate for £16,500 in 1860 and added a tunnel under the ancient Saxon Road to his boathouse beside the Thames. The entrance, long since sealed off, may still be seen in the brick wall that fronts the river road. The size of the estate had been enlarged in 1855 by the purchase of additional land from the parish, with the Vestry insisting on the retention of a public footpath through the new area, known as the Markway, which is still maintained to this day.

The last private owner was a Victorian gentleman of considerable wealth and achievement, Lieut-Colonel William Horatio Harfield, whose name is preserved in Harfield Road, which forms the Eastern boundary of the present estate. During his ownership, in 1877, there was a disastrous fire, damaging both wings but leaving the central section intact. The house was subsequently enlarged by the owner, with wings added to the east and west of the central block and the porte-cochère built at the western end. The additions were constructed to match the style of the original building. They contain the present library and conference room.

After Harfield's death, the house became a country club for a period, but in the early years of the 20th century it failed. The property was then left empty and derelict for a time. The estate was divided and Harfield Road was built. In 1925 the house and fifty acres of the estate north of the road were put up for auction, which the Salvation Army bought for £10,500 as a conference centre.

After its acquisition, The Salvation Army provided an addition to the rear of the main block, which was subsequently replaced in 1986 with the present fully glazed extension. The bedrooms to the main house were provided with en-suite facilities in 1992. A separate building, the annexe, had already been erected in 1969 to provide additional sleeping accommodation with 28 bedrooms, all with en-suite showers.

In a pamphlet on its history Mike Ungersma wrote the following in 1978:

It is a tribute to the foresight of The Salvation Army that Sunbury Court stands today not only as a living monument to a rich national heritage, but also as a working institution providing unexcelled conference facilities for thousands of Christians from around the world.

Visitors dine in the mansion's 250-year-old drawing room, surrounded by the artistry of Elias Martin, the Swedish painter who came to study in London and found himself decorating the homes and palaces of the wealthy. These paintings were restored some years ago to their original brilliance through the co-operation of the Swedish Institute of Stockholm. These priceless frescoes are now just as they were seen when Martin painted them directly upon the plastered walls, more than two centuries ago.

In the hallway that separates the dining room from the lounge, visitors pass under the graceful moulded ceiling and skylight. Like the Martin paintings, these simply proportioned designs are part of the original 18th century building. This hallway is an appropriate introduction to the octagonal shaped lounge. Once a music salon, this room features one of the most noticeable objects in the building, a 3,000 piece crystal chandelier,

152. Sunbury Court Main House.

thought to be an artefact of the original mansion. Here too are marvellous examples of Victorian mirrors, gilt work and a late 19th century fireplace of marble.

One of the most attractive features of the house is the curved main staircase. Visitors see it today much as it was when the mansion took shape in the early years of the 18th century. A staircase that they don't see, however, is the winding spiral of ironwork topped by a skylight and located near the entrance to the Conference Room. While the stair itself is probably Victorian, the well in which it is built has been used by the staff for access to the kitchens and storerooms for more than two hundred years.

The Victorian wings added by Colonel Harfield in the late 19th century are integrated faithfully into the older core of the building. Harfield even used the expensive but novel device of false windows that are fully glazed with black glass but have no interior opening. Their only purpose is to preserve the balance of the exterior façade.

The wing to the east, housing the library, the reception hall and a small meditation room is noteworthy for its black and white marble floor. But it is the west

wing, with its massive, high ceiling conference room and elaborate coachman's entrance that is of special interest to Salvationists. Mention Sunbury Court to a Salvationist anywhere in the world and chances are they will respond: '*Oh yes, that's where they elect the General.*' It is here that the first Salvation Army High Council gathered in 1929. The next two High Councils took place at Clapton, but the Army's Generals from 1946 until 1999, when a new conference centre was opened, were elected in this impressive hall by Salvation Army leaders assembling from their posts around the world.

A separate youth centre in the grounds was opened on 6 June 1938 by General Evangeline Booth. The facilities include an open-air swimming pool, sports pitches and a camping site. The original huts were subsequently replaced by the present range of timber buildings.

The new conference centre in the grounds of Sunbury Court, opened in 1999, incorporates 'state of the art' conference facilities and is now used for the meeting of the High Council, and for many other conferences. The layout of the main conference room is octagonal in shape with a central roof light incorporating the colours of the Salvation Army flag in the glass, arranged in a star motif.

Sunbury Court has a truly international reputation. Over the decades it has been the focal point for some of the most important moments in the Army's history. It has served the Army well, as a gathering place for young and old, as an eventide home, a recreation and relaxation facility for soldiers, sailors and airmen during the war and as a conference centre for young people, home league members, youth leaders, local officers of various sections, and councils for staff and corps officers. There are no ghosts at Sunbury Court, but there is a spirit, a spirit that links its past with its present, and each visitor to its enchanting heritage.

153. Sunbury annexe.

154. *Sunbury new conference centre – external and internal views. (Left and below left)*

155. *Youth Centre dining hall. (Below)*

156. Sunbury Court conference centre – floor plan

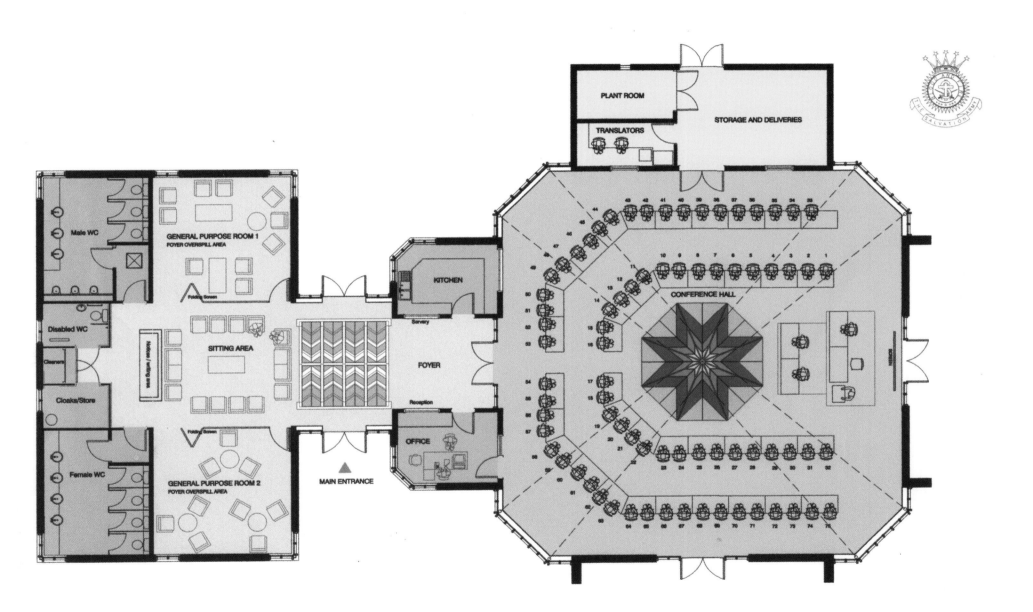

157. Sunbury Court conference centre – cross section

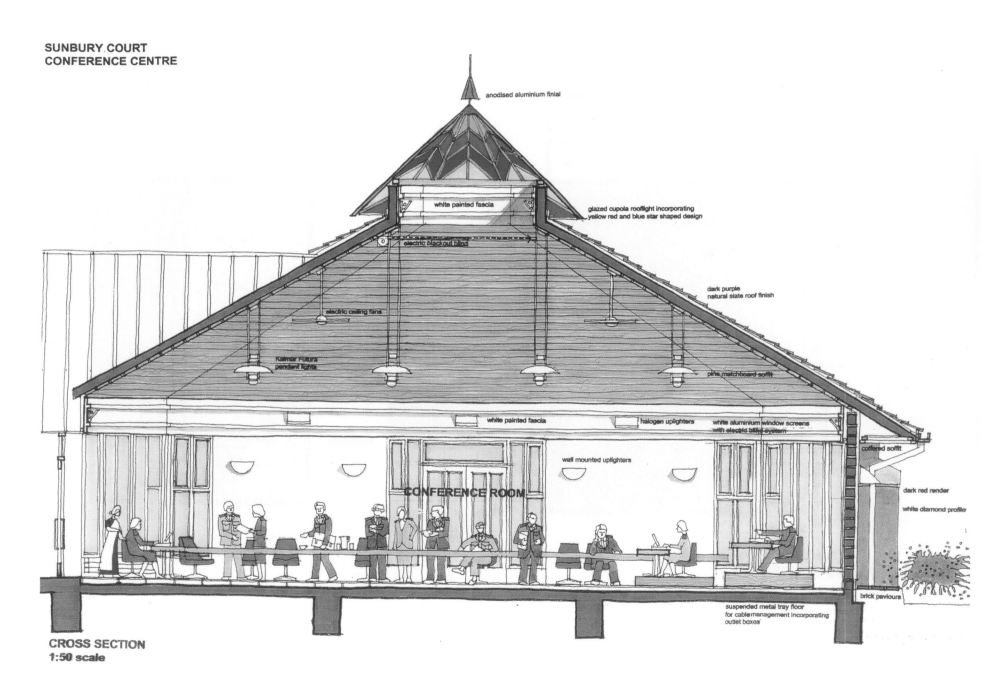

SUNBURY COURT
CONFERENCE CENTRE

anodised aluminium finial

white painted fascia

glazed cupola rooflight incorporating
yellow red and blue star shaped design

electric blackout blind

dark purple
natural slate roof finish

electric ceiling fans

Kaiser Futura
pendant lights

pine matchboard soffit

white painted fascia

halogen uplighters

white aluminium window screens
with electric blind system

coffered soffit

wall mounted uplighters

CONFERENCE ROOM

dark red render

white diamond profile

brick paviours

suspended metal tray floor
for cable management incorporating
outlet boxes

CROSS SECTION
1:50 scale

158. Notintone Place courtyard and museum.

Notintone Place

Number 12 Notintone Place in the district of Sneinton in Nottingham is the house where, on 10 April 1829, William Booth was born. This house and those on either side originally stood on their own but in the 1830s they became part of a terrace of three-storey houses along Notintone Place. In 1913 these houses stood in a tree-shaded cul-de-sac, built back from the road and guarded by tall railings and a low brick wall. On 25 October 1939, just days before her retirement, General Evangeline Booth unveiled a brass plaque in the room where William Booth was said to have been born. In the previous year, the house had been used by the Army as a hostel for stranded girls, providing emergency accommodation for six people.

At the start of the Second World War cadets were moved away from London for their safety. Twenty five women cadets, with their sergeants and training officers, were accommodated in these three houses from September 1939 until March 1940, when they were able to return to the William Booth College to complete their training. After their use for training purposes ceased, these houses became a Goodwill Centre.

In the late 1950s the three houses were acquired under a compulsory purchase order by the City Council, as part of their slum clearance programme, but then re-let to the Army at a nominal rent. In 1959 they were put to use as a museum to maintain William's birthplace as a visitor attraction, with a resident caretaker installed in one of the other houses. In 1963 it was announced that the house would be spared from a slum clearance scheme and be transferred to the Army. By 1965 the surrounding properties had all been demolished, so the three properties stood in splendid isolation in a sea of rubble.

The Salvation Army then acquired this site and surrounding land. The site was redeveloped to provide a

new complex of buildings including an elderly care residential centre, a hostel for homeless families and a Goodwill Community Centre. Thus the redeveloped site has become a living memorial to the life and work of William Booth. The three original houses were carefully restored with new gable walls and chimney stacks, new roof, floors, doors and windows. The original brickwork to the main flank walls was retained, but some of the facing to the bricks had deteriorated. As it was impossible to match the original facing bricks, those damaged bricks were individually cut out, turned around and put back into the walls with the undamaged inner face now on the outside. Two of the houses were turned into an exhibition about the life of William and Catherine Booth as well as of the development of The Salvation Army. The whole exhibition is set out in chronological order.

One of the former bedrooms, being the actual birth place of William Booth, has been restored and furnished in the fashion of the early nineteenth century. Several items of furniture belonging to William Booth have been placed in this room as well as Booth's christening robe and his wedding waistcoat which are also displayed in a showcase here. In the courtyard at the front of the house stands a statue of William Booth, alongside some trees and a flag pole.

The whole complex of buildings and the exhibits were designed by the IHQ in-house Architects Office with David Greenwood being the project architect. They were built by Simms, Son and Cooke and opened on 1 October 1971 by Sir Keith Joseph MP, Secretary of State for Health and Social Services. General Erik Wickberg and Commissioner Catherine Bramwell-Booth, the grand-daughter of William Booth were both present. The

scheme received a Civic Trust Award in 1972.

Now, almost 40 years later, it is being refurbished. The enlarged museum section should re-open in 2011.

Comments on special buildings

These four special buildings have a historical and symbolic significance probably greater than any other Army buildings. The William Booth College, although built after William Booth's death, being the fulfilment of his dream for a University of Humanities and of course was built as a memorial to him. It was originally named the International (William Booth Memorial) College and many cadets from around the world have received at least part of their training there. The International College for Officers (The Cedars) was similarly part of William's dream, which he commenced in 1905 as his Staff Training College initially located in Clapton, London. It promotes and symbolises the international nature of The Salvation Army.

William Booth nominated his successor as General, so that after his death his son Bramwell succeeded him as the international leader of the Army. In 1929 when Bramwell was too ill to fulfil his duties, a High Council of Army leaders was called to elect a new General. That historic meeting took place at Sunbury Court and most new Generals since then have been elected there. Notintone Place in Nottingham is of course William's birth place and now contains a museum and exhibition of William and Catherine's life together with a sequential historical account of the international development of The Salvation Army. It attracts visitors from around the world and is an essential and inspirational part of the I.C.O. delegates experience on coming to England, the birth place of the Army's founder.

159. Bedroom where William Booth was born – now part of Notintone Place museum.

HEADQUARTERS BUILDINGS

160.
*International
Headquarters,
London.*

International Headquarters

William Booth's first evangelical meetings took place in the street, then in a tent on a disused Quaker burial ground. Even when the work expanded, he just required rented premises to use for meetings. However, in 1867 Booth purchased a former public house, the Eastern Star, number 188 Whitechapel Road and turned it into the headquarters of the 'East London Christian Mission'.

By 1869 the movement had become the 'Christian Mission' and Booth purchased the People's Market, 272 Whitechapel Road. The cost was £3,500 and Booth turned it into the People's Mission Hall which was used as a place of worship, a cheap food shop for the poor and his headquarters' offices. These premises remained Booth's Headquarters when in 1878 the Christian Mission became The Salvation Army.

However, William and his son Bramwell, by now his chief of staff, had been increasingly exercised by the need for more suitable and spacious accommodation for their headquarters. When returning together from some business calls along Queen Victoria Street they saw a notice on the other side of the road *'These desirable promises to let'*. It aroused their immediate attention and Bramwell exclaimed: *'There's our new headquarters'*.

A quick 'peep through the door' confirmed their opinion that the spacious front and back rooms would afford excellent accommodation for a meeting room and offices. The building had previously been used as a billiards club. Leaving post-haste for Whitechapel, the Booths gathered their staff and told them of their discovery. They urged them to pray about the matter and hurried off to talk to Thomas A. Denny, a generous benefactor. Mr Denny offered to pay the first year's rent. A copy of the original lease containing William Booth's signature and wax seal dated 15 December 1882 is retained within The Salvation

Army Heritage Centre archives. Little did Booth realise at that time that some 10 years later he would be able to purchase the freehold outright for £70,000 – due this time to the generosity of a Scottish friend Mrs Elizabeth Orr Bell. The transport of the effects of that early-day Army Headquarters required only two trips in a fruiterer's horse-drawn van and a handcart.

One amusing episode was that half way to the new City offices one of the wheels fell off the handcart. Cadet William Whattam attempted to fix it, while his colleague, another cadet known as 'Zulu George', held off the roughs by threatening them with the flagpole that formed part of the precious cargo. The rest of the journey was made on one wheel, with one perspiring cadet pushing while the other held up the handcart on the side without a wheel.

Thus, since 8 September 1881 the International Headquarters of The Salvation Army has been located at 101 Queen Victoria Street within the prestigious square

161. View of 1881 IHQ building on Queen Victoria Street.

mile of the City of London. On that date no formal ceremony took place but some two weeks later a noon-day prayer meeting was held, led by William Booth himself, to thank God for the provision of their new headquarters.

The original building purchased in 1881 was destroyed by fire during the Second World War, following German bombing. That building, however, had been the scene of many significant historic events:

162. Site of IHQ after destruction by enemy bombing in 1941.

- From 101, The Salvation Army sent out its first missionaries to pioneer the Amy's work in India – surely one of the City of London's finest export drives.
- At 101, the City Chamberlain conferred with *Pall Mall Gazette* editor W. T. Stead and Bramwell Booth about the iniquitous traffic in child prostitution which was

rife in London. The action they decided upon resulted in the passing of the Criminal Law Amendment Act of 1885, raising the age of consent to 16 years of age.
- In 1905, William Booth was escorted from 101 to the Guildhall where he received the Freedom of the City of London.

Seven years later, in 1912, his funeral procession blocked all traffic in the City for most of the day. Thousands of Salvationists marched past the Mansion House, where the Lord Mayor took the salute, en route to Abney Park cemetery, in what seemed like a state funeral. Similar scenes were repeated in 1929 with the promotion to glory of his son, General Bramwell Booth.

The devastating air raid of 11 May 1941 and the subsequent fire destroyed the original 101 building. General George Carpenter, the Army's international leader at the time, pledged to rebuild the headquarters and described the Army centre as *'no ordinary commercial house, nor merely the administrative centre of a worldwide organization. It was a spiritual centre which united people of more nations than any other building in the City of London'*. He also stated *'that 101 will rise again'*. City authorities evidently felt similarly, as among the first to express profound regret at the Army's loss was the Lord Mayor of London, Sir George Wilkinson. He told General Carpenter that the City Corporation was *'most anxious to find a way of rehousing the movement's administration in its old location'*.

With such assurance to encourage them, The Salvation Army began the daunting task of raising £1,250,000 necessary to build the new international headquarters. Thanks to the generosity of Salvationists and friends from around the world, the task was eventually accomplished. The Salvation Army had already acquired the freehold of numbers 101 to 107

Queen Victoria Street and the City of London Corporation, in accordance with their earlier expressions of help, agreed to add to the site by selling to The Salvation Army the freehold of numbers 97 and 99. The total cost of the final scheme was about £1,450,000 including a purchase cost of £52,500 for the additional areas of site and furnishing costs of £37,000. The builders, Humphries Ltd, carried out the construction after winning the contract through competitive tendering.

On 13 November 1963, Her Majesty Queen Elizabeth the Queen Mother opened the new IHQ building. The 'welcome home' given by the civic dignitaries to the Army left its leaders in no doubt that they had made the right choice in electing to return to this historic site.

Design of this building had been entrusted to Hubert Lidbetter and his son, Martin. Hubert Lidbetter, an architect of renown, had served as vice-president of the RIBA from 1942-1943. He was best known for his designs of Friends Meeting Halls for the Quakers and had been awarded a RIBA London Architecture Bronze Medal for his design of Friends House in Euston Road. He was also well known for his domestic architecture as well as for schools and non-conformist churches.

General Wilfred Kitching was the leader of The Salvation Army during the time of the building of the new IHQ. He later wrote in *The Friend* (a Quaker publication) dated 4 March 1966:

Among the names submitted for my consideration was the name of Hubert Lidbetter. Apart from his high qualifications and established reputation, I was interested to learn of his Quaker connections. In finally accepting his services, I felt that he should discover an approach, which he would have to the requirements of The Salvation Army that would be sympathetic, even spiritual. We found Hubert Lidbetter a man of patience and good will. Many difficult negotiations and unexpected problems were faced and it would be impossible to estimate the invaluable help and advice given by him and his partner. At the opening ceremony on 13 November 1963 I presented him to Her Majesty, the Queen Mother. As he escorted the Queen Mother and myself around the building, I felt that in every way he was worthy of the expressions of commendation that she offered to him as the architect. One important city official said to me after the opening: 'In the midst of new buildings that speak of material ways of life, yours is a building that has a spiritual mark upon it, and much of the credit for that estimate must go to Mr. Lidbetter.

General Wilfred Kitching himself had a Quaker background and hence had a great affinity with the architect.

The building design was for a six-storey façade fronting directly on to Queen Victoria Street and Peter's Hill, reducing to five stories part way along the façade on to Lambeth Hill. The plan form for the main five and six-storey offices was arranged around an open courtyard facing south. The street level at the back of the building onto Upper Thames Street was considerably lower than onto Queen Victoria Street. This made possible an additional lower ground floor level as well as a basement on this frontage. A single storey office block at the lower ground floor level occupied most of the open courtyard at the rear. The basement level provided extensive car parking, boiler room and storage. The buildings occupied most of the site but a temporary public road had to be maintained through the site for a period of 10 years after its completion. This provided part of a one-way system linking Upper Thames Street to Lambeth Hill. This road necessitated a two storey high opening through the east wing of the building. Following the closure of this road and the infill of the building aperture, the remainder of that road was named Booth Lane and the section of it retained within the site became additional car parking. Later improvements to Upper Thames Street and Lambeth Hill, as well as the creation of Castle Baynard Street, made that temporary road obsolete.

The height of the building was restricted by the views of St Paul's Cathedral from the south. In order to meet this requirement, the passenger lifts within the building did not travel to the uppermost floor level, as the motor rooms above roof level would have contravened that restriction.

The building was designed to house the staff of The Salvation Army International Headquarters and those of the National Headquarters as well. While there was no physical division within the building, two separate entrances were provided. The IHQ entrance was from Queen Victoria Street and the NHQ entrance was from Peter's Hill.

The IHQ entrance had many notable features:

164. Bramwell Booth hall, under Vista Way in 1963 building.

- Two halves of a global map of the world were mounted on the east and west walls, each with a slogan under them reading: 'The world for Christ' and 'Christ for the world'.

- A carved profile of both William and Catherine Booth.
- The names of all the generals of The Salvation Army from William Booth up to John Gowans, carved into the polished marble walls and filled with gold leaf.
- Both entrance halls were two stories in height with first floor balconies.

One unique feature of the building was the Bramwell Booth Memorial Hall. This large meeting hall was constructed at basement level and located under Peter's Hill, which is now the Vista Way between the Millennium Footbridge over the Thames and St Paul's Cathedral. The Bramwell Booth Hall was used for weekly prayers for all staff and for special occasions, including the occasional solemnization of marriages. The walls were lined with cedar wood panels and the floor was laid with cork tiles. Tiered seating and acoustic treatment to the walls, floor and ceiling made the hall an excellent auditorium for most occasions. Later, portraits of all former generals were moved from Denmark Hill, where they had graced the Assembly Hall of the Training College, and hung

around the walls of the Bramwell Booth Hall, with the exception of William Booth, whose portrait still hangs in the Assembly Hall of the College, built in his memory. A bronze bust of Bramwell Booth was located at the top of the entrance stairs to the meeting hall and a plaque inside the hall acknowledged that funding for the hall came from Salvationists of the Canada and Bermuda Territory.

Another feature of this building was the central location of the General's suite of offices on the second floor with a large, curved bay window to the General's personal office. During periods of redevelopment on adjacent sites, the General enjoyed unrestricted views of the River Thames.

The building also housed two Salvation Army companies, Reliance Bank and Reliance Travel; each located adjacent to one of the two entrances. A dining room for all staff was located in the East Wing on the third floor. A three-bedroom flat was also provided at roof level for the caretaker. Similar flats on later adjacent buildings, described as penthouses were sold for £1 million each.

During construction of the basement a graveyard was unearthed, apparently belonging to a church of St Peter and St Paul the Lesser, which had been erected in the 12th century and destroyed in the Great Fire of London in 1666. The bones in the graveyard were exhumed and re-buried elsewhere. Along the boundary of the site, near the Thames, remains of St Paul's Wharf were found. This was a Roman wharf built in the first century and some of the original oak piles were found well preserved, having being embedded in the river silt. Foundation stones of a large Roman auditorium were located at the west end of the site. The remainder of the foundations to that building were later discovered when the adjacent City of London School was being built.

The new IHQ building was completed in 1963 and was the first purpose-designed suite of offices for The Salvation Army International Headquarters. It served the IHQ and THQ administrations well for almost 40 years during which period the building underwent a major refurbishment only once, between 1990 and 1992. During the seventies and eighties major redevelopment work took place on all the sites adjoining IHQ. Most of the foundations to those buildings required driven piles, so that by 1990 the IHQ building had substantial cracks in its plaster finishes. The increasing demands of IT facilities and additional electrical loading necessitated a major refurbishment programme including new cable trunking, extensive plaster repairs and redecoration. This work was carried out over a two-year period while the building remained almost fully occupied. The work was arranged in 16 phases, each phase lasting six weeks with the occupants moving temporarily into two-storey porta-cabins located on the flat roof of the single-storey block at the rear, while a small number of staff moved over to the Training College to provide extra flexibility. Each phase was completed on time due to the organizational expertise of The Salvation Army in-house project manager as well as an efficient contractor, namely Higgs and Hill. The total cost of the work was £3.3 million including fees and VAT. This was more than twice the original cost for the complete new IHQ building in 1963. The refurbished buildings continued to serve the Army well until complete redevelopment was necessitated, due in part to relocation of The Salvation Army Territorial Headquarters administration.

In the 1990s, The Salvation Army reorganised its central administration, dividing the functions of its international and national activities into two separate headquarters. The Territorial Headquarters, for national activities, then moved its staff, previously housed at the offices in Queen Victoria Street, to a building at the Elephant and Castle, South of the River Thames. The remaining staff found themselves occupying little more than half a building measuring 80,000 sq ft (7,430 sq m). The charity had owned the site since 1881 so they instructed architect John McAslan to obtain planning permission for maximum development of the site for offices. He was able to obtain planning permission for a much larger building of 120,000 sq ft (11,150 sq m) which would utilise the whole site.

Following discussions with Healey and Baker (now Cushman and Wakefield, Healey and Baker) General John Gowans asked them to explore how complete redevelopment of the site might fund a new international headquarters building by selling a long leasehold on part of the site. They introduced Andrew Chadwick of Chadwick International, an architectural practice specialising in 'space economy'. Chadwick devised an office layout that would enable the remaining staff to fit comfortably into just 35,000 sq ft (3,250 sq m). This created enough surplus space on the site to enable the Army to do the deal it wanted.

Discussions took place with a number of development partners before Michael Glatman of Abstract Securities

165. IHQ 2004 building at night – view from Queen Victoria Street.

was finally appointed in March 2001 as the Army's development partner. He worked with architect Sheppard Robson to prepare a design for both buildings based upon the client's brief prepared by Andrew Chadwick and Healey and Baker. A task force appointed by the General, which included in-house technical expertise of an architect, surveyor and solicitor were given the responsibility of vetting the designs and negotiating the technical specification.

The financial services group, Old Mutual, had been lined up as a pre-let for the commercial building of 90,000 sq ft (8,360 sq m) of offices, which would effectively fund the whole development. Old Mutual had been in detailed discussions with Abstract, but they pulled out after the events of 11 September 2001 in the United States of America when the twin towers of the World Trade Centre were destroyed by terrorist action, and the consequent loss of confidence in the property market.

Abstract was able to save the situation by selling the development package to US developer Hines, who were signed up in March 2002. The company was new to the London market and eager to strike its first deal. Hines agreed to develop the commercial site speculatively and provide a new International Headquarters for The Salvation Army as part of the agreement. The completed speculative office building comprises seven floors of space totalling 90,000 sq ft (8,360 sq m). It is located next door to The Salvation Army IHQ and its address is 99 Queen Victoria Street, with the Army retaining the 101 address. The entrance to IHQ is actually off Peter's Hill, the pedestrian thoroughfare leading from Tate Modern across the Millennium Bridge to St Paul's Cathedral.

The new IHQ building and the commercial offices are designed as completely separate entities, although immediately adjacent, with separate structures and services. This will allow either building to be replaced independently should the need arise due to such factors as a change in the demands of the commercial office market.

This property deal took several years to come to fruition but upon completion the comments from the professional press were very complimentary, as shown by this extract from *Property Week*, 5 November 2004, entitled 'The Army's Salvation' and written by Mark Jansen:

A canny property deal has given The Salvation Army a new headquarters in the heart of London free of charge. It is the kind of property deal that most occupiers dream about. First, an owner-occupier drastically reduces the amount of space it needs. Then, it sells a long lease on the space it has vacated to a developer for £15.4m. The developer transforms the entire site into modern offices. The money raised from the sale of the lease funds the construction of a new headquarters on the same site for the owner-occupier.

The developer also agrees to pay ground rent to the original occupier, which remains the freeholder, providing a minimum of £200,000 a year in extra income. The lucky or clever occupier in question is The Salvation Army. It may be a charitable Christian organisation but it is not naïve when it comes to making property deals, as the partners who worked with it will testify.

The Princess Royal officially opened the new International Headquarters on 9 November 2004. The building overlooks the Thames and faces on to the Millennium Walkway, the route used by thousands of tourists every day as they cross the footbridge that spans the River Thames connecting Tate Modern Art gallery on the south bank to St Paul's Cathedral on the north.

166. View of Peter's Hill from Millennium Bridge.

The openness and transparency of the façade provide the opportunity for the new IHQ to be a window to the world, reflecting the nature of The Salvation Army. The glass façade has also been inscribed with Biblical texts to reinforce the spiritual nature of the Army's motivation. Passing tourists are able to look through this glass frontage to see some aspects of the workings of IHQ, as the meeting hall and main board room are located on the ground floor. The location of the entrance on Peter's Hill is an open invitation to the passing crowds to use the

167. IHQ Chapel at first floor level.

168. IHQ Board Room at ground floor level.

169. IHQ entrance area showing the circular boardroom (left); 170. glass-picture panels (middle); 171. basement cafe (right).

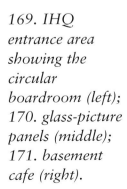

from the pavement although located at basement level. The entrance route to the offices is arranged across a bridge over this void. In the public restaurant is one of Rosa Branson's oil paintings depicting the Salvation Army in action around the world. The scenes portrayed are ones which the artist saw for herself as she travelled around the world, at her own expense, to witness first hand the Army with its 'heart to God and hand to man'. The painting which measures 8 feet by 5 feet was completed and framed by this famous artist herself as a gift to The Salvation Army, similar to the other twelve paintings that she has completed specifically to publicise the Army's work.

The centrepiece of the building is a small glass chapel suspended over the entrance onto Peter's Hill and protruding from the main frontage. It radiates coloured light and serves as a night-time beacon. It appears as an extension of the common space, as it juts out of the façade, forming a portico over the entrance. The chapel was designed by a sculpture/architect partnership and has amber glass side walls. It radiates coloured light and glows at night as a night-time beacon, not only emphasizing the location of the entrance but the spiritual nature of the building. Inside the chapel the front façade's glass louvres reflect passing clouds on a clear day, while the amber sidewalls infuse it with what some have described as a 'soft religious light'. The simple wooden

public restaurant where they can mingle with Salvationists and view an exhibition about the Army's worldwide work. The ground floor slab is set back from the pavement line so that the restaurant is clearly visible

mercy seat and cross add to the atmosphere of a place which is ideal for prayer and contemplation and where the presence of God can be easily realised.

Major Charles Swansbury, who co-ordinated the project and had worked in the construction industry before joining The Salvation Army, said: *'It is very modern and innovative; the old building had an insular, introspective feel, whereas this is open and transparent and visible, and we're very excited about that.'* Commissioner Harry Williams writing in The Salvation Army's *Officer* magazine in 2004 described the new IHQ building as a *'Crystal Palace for The Salvation Army'*.

At the conceptual stage of the design, the stated aims for the new building were that it had to be:

- Modern in design
- Frugal in operation
- Evangelical in purpose

General John Gowans's vision for the new International Headquarters was expressed as follows:

- *I have always felt that this new building should be able to speak for itself*
- *It has to be a welcoming place where people feel immediately at ease, nothing of the barricade about it; not a hiding place but transparent, cheerful and disarming.*
- *It should say any work undertaken in God's name deserves the best and most efficient equipment that modern technology can provide.*
- *It should not suggest extravagance or draw attention to itself; its mission matters most.*
- *It should suggest at once that it does not exist for itself but to serve everyone and particularly those in trouble or who have a problem.*

- *It should be obvious that it is dedicated to the service of Salvationists in the 109 countries where we are at work; its ability to speak many languages should be obvious.*
- *It has to offer information concerning the Army's philosophy, its history, its present projects and its needs.*
- *It should be clearly determined to help the Army achieve its basic ambitions: to announce the good news that is personified in Christ, to produce Christ-like people, to serve suffering humanity without discrimination of any kind.*
- *Without any air of the sanctimonious, the visitor should sense the presence of God in the place, even though it may not be recognised as that.*
- *The mercy seat as the symbol of God's presence, of His love and compassion... should take its place in the heart of the building with an open invitation to prayer.*

Upon completion he said: *'The optimism the new building generates is a vital thing. Yes, I am happy'*. The translation of so many spiritual objectives into a building design may seem to have been an impossible task, but the design architects were delighted to have such a clear mandate expressing the symbolism required. They stated: *'this client's brief was an architect's dream.'*

By the time the building was opened General John Gowans had retired, but his successor General John Larsson supported and complemented those views in his message reported in January 2005 in the RIBA Journal, as follows:

- *We wanted to make people aware that The Salvation Army is a forward-looking dynamic movement. It is bigger now than it has ever been in its history. This is*

172. IHQ General's office – exterior and interior views; General John Larsson and Commissioner Freda Larsson.

interesting considering how church attendances are declining generally.

• *We wanted the building to be welcoming and transparent, and to make people realise that it is not just an ordinary office block. The Salvation Army International Headquarters is the centre for a movement which is part church and part social organisation. We wanted the building to speak of that, with the crosses and the text on the walls. Judging by the number of people who stop and look at it, we have achieved that.*

173. Rosa Branson's oil paintings depicting the international work of The Salvation Army – hung in IHQ cafe area.

• *This is not a building for public worship, but we wanted the chapel to be the spiritual centre of The Salvation Army world, where people could meet and pray. We also wanted the General's floor to be accessible, and linking this to the chapel by placing workspaces either side of it seems to give a focal point to the building.*

• *It took various attempts to get the commercial relationship with the developer right but once we were working with Hines it went very smoothly indeed. This really is a model of how to make good use of a site. Reducing your own requirements obviously goes a long way to making sites viable for developers. There are other places where we have rented out lower level spaces and used the upper ones ourselves. While the actual principle is not new, the International Headquarters has been the most outstanding example of it.'*

Territorial Headquarters

From the commencement of The Salvation Army, its administrative functions in the United Kingdom and the Republic of Ireland were part of International Headquarters, with the General having direct responsibility for this work, in addition to his or her international role. Some aspects of the work, such as the Field (evangelical) work in England and in Scotland as well as the Men's and Women's Social Services had their own headquarters but each was responsible directly to IHQ. The business functions such as finance and property services as well as the Editorial, Literary, Music and Public Relations Departments were an integral part of the IHQ administration.

In 1989 General Eva Burrows appointed Colonel John Larsson to carry out an administrative revue of the functions of IHQ in order to put the work in the United

Kingdom on the same footing as that in other territories and restrict the functions of IHQ solely to its international role. In 1990 the recommendations of the review were adopted and a separate United Kingdom Territory was formed. Commissioner John Larsson was appointed as its first Territorial Commander. The remaining functions of IHQ meant a much reduced number of staff. While the two administrations remained in the same building at 101 Queen Victoria Street for a while, it was inevitable that separate buildings would now be required. In 1998 the Territorial Headquarters administration moved from 101 Queen Victoria Street in the City of London to 101 Newington Causeway near the Elephant and Castle, in the London Borough of Southwark. This left the IHQ building in the City greatly under-used and prepared the way for redevelopment of the whole site and the new IHQ building – described earlier.

THQ purchased a relatively new building, built in 1986 and previously used by a QUANGO (a quasi-autonomous non-government organisation). It was in an excellent location, close to both main line and tube stations and on numerous bus routes. It has a striking appearance with gold coloured reflective glass over most of its façade onto Newington Causeway. The layout was

174. Teritorial Headquarters – 1998 building. (Left)

175. Rosa Branson's oil painting depicting UK work of The Salvation Army – hung in THQ entrance foyer. (Left)

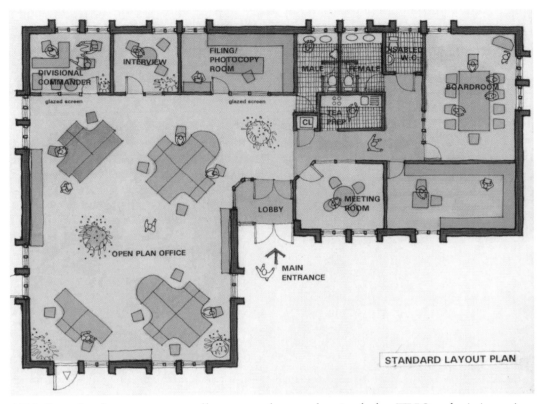

176. Standard floor plan for new divisional headquarters offices. (Above)

177. New Liverpool DHQ. (Right above)

178. New South and Mid Wales DHQ. (Right below)

generally open plan and suited the THQ administration well, with relatively few alterations necessary. The building cost £5million to purchase and a similar amount was spent on refurbishment. The building was however opened in 1999 debt free, because the whole of this cost was met by a grant from IHQ for National Headquarters' equity interest in the City of London site and by the sale of a leasehold property in Judd Street, Kings Cross, formerly occupied by the Salvation Army Social Services Headquarters and SP&S Ltd. In the entrance foyer is yet one more of Rosa Branson's oil paintings depicting the Army's work in the United Kingdom with over 30 other more general oil paintings by Rosa Branson decorating the office walls throughout the building.

Divisional Headquarters

Following the re-organisation of IHQ and THQ, the UK Territorial leaders decided to carry out a review of the divisional (regional) administrations. The result was a decision to reduce the number of divisions from 25 to 18. The new divisional headquarters generally needed to be re-located and they also required larger buildings. A standard administrative model was formulated and a standard building design prepared by the in-house architects, which was used for about half the new DHQ buildings in their new locations. Liverpool with South and Mid Wales Divisional office buildings are illustrated as typical.

Salvationist Publishing and Supplies

After the compilation of The Salvation Army's first hymn sheets and pamphlets other publications, such as *The War Cry*, and a full Salvation Army hymn book soon followed. When The Salvation Army developed uniforms they found that Salvationists' requirements were boycotted all over the country. Tailors would not make the Army uniforms and dress-makers 'turned up their noses' at the thought of making plain blue serge dresses for Salvationist lasses. With typical pragmatism, the Army set up its own Trade Headquarters to make and supply uniforms, publish magazines and books, as well as produce all the other articles that the Army would need for the 'Salvation War'. The Trade Department or SP&S, as it later became known, commenced on 31 December 1884 as part of the International Headquarters at 98 and 100 Queen Victoria Street, London. The business quickly expanded requiring additional premises in London at 96 Southwark Street and at 100 Clerkenwell Road with the Southwark Street premises housing The Salvation Army's own printing works.

On 17 June 1911 new business premises were opened in Judd Street at Kings Cross for the Trade Headquarters. These new premises were necessary to house all the various trade departments which had developed by then. From a later account in *The War Cry*, this was only just in time as they previously occupied a building in Fortess Road, north London, which was alongside stables. Not only did the customers and employees have to endure the various smells, especially from the manure heap, but the foundations of the building began to subside to the point of collapse while it was still occupied.

The new purpose-built SP&S headquarters building provided 40,000 square feet of floor space and was designed by The Salvation Army's own architects and

built by Gluyas of Bristol at a total cost of £20,000. It was four stories high plus a basement which was lit by natural light due to a light well all around the building. The apparent height of the building appeared reduced due to the use of a mansard roof and the skyline was improved with the introduction of dormer windows. The ground floor walls were clad in limestone blockwork and the walls of the next two floors were finished in red facing bricks. The imposing entrance was on the corner of the building facing towards St Pancras station and it was surmounted at roof level by a lead-covered tower and flag pole. The building symbolised the confidence and success of this Salvation Army business venture, established in a hostile social and commercial environment.

In addition to the new headquarters at Judd Street, The Salvation Army moved its own printing works to Camp Road, St Albans where the building was called the Campfield Press. The building also housed The Salvation Army's own brass instrument manufacturing factory to

179. Painting of SP&S 1911 building. (Above left)

180. SP&S 1995 building. (Above)

supply the large number of corps bands around the country.

The Judd Street Headquarters building, which contained its own bonnet factory, was substantially renovated in 1977 after the combined Social Headquarters was moved into another part of the same building. In 1995 the SP&S operation was moved to Tiverton Street into purpose-built premises at the back of the new THQ building at the Elephant and Castle and the Judd Street premises were sold.

The profits from the operation of SP&S together with other Salvation Army business operations, such as Reliance Bank and Reliance Travel have helped finance the Salvation Army's evangelical and social work from their inception. The officers and soldiers who have been appointed to work in these business operations have perceived their roles to be just as essential as those serving in corps or social centres in their contribution to the work of The Salvation Army. SP&S have now been incorporated into the Salvation Army Trading Company which also includes its numerous charity shops and textile recycling business.

Archaeological History

One of the great things about walking around the City of London is that wherever you go, you know that just beneath your feet lie layers and layers of history: day to day lives, momentous events and entire civilizations from millennia of human existence; all mapped out for us in stone, soil-marks, relics and rubbish. The landscape around still echoes the shape of this history.

During Roman times the River Thames was much wider than it is today. On the South side, Southwark was an expanse of marshland and channels. On the north side the river's edge within the City of London was some 100 metres further north than it is now, reaching right into the southern boundary of the present IHQ site. Since then the river has been narrowed, the North Bank moving ever southwards as land was reclaimed over the centuries, driven by the need for more space.

The Salvation Army is naturally proud of its history and its association with this site over the last 130 years or so. The use of the IHQ site for significant buildings, however, goes back at least 1,750 years, as was found during archaeological excavations carried out by the Guildhall Museum during the rebuilding of the previous IHQ building and during the more recent redevelopment of the site. These activities and similar excavations during the rebuilding of adjoining sites and roads revealed some interesting artefacts. The excavations revealed a sequence of building on this site and those adjoining it from the third century to the present time.

When the City of London School, on the next door site, was being built the opportunity arose to explore more of this area of archaeological interest. Huge foundations were discovered and evidence of a courtyard, suggesting a very large and high-status Roman building covering much of the site. It was an unfinished construction dated from around 294 AD, a similar date to the building remains found underneath IHQ. It has been suggested that this was a palace or a very high-status building being constructed by someone of considerable wealth and importance, but for some reason the construction was abandoned before completion. Historians have tried to tally the archaeological evidence with known historical records and have even come up with suggestions for the owner of this building. Someone who rose to prominence in the late third century began to construct a palace in this corner of London, but something dramatic happened around AD 294 which meant this grand project was left incomplete. The name suggested for that person was Allectus.

181. Aerial view of the City of London showing River Thames, Millennium Bridge, City of London School and St Pauls in relation to the IHQ site.

Allectus was either the finance secretary or an adviser to the rebel emperor M. Mausaeus Carausius. After a dispute with Rome, Carausius had declared himself Emperor of the British provinces, somewhere around the year AD 286. Allectus later assassinated his boss and assumed the position of self-declared emperor himself. Constantius, appointed 'Caesar' by Rome, sent a fleet to recapture the British Isles. Allectus did not have the military experience of his predecessor and his defence of

his kingdom ended disastrously. The Roman legions recaptured the island with hardly the loss of a single soldier. Allectus therefore met his end about 296 AD somewhere near Silchester.

The sampling of the tree ring dating in the oak piles identified two distinct periods of building on the IHQ site during the Roman occupation of Britain. The first period was between AD 172 and 250 and the second period AD 293 to 295. There was also evidence of a later development during the Saxon-Norman period, when of course the medieval Baynard's Castle was built on a nearby site. Evidence was also found on the IHQ site of later buildings destroyed during the Great Fire of London in 1666 as well as evidence of even later buildings of the Victorian period. The present IHQ site has obviously been in continuous use for the last 2,000 years to house the living and the dead, as disclosed in the burial remains, while The Salvation Army has only occupied it for the last 130 years.

Other artefacts found during foundation excavations included some remnants of the distinctive Pingsdorf pottery of the 11th and 12th century, imported from the Rhineland where it was originally manufactured. A plaque that was originally placed on the IHQ building was provided by the City of London Corporation. It confirmed further historical interest, as it indicated that the 'Curriers Hall' occupied the site in 1583.

During the building process on other Army sites, archaeological artefacts have often been discovered, which speak of former occupants as described here. In recent years The Salvation Army has sometimes built in 'time capsules' containing Army memorabilia into their new buildings, so it is interesting to ponder what

messages Army buildings and their artefacts will convey to future generations. Whatever the future of The Salvation Army, the archaeological evidence of the last 2,000 years gives some support to the belief expressed in the hymn 'Onward Christian Soldiers'

Crowns and thrones may perish, kingdoms rise and wane,
But the Church of Jesus constant will remain'

Another site, in the City of Westminster, was being excavated for a new Salvation Army hostel to replace the former Great Peter Street hostel building when an interesting artefact was discovered. It was an unbroken Bellarmine Jug in perfect condition. On its neck the jug portrayed the stylised likeness of the Italian Jesuit priest, Robert Bellarmine, a friend of Galileo. He was known for his tendency to rail against the evils of drink, so the potters of the Rhine Valley, where the jug was made, expressed their disapproval of him by putting his image on their beer mugs. The jug is now preserved in a showcase at the entrance to the chapel in the hostel. It is ironic that this artefact, which seeks to ridicule a campaigner against alcohol, should be found on the site of the original Army hostel, which was opened in 1911 by William Booth, another campaigner against drink.

Comments on Headquarters buldings

The various headquarters buildings have always been a reflection of the way in which The Salvation Army has chosen to organise its administration to support and direct its front line activities. Each of the various head-quarters has a range of business sections within them related to its mission. However, separate business enterprises, such as SP&S have been developed in their

182. Pingsdorf Pottery. (Right)

183. Bellarmine Jug. (Far right)

own premises after an initial start within the Army headquarters. This is also true for other Salvation Army business enterprises, such as Reliance Bank and the Salvation Army General Insurance Corporation (SAGIC), which now also enjoy physical separation with their own premises at Faith House in 23/24 Lovat Lane within the City of London.

The property deals, especially for its office buildings, which the Army has concluded have shown business acumen that has surprised many people in the property world. The buildings have not only been excellent functionally but have been acquired at minimum cost to Army funds, often providing a substantial profit. Surprisingly the Army has not sought to raise money by loans or mortgages for any of these developments, so that contrary to the current financial climate The Salvation Army does not have outstanding debts against buildings in its extensive property portfolio. This is due to the excellent property and financial advisors whom the Army has used, both from within their in-house staff and from selected external consultants.

Some might question the need or wisdom of a charity

owning its buildings. However, after an initial period of renting properties, William Booth decided that The Salvation Army should purchase or build the properties it needed for its mission, which gave to the work a sense of permanence. The policy of acquiring the freehold or long leases on land has served the Army well over the years from a business point of view, because as land and property prices and values in the UK have soared, the Army has always had valuable property assets to use in any negotiations. This principle has enabled corps, social centres and headquarters especially, to relocate or rebuild when existing buildings were compulsorily acquired by local authorities or where they were desired by private development companies. During the 1960s and 1970s especially, the Army was paid equivalent reinstatement value by local authorities for their properties plus a free site, when redevelopment plans for inner city areas included an Army site. The IHQ deal is a spectacular example of the kind of benefit that this policy has provided but many other new buildings for corps and social centres have been funded in similar ways.

FINAL THOUGHTS

The story of the development of The Salvation Army in the British Isles since it commenced in 1865 as the Christian Mission is a fascinating one when told from any perspective. This narrative has sought to illustrate it and describe it through the buildings that it erected and used, developed to the 'Glory of God'. While the book contains much historical information about Salvation Army buildings, its story is essentially a spiritual one, which has resulted in many changed individual lives and affected some significant aspects of British society.

Scriptural teaching makes it clear that the Christian Church is the people, not the buildings. In recent television and radio programmes examining the efficiency of different organisations, mention has been made that The Salvation Army is considered to be the most efficient charitable organisation in the USA. In discussions regarding the work of the Army in the UK, no conclusion was drawn on this issue, in spite of many complimentary comments about its work. However, the commentators concluded that any organisation would envy the dedication and commitment of the Army's personnel to its mission. This historical story of the Army has demonstrated these qualities in plenty plus great energy, imagination, flexibility and pragmatism in overcoming countless difficulties. Such qualities have been shown not only by those engaged in 'front line' duties but those working behind the scenes in various administrative and support roles. Certainly the Army's ability to meet each new challenge throughout its history would not have been possible without such people.

Throughout all the changes necessary in its programmes and buildings, each new challenge has illustrated the importance that the Army still places in responding to the love of God, by showing love in word and action to others, especially to the poor and 'down trodden'. The large portfolio of Army buildings which are specifically dedicated to social work and especially those for housing homeless people also testify to the equal emphasis placed on loving ones neighbour as to loving God. While Salvation Army buildings today have greatly changed to reflect changes in society at large they clearly still reflect and symbolise the values, ideals and priorities that were the driving force when William and Catherine first commenced their spiritual warfare. It has been necessary for each new generation to rediscover the principles set out in Booth's *In Darkest England and the Way Out* and apply them to each new situation. The recent labelling of the hostel programmes and buildings as 'Hostel Plus', and even more recently as 'Lifehouse' illustrates that Army goals go far beyond just housing homeless people. Similarly the development of 'Employment Plus' programmes and enterprises in the United Kingdom reflects a revival of the principles of Booth's vision as expressed in his elevator system.

While the Army has maintained its emphasis on developing holy people rather than sacred buildings, the quality of the physical environments created for both worship and service show their awareness of the contribution that good buildings can make to the success of their mission. The Army's social services buildings, in particular, illustrate that a 'good fit' between service programmes and the design of the buildings make the work so much easier and more effective.

The transition from a mission to an army and then into a church is visually apparent in the external treatment of the corps buildings as well as in the increase of the facilities provided. The separation of different aspects of corps functions and their later reunification is also reflected in the design of corps buildings. While Salvation Army corps buildings still reflect many unique aspects of its worship and service, the previous avoidance of church symbols and terminology seems to have largely disappeared. This may be because of a growing awareness that a large portion of the UK population seem to be unaware that The Salvation Army is a church. This is one of many ways in which The Salvation Army has had to adapt to changes in society. Another of these ways is the gradual delegation of authority and responsibility from headquarters to corps level, which has resulted in such a variety of forms of worship and service. This, again, is reflected in the wide variety of architecture evident in corps buildings.

The Salvation Army's social buildings have undergone radical changes as well due to greatly increased financial resources and the requirements of central and local governments, as well as the expectations of society. The quality of the physical environments provided owe much to the application of dedicated creative minds informed by continuous social research and guided by the Holy Spirit, especially in the facilities for homeless people.

The need to place needy people in suitable physical and social environments for their rehabilitation was first part of William Booth's concept in his 'elevator system'. This concept is still evident in the latest social centres where the design of both the facilities and social programmes seek to provide therapeutic environments for the care and healing of their residents. William Booth's use of research data to help him in his action plans for social change are still continuing in the present use of research information to assist in the formulation of new directions for the Army in its fight for social justice. Salvation Army buildings have always been dedicated 'to the Glory of God'. It is anticipated that the worship and service provided in them will continue to have the same aim.

Every building development is a tribute to the faith and works of so many people. In every age, building projects could not have been realised without the vision and faith of many individuals and groups of people, who were undaunted by seemingly impossible difficulties. The Army has always been a church *'with its sleeves rolled up'* and funding for these schemes has been raised in so many ways, from jumble sales to major donations. Most people who voluntarily contribute to the Army's work do so because they have been impressed by the dedication and commitment of individuals whom they have met or heard about. The personal integrity of officers, such as Brigadier Laurie Johnson, have resulted in the Army receiving millions of pounds in land and cash, long after they have been promoted to glory. Youell Court flats for retired officers in Bournemouth and Youell Court residential care home in Coventry are tributes to that man's integrity.

Some people who made important contributions to the realisation of building projects, did so by being able to influence and impress wealthy individuals or government officials as to the value of the Army's work. Brigadier Ken Nutty was able to get close to wealthy individuals for the benefit of the Army, for instance Sir Charles Haywood, who provided substantial funds for the new halls at L'Islet in Guernsey. Edward Alsop, the late Chief Executive of SAHA was able to secure capital funding for the new hostel in Westminster, which now bears his name. The 1960s and 1970s were periods of intense redevelopment of inner city areas of towns and cities in post-war Britain, which involved many Salvation Army buildings. Ernest Lipscombe, the Army's Chief Surveyor during this period, used his considerable skill and experience in negotiating replacement sites and equivalent reimbursement funding, making many of the new Army corps and social buildings possible. The creative qualities of the architects involved in designing each scheme made their own contribution. These are just a few individuals of many whose devoted service has contributed to these projects. The symbolism of all Army buildings lies not only in the qualities of the organisation but in characteristics of the individuals who made them possible. The 34 oil paintings given to the Salvation Army by artist Rosa Branson, including thirteen of them specifically commissioned to depict its work, adorn the walls of many of its buildings providing considerable interest in the stories and in the symbolism portrayed. They represent one person's admiration for the Army's work and her willingness to dedicate her talent to the glory of God, rather than seeking financial rewards for her God-given creative talent.

During the opening ceremony of Bradbury Home, a new Army residential care home for elderly people in Southend, the local Member of Parliament Sir Teddy Taylor recounted his own experience of The Salvation Army while visiting Pakistan. Following the invasion of Afghanistan by the Russian Army, thousands of Afghan refugees fled across the border into northern Pakistan. The Salvation Army, along with other relief organisations, organised refugee camps and administered necessary aid. This was despite the fact that the Salvation Army uniform with its red flashes and epaulets was unfortunately rather similar to the Russian Army uniform, so the Salvationists had to change their uniforms for their own safety. Sir Teddy was so impressed with the efficiency of the organisation and the compassionate care offered by the Army to people of a different faith, that he exclaimed: '*God knows that the world should know about the work you are doing here*'. The officer in charge, Major David Burrows, responded: '*Well if God knows, that is all that matters*'. Those responsible for raising funds for the Army's work might wish that the world would know about it, but David's remark shows that in his opinion the purpose of the Army's work is not to bring honour and glory to the organisation but to bring glory to God.

Many people will be familiar with the Alpha course, which explores the meaning of life from a Christian point of view, which has been developed and promoted principally by Reverend Nicky Gumbel, the vicar of Holy Trinity Brompton Church in Kensington, London. Not only has the course been used throughout the United Kingdom but across the world. One of a number of follow-up courses to Alpha, created by Nicky Gumbel is entitled 'A Life Worth Living', based upon St Paul's letter to the Christians at Philippi. It explores how many of the fundamental aspects of life become different, described as new, when a person becomes a Christian. When it comes to ambition it suggests that there are basically only two motivations for everything we do; '*Either to live for our own glory or to live for the glory of God*'.

Those words, *To the Glory of God*, on the foundation stones or opening plaques of Salvation Army buildings are not just nice-sounding phrases, nor do they relate only to the purpose for which the buildings were erected, but they reflect the reason for all that The Salvation Army does and why it was brought into existence. However, preposterous it may sound, the teaching of Jesus is that the reason why we were all created was for that sole purpose, so that our lives should bring glory to God.

Commissioner Elizabeth Matear in a letter from Rome in May 2007 wrote:

'The stones of the eternal city had many stories to tell. They exuded power, conquest and authority. They made a virtue of and idolised man-made achievements and made God in man's image. The mausoleums contained dead men. However, grand the structure, dead is dead.

Praise God the foundation of our faith is in a living Saviour, 'the Living Stone' (1 Peter 2:4) and we are 'living stones, being built into a spiritual house' (2 Peter 2:5). The monuments and ruins of ancient Rome have been added to over the centuries. Christian Rome with its array of treasures and church architecture are motivators for many who visit Rome. The legacy and genius of artists and craftsmen bring tourists and purists to admire. In my musing, I say 'They don't build like that any more!' Some of our buildings have failed to last a single generation, indicting testimony to lack of stewardship; others are standing and give a testimony to the glory of God.

Yet here is the greatest and most glorious truth that the building we are engaged in is eternal and spiritual, 'living stones'. The building we are engaged in is not about structure and monuments to ourselves. 'The result of our ministry, written not with ink but with the spirit of the living God, not on tablets of stone but on tablets of human hearts; for what was glorious has no glory now in comparison with the surpassing glory'(2 Corinthians 3: 10).

Our history as a Salvation Army is always connected - back down the millennia and in recent history we name the names - the converts, the soldiers, the officers, their children, grandchildren from generation to generation - living stones all to the glory of God, standing as testimony to the grace and faithfulness of God. Let no one decry such a heritage and may we not be silent in our witness 'if they keep quiet, the stones will cry out' (Luke 19:40).

'God is the builder of everything ... we are his house, if we hold on to our courage and the hope of which we boast' (Hebrews 3: 4-6) (1 Corinthians 3:10, 11). It is a strong reminder that while all that we do as Christians should be to the Glory of God, only the spiritual things will last forever.'

Those words are a reminder that some Salvation Army buildings may last for 100 years or more and our cathedrals last for 1,000 years or more, but these structures have a finite life. However, the transformed lives of individuals brought about by the grace of God and the work of God's Holy Spirit have a quality of infinity about them, as their spirits are promised eternal life.

At the Centenary Celebrations of The Salvation Army on 24 June 1965, Michael Ramsey, the Archbishop of Canterbury said:

There's the gift that I believe every Salvationist has in a wonderful measure and that is the gift of joy. I've seen many odd things in my time but I don't think that I have ever seen a gloomy member of The Salvation Army. The gift of joy is very wonderfully yours and may that gift go on being yours. It isn't only that we convert people to Christianity and that they cheer up and discover in our holy faith what a deep secret of joy there is.

No, isn't it also the other way round? That by the sheer joy of Christian character and Christian life other people are affected and led to come and join in something that is full of cost, full of deep sacrifice, but also the most joyful thing in this world and the next.

Finally, for a church that initially started as a mission, here are some final thoughts from a quotation which was intended as a challenge for the universal Christian Church:

• 'You must die as a church and be reborn as a mission.
• The Kingdom isn't a programme, but men and women, living radically for Christ.
• The Christian life has to be demonstrated and not just explained.
• Evangelism is to grow the Church rather than to grow my church'.

May The Salvation Army continue in the future to demonstrate with infectious joy the love of God, as it responds to the needs of each new generation under the guidance of the God's Holy Spirit and may it offer new opportunities for worship and service to the Glory of God.

BIBLIOGRAPHY

The Salvation War 1982

Orders and Regulations for Divisional Officers 1885, chapter 15 on Property

In Darkest England and the Way Out 1890 by William Booth

Nottingham Guardian 18 July 1914

RIBA Thesis on Evangelical Centres by Gerald Norwood, 1954

The History of The Salvation Army, volume 3, chapter 20, Robert Sandall, Nelson 1955

RIBA Thesis on Salvation Army Halls by David Blackwell 1956

Tragedies of Affluence 1965

Paper on Architectural Development for Salvation Army Buildings and Camps by Lieut-Colonel George F. Russell – presented to the Executive Officers Councils of the USA Eastern Territory on 16 November 1966.

Gods Army Cyril Barnes, SP&S, 1978

Today in Darkest England, chapter 7 'Home and Dry' by Caughey Gauntlett.

Building Design 25 January 1986

Property Week 5 November 2004

Hadleigh Salvation Army Farm – A Vision Reborn by Gordon Parkhill and Graham Cook 2008

After-Sight and Foresight by Denis Hunter

How to Read a Church by Richard Taylor 2003. published by Ryder Books

Open University Course Video for the Arts Foundation Course on Religion and Society in Victorian Bristol presented by John Kent

Christian Mission Historical Association publications in various papers as follows:

> *Building The University of Humanity in Camberwell* by Tony Wilson
>
> *Hadleigh Farm – A Vision Reborn* (no name)
>
> *L'Islet Fortress, Guernsey 1883 – 1982* (no name)

RIBA Journals – dates given in text

Extracts from Salvation Army publications including the War Cry and All the World

DOE Interim Lodging House Standards

Guildhall Museum of London papers on archaeological history

This is International Headquarters booklet by James Northey

RIBA Library

Society of Friends Archives

Records at William Booth College and Sunbury Court

The Salvation Army International Heritage Centre Archives

LIST OF ARCHITECTURAL AND DESIGN AWARDS ON SALVATION ARMY BUILDINGS

1972 Civic Trust Award for the William Booth Memorial Centre, Notintone Place, Nottingham.

1975 Heritage Year Award by Civic Trust for the Conversion of Mortimers Hotel, St. Giles Street. Norwich to a Salvation Army Community Centre.

1986 City of Stoke-on-Trent Good Design Award for Salvation Army Hostel.

1987 Conservation Society Commendation for Salvation Army Leamington Spa Hall

1987 City of Hereford Conservation Area Award for Salvation Army Hereford Corps Hall.

1988 Civic Trust Award for Bristol Citadel Corps building.

1989 RIBA East Region Design Award and the Ipswich Society New Building Award for Salvation Army Lyndon House Hostel in Ipswich.

1994 Southend-on-Sea Borough Councils Design Award for Salvation Army Bradbury Residential Care Home.

1994 Southend-on-Sea Borough Design Award Commendation for Shoeburyness Salvation Army Hall.

1994 The Ipswich Society Commendation for Ipswich Citadel Salvation Army Hall.

1995 Quality in Urban Design Award by the Royal Town Planning Institute for Salvation Army Development at Soho Street, Shildon, County Durham.

1996 Borough of Spelthorne Design Award, both the overall winner and for disabled access, for Salvation Army Staines Corps Hall.

1999 Borough of Spelthorne Design Award, both the overall winner and for disabled access, for Salvation Army Sunbury Court Conference Centre.

2006 New City Architectural Award by the Worshipful Company of Architects for the Salvation Army International Headquarters Building.

2009 RIBA Awards – Community Architecture Award and East of England Building of the Year as well as the ASCE/RIBA Award for Religious Architecture of the Year for Salvation Army Chelmsford Corps Hall.

2011 Winner in Garden City Heritage Awards – The Salvation Army Community hall in Letchworth.

LIST OF ILLUSTRATIONS

Front cover: Painting by Michael John Ewins of significant events & buildings throughout SA history.

1. Example of foundation stone: 'To the Glory of God'
2. Slimbridge Village Church Spire
3. London's Canary Wharf
4. Aerial view of St Paul's Cathedral with the Salvation Army International Headquarters (1963 building) in the foreground
5. Durham Cathedral
6. Liverpool's Anglican Cathedral of the Church of Christ
7. Nave of the Church of Christ Cathedral
8. Liverpool's Roman Catholic Metropolitan Cathedral of Christ the King
9. Huge lantern over altar to Christ the King Cathedral
10. Original design drawing for York Citadel – 1882
11. Original drawing by Sherwood for a standard hall design
12. Original design drawing by Oswald Archer of Nottingham Memorial Halls
13. Aberdeen Citadel
14. Drawing of open-air meeting led by William Booth
15. Drawing of Effingham Theatre
16. Drawing of meeting in Portsmouth Music Hall
17. Eastern Star 1867
18. Railway Arch Meeting Hall attacked by opponents of the Mission
19. People's Market converted to People's Mission Hall 1870
20. Drawing of Bristol Circus exterior
21. Drawing of Bristol Circus interior
22. Converted Skating Rink at Oldham, Lancashire
23. Tunnel entrance to Regent Hall
24. Regent Hall interior
25. Rosa Branson's oil paintings symbolising Regent Hall Corps activity. (Only two shown of the six donated for use in entrance tunnel.)
26. Clapton Congress Hall and National Training Barracks
27. Drawing of the Eagle Tavern, after takeover by The Salvation Army 1882
28. Edmonton Citadel front facade
29. Sheffield Citadel Hall
30. Rochdale Citadel Hall
31. First floor plans of Sheffield and Rochdale Citadel Halls
32. Camborne Hall, Cornwall
33. Drawing of front Façade of Bristol Citadel 1896
34. Floor plans of Bristol Citadel – circus shape?
35. Interior Bristol Citadel
36. Aberdeen Citadel
37. Main Hall interior Aberdeen Citadel
38. Manchester Star Hall interior
39. Brighton Congress Hall (with entrance porch added and parapet reduced)
40. Tottenham Citadel
41. Grantham Hall
42. Cirencester Hall – 'temporary home' for 51 years!

103. Great Peter Street Hostel with dormitory and entrance shown below
104. Aerial view of Edward Alsop Court, Westminster Abbey and Houses of Parliament.
105. Booth House after renovations
106. Rosa Branson oil painting illustrating SA work with homeless people
107. Lyndon House, Ipswich
108. Self-contained training flats – Ipswich
109. Tom Raine Court, Darlington
110. Davis House, Swindon
111. Hope Town Hostel – 2006 building
112. Ann Fowler hostel – 1980 building
113. The Mothers' Hospital
114. Strawberry Field original building
115. Thorndale House, Belfast
116. Copper Beeches Nursery, Leeds
117. Shepherd's Green Family Centre, Birmingham
118. Hyrstlands Approved School, Batley
119. Hyrstlands new study centre
120. Hyrstlands new classroom/main hall with security link to main house
121. David Gray House, Isle of Man
122. Grenville, Godalming, Surrey
123. Wickstead Hall, Whitchurch in Shropshire
124. Bradbury Home, Southend-on-Sea – views from road and garden
125. Youell Court, Binley in Coventry, with aerial view shown below
126. Greig House Treatment Centre, Docklands, London
127. David Barker House Annexe, Blackfriars
128. George Steven Day Centre, Kilbirnie
129. Youell Court Flats, Bournemouth
130. David Barker House, Blackfriars
131. Riverside House, Docklands
132. Ty Gobaith, Cardiff in Wales
133. Some of the original farm activities, including tending the orchard, making bricks, feeding the chickens and using the heavy work horses
134. Hadleigh New Tea-rooms
135. Appeal brochure painting of The Pleasance Men's Hostel, Edinburgh
136. Lyndon House Men's Hostel, Ipswich, floor plans
137. Edward Alsop Court – ground floor plan
138. E.A.Court – first floor plan
139. Hopetown 2006 Women's Hostel – upper floor plan
140. Greig House Substance Treatment Centre – ground & first floor plans
141. Youell Court Residential Care Home, Binley – upper floor plan
142. Eva Burrows Residential & Day Centre, Glasgow – perspective drawing
143. Sunbury Court
144. Gilbert Scott's axonometric drawing – William Booth Memorial Training College
145. William Booth College administration block and tower
146. William Booth's statue and entrance foyer to college
147. College Assembly Hall
148. New block of flats for cadet families
149. The Cedars, Sydenham Hill – view from road
150. The Cedars – view from rear garden
151. Rosa Branson's oil painting representing the essence of the Salvation Army's message
152. Sunbury Court Main House
153. Sunbury annexe
154. Sunbury new conference centre – internal and external views
155. Youth Centre dining hall